In Search of the Good Life

In Search of the Good Life

Through the Eyes of Aristotle, Maimonides, and Aquinas

Corey Miller

⌘PICKWICK *Publications* • Eugene, Oregon

IN SEARCH OF THE GOOD LIFE
Through the Eyes of Aristotle, Maimonides, and Aquinas

Copyright © 2019 Corey Miller. All rights reserved. Except for brief quotations in critical publications or reviews, no part of this book may be reproduced in any manner without prior written permission from the publisher. Write: Permissions, Wipf and Stock Publishers, 199 W. 8th Ave., Suite 3, Eugene, OR 97401.

Pickwick Publications
An Imprint of Wipf and Stock Publishers
199 W. 8th Ave., Suite 3
Eugene, OR 97401

www.wipfandstock.com

PAPERBACK ISBN: 978-1-5326-5321-6
HARDCOVER ISBN: 978-1-5326-5322-3
EBOOK ISBN: 978-1-5326-5323-0

Cataloguing-in-Publication data:

Names: Miller, Corey, 1972–, author.

Title: In search of the good life : through the eyes of Aristotle, Maimonides, and Aquinas / by Corey Miller.

Description: Eugene, OR : Pickwick Publications, 2019 | Includes bibliographical references.

Identifiers: ISBN 978-1-5326-5321-6 (paperback) | ISBN 978-1-5326-5322-3 (hardcover) | ISBN 978-1-5326-5323-0 (ebook)

Subjects: LCSH: Ethics. | Happiness. | Aristotle. | Maimonides, Moses,—1135–1204. | Thomas,—Aquinas, Saint,—1225?–1274.

Classification: B491.E7 M55 2019 (print) | B491.E7 M55 (ebook)

Unless otherwise noted, Scripture quotations are taken from The Holy Bible, New International Version®, NIV®. Copyright © 1973, 1978, 1984, 2011 by Biblica, Inc.® Used by permission. All rights reserved worldwide.

The Scripture verse marked NASB is taken from The Holy Bible, New American Standard Bible®, Copyright © 1960, 1962, 1963, 1968, 1971, 1972, 1973, 1975, 1977, 1995 by The Lockman Foundation. Used by permission.

Manufactured in the U.S.A. 09/27/19

To my children, Parker, Sadie, and Dacey.
May you forever know the good life.

Contents

Introduction | ix

1. A Common Teleological Background: Aristotle | 1
2. Maimonides and the Good Life | 36
3. Aquinas and the Good Life | 79
4. Maimonides and Aquinas in Dialogue | 127
   Conclusion | 182

   Bibliography | 187

Introduction

This project is a comparative exploration of the good life from the standpoint of two of the greatest medieval philosophers. As Moses Maimonides (1135/8–1204) is the greatest Jewish philosopher of the medieval period, so Thomas Aquinas (1225–74) is the greatest Christian philosopher of that period. Yet it has been said that "Maimonides without Aristotle is unthinkable,"[1] and, "without Aristotle, Thomas would not be."[2] These statements convey the enormous influence Aristotle has had on the two medievalists and continues to have on their respective traditions through their writings, such that the views of these latter thinkers' come to light best when understood in light of their historical sources of influence.

Given that Aristotle was the major (though certainly not the only) philosophical influence on these two thinkers, it makes sense to begin this exploration by attending to his views, which are germane for shaping some of the background of their respective positions on important issues. While noting the common structure that the medieval thinkers share with their ancient philosophical forebear, indeed with much of the classical tradition altogether, my central concern in this research will be to identify certain important features that seem to be lacking in Aristotle but are accounted for in either Maimonides or Aquinas or both and which do philosophical work throughout their respective projects. These features serve to distinctly illuminate the common Maimonidean and Thomistic accounts on the nature of the good life over the Aristotelian account, as understood through an exploration of the three respective views on the fallen human condition and human perfectibility. In the same spirit, a comparative approach of all three gives us greater clarity of the significant points of interest than we would have without the comparison. While there are other

---

1. Frank, "Introduction," 3.
2. McInerny, *Thomas Aquinas*, xxxiv.

works comparing Aristotle and Maimonides,[3] Aristotle and Aquinas,[4] and Maimonides and Aquinas,[5] precious little has been done on all three, particularly with the *foci* of this dissertation. Yet still, the emphasis is on the medieval thinkers as they adopt and adapt Aristotelian thinking and maneuvers. It is in this comparative religious dialogue and in exercising the age-old quest of the relationship between Athens and Jerusalem that these thinkers' views are best illuminated.[6]

Chapter 1 provides a broadly characterized Aristotelian view of the good life to set the philosophical background of the problem(s) in our exploration. Chapters 2 and 3 provide the respective Maimonidean and Thomistic accounts, revealing their indebtedness to, but also their significant departure from, Aristotle on the good life by exploring their philosophical and religious accounts of the fallen human condition and human perfectibility. Chapter 4 explores the important differences between the medievalists' respective positions by direct comparison in a sort of dialogue, the implications each has for one another relative to the good life, and an extended discussion of Aquinas's view of spiritual formation.

---

3. Frank, "Humility," 89–99; "Anger," 269–81; "Defining Maimonides," 231–34; "Maimonides and Medieval Jewish Aristotelianism," 136–56; Jacobs, "Plasticity," 443–54.

4. Jaffa, *Thomism*; Kenny, "Aquinas," 15–27; MacDonald, "Ultimate Ends," 31–65; MacIntyre, *Whose Justice?*

5. Broadie, "Maimonides and Aquinas," 224–34; Burrell, "Philosophical Foray," 181–94; Dobbs-Weinstein, *Maimonides and St. Thomas*; Fox, "Maimonides and Aquinas on Natural Law," 10–26.

6. Tertullian, *Prescription against Heretics*, 7.

1

A Common Teleological Background: Aristotle

The purpose of this chapter is to set up the philosophical background and problems in Aristotle that Moses Maimonides and Thomas Aquinas endeavor to resolve or improve on by suitably adapting Aristotelian thinking for their purposes. To do this, I will provide a plausible and broadly characterized Aristotelian view of the good life—an account of Aristotle's understanding of human perfectibility roughly shared or taken for granted by both thinkers.

First, I will trace the basic Aristotelian structure of the human good by considering raw human nature, its ultimate end, and how to get from man as he is in the raw to man as he could become. Second, I will address certain problems the account raises that have the effect of rendering the human end elusive for most people to obtain given certain preconditions necessary for the good life. That is, on this account, there are certain things that disqualify most people from ever reaching the prize, the good life. Third, I will look at the narrow gate through which a few might pass to experience the good life; finding that, even while elusive for most, it becomes elusive even for the best of men as a mere human idealistic façade or else quite rare and episodically unsustainable. In essence, I will show that Aristotle's eudaimonistic view of human perfectibility ends with a whimper rather than a bang as one cannot be optimistic about the attainability of the good life. The Aristotelian account lacks certain necessary features of the best life for man, even the best of men (much worse for the worst of them), which is where the medievalists will make their advance.

In addition to observing the structure, problems, and a possible way through to attaining the good life, we will see Aristotle setting the stage for the Aristotelian move made by the two medievalists. Most interesting, as Aristotle's view on human perfection is developed and understood by an individual's philosophical speculation and relevant activity, it reveals a striking two-tier notion of moral virtue (a necessary precondition to the ultimate perfect life of intellectual virtue).

Ironically, the moral bifurcation Aristotle makes between *fully* virtuous acts and *merely* virtuous acts winds up itself being just one part of the additional bifurcation that both Maimonides and Aquinas are committed to in their respective philosophies, given a certain nexus that without which the virtues are less than virtuous and virtue itself is less accessible than even Aristotle's scheme supposed. This nexus of key features becomes all the more important to obtaining the good life. Indeed, without it, to use Aristotelian idiom, the virtues become like matter without form. As Aristotle's perfect life is found lacking (i.e., an exhibit of Aristotelian privation), it is here where the medievalists seek to supply the form, and where the Maimonidean and Thomistic man (given their richer ontology) will always be in an advanced state relative to the good life over the Aristotelian man.[1]

The Basic Structure of the Human Good

Aristotle's vision of the human good is eudaimonistic, teleological, and intellectualist. Eudaimonism is the view that happiness is the ultimate justification of morality.[2] It is the well-lived life favored by a god. Aristotle is also, from a contemporary viewpoint, an ethical naturalist (ethical terms refer to natural properties and are therefore defined via factual terms).[3] As an ethical naturalist, he holds that nature determines normalcy. In some respects, Aristotelian ethical structure seems to fit our moral experience, a structure that dominated the schemes of both the classical and most prominent Western theistic traditions. It is fundamentally the Aristotelian teleological structure of the world that the major theistic traditions in the West were more than willing to co-opt for their own projects in philosophical theology.[4] This structure was analyzed by Aristotle in the *Nicomachean Ethics* (NE).[5]

---

1. The term *man* is used throughout this work in a gender neutral sense and is intended to denote a typical representative of humankind more generally. This usage is largely consistent with the usage found in Aristotle, Maimonides, and Aquinas.

2. Annas, *Morality of Happiness*, 43–44.

3. Pojman, *Ethical Theory*, 737.

4. In addition to major Jewish and Christian thinkers like Maimonides and Aquinas, Averroes is of particular note in Islam. See Taylor, "Averroes," 180–200.

5. Aristotle, *Nicomachean Ethics*. Unless otherwise noted, regular textual references will be from Aristotle, *Complete Works*, edited by Jonathan Barnes, and will be referenced in footnotes as *NE*.

On a fundamental level we see a stark contrast between man as he actually is in his raw, uncut, and otherwise untutored form, and man as he could become if he only realized his potential that is grounded in the essence of human nature. Accordingly, then, ethics is the field of thought that informs man on how to make the transition from one state to the next via practical reason. It presupposes some account of potentiality and actuality as elaborated by Aristotle: man as he is "in the raw" (human nature), and man as he may become if he understood his human *telos*, a term often translated "end," "goal," or "purpose." This teleological structure of Aristotle's view of human nature is a microcosm of his view of all of nature, which is likewise teleological.

In short, ethics informs us as to what one ought to do, ethically, if one is to attain the good life. We thus have the threefold and interrelated schema: raw and untutored human nature with attending capacities, principles of rational ethics prescribing how humans ought to live to attain the good life, and the fully developed human in the form of the good life.[6] To say what one ought to do according to this view is to say what will in fact lead to one's *eudaimonia*, one's flourishing, according to the natural kind of thing it is.

While someone may object that this is guilty of the 'is-ought' fallacy, a modernist charge, the classical and theistic picture denies the modern fact/value dichotomy according to which it is fallacious to derive an 'ought' conclusion from an 'is' premise, value from fact. This objection ignores that there are some cases where it is legitimate to do so, those cases in particular where there is a functional concept employed.

For instance, from the proposition, "This watch fails to keep time well," we can infer a value statement, "This watch is a bad watch," where we define *watch* in terms of its purpose or function. The criteria for defining a watch and for a *good* watch are similarly factual criteria. The way something is in its nature defines how it ought to function. Thus, in some instances, to call something good is to make a factual statement. And the good for man is grounded in that which is most salient about human nature wherein man functions well or good when he functions properly, the way man ought to function in order to flourish. In any case, we are simply representing the historical view.[7]

---

6. MacIntyre, *After Virtue*; Hare, *Moral Gap*.
7. Searle, "How to Derive 'Ought' from 'Is,'" 43–58.

Human Nature and Its Natural Capacities

Aristotle's ethical theory, and his overall theory of the human good, rests (in part) upon his view of human nature as such. In considering the good life, we should first want to know what sort of life it is and then inquire about the good for that sort of life. Thus, it is appropriate to consider Aristotle's metaphysical and psychological grounding for ethics.[8]

Basic to Aristotle's ontology is substance, the subject of predication (e.g., "Socrates is white," where Socrates is the subject), as discussed early on in the *Categories*. Later, after he discovered the distinction between form and matter, it became common for Aristotle to describe natural substances in hylomorphic terms.[9] That is, an individual substance is a unified matter-form composite. This is true of humans, where body is to matter what soul is to form. What makes matter what it is specifically is its form. Aristotle believed that living things have a nature, and humans have a specific nature and thus a specific form. To identify the form of something is to identify the natural kind to which it belongs (e.g., human, lion, etc.) In *Physics* II, Aristotle ties form and function together by contending that a natural organism is its form, arguing that its functional properties are the essential explanatory properties of its activity or behavior.[10] If we can discover the characteristic activity of the organism, its soul will be the power to engage in that particular activity thereby expressing certain capacities.

Aristotle begins his *Metaphysics* with, "All men by nature desire to know."[11] But what do we desire to know, and what is it that explains this desire? Man's distinct nature is a unique inner principle of change such that his overall function is to live a robust active life expressing that nature.[12] In accounting for change, Aristotle further developed the notions of matter and form, where matter is potentiality and form is actuality. This potentiality-actuality distinction is the subject of Book IX (Theta). Things have certain potentialities grounded in the sorts of things that they are, and they function best when they actualize those potentialities. He says that soul is in some sense the first actuality of a living body, whereas its second actuality

---

8. Irwin, "Metaphysical and Psychological Basis," 35–54.

9. Aristotle, *Metaphysics* VII.7–9. See also Code, "Aristotle," 411–39; "On the Origins," 101–131; Witt, "Hylomorphism in Aristotle," 673–79.

10. He goes on to describe the four causes—formal, final, efficient, and material—which are used to explain a thing.

11. Aristotle, *Metaphysics* I.1.

12. Aristotle, *On the Soul* I.1–2; II.1–1.2; III.2–4, 5, 9–13; *NE* III.1–5; VI; *On the Movement of Animals* VI–VII.

is fulfillment.[13] When observing the characteristic activities of things, we discover that the powers that constitute soul form a hierarchy. That is, various kinds of souls (e.g., nutritive, perceptual, and intellectual) form a kind of hierarchy. While any creature with reason will also have perception, and any person with perception will also possess the abilities of nutrition and reproduction, the converse does not hold. Man distinguishes himself by his ability to engage in both practical and theoretical reasoning. Aristotle describes mind (*nous*, often rendered as "intellect" or "reason") as "the part of the soul by which it knows and understands,"[14] which is thus characterized in broadly functional terms. Plainly, humans can know and understand things, and we want to know and understand things because it is in our nature.[15] Whereas possessing sensory faculties is essential to being an animal, possessing mind is essential to being a human. But beyond simply understanding, it is equally essential to the human being to plan and deliberate courses of action toward some end. Aristotle distinguishes the "practical mind" ("practical intellect" or "practical reason") from "theoretical mind" ("theoretical intellect" or "theoretical reason").[16] In all this, investigating this capacity of the soul has a special significance for him. In investigating mind, he is, in fact, investigating what makes humans human.

Humans are not born good or bad but are ethically neutral.[17] However, we can become good or bad, virtuous or vicious over time. Human nature resides in its psychic abilities, abilities which distinguish the human soul from all other species as was said previously. In *NE* I.7, Aristotle defines the human good by reference to the proper functioning of these particular human rational abilities by virtue of which humans can achieve their *telos* in ethical matters and beyond. So if one is not functioning properly so as to achieve one's *telos*, this dysfunctionality may be linked either to some defect in the original design or to, at some point along the path, impeding the actualization of one's nature and requiring an adequate remedy (to be considered in chapters 2 and 3). To know what the human good is we must first gain an understanding of the human soul.[18]

Aristotle makes arguments for *eudaimonia* being both practical and theoretical, two ways of understanding how to perfect the human soul

---

13. Aristotle, *On the Soul* II.1, 4412a27–28, b5.
14. Aristotle, *On the Soul* III.4, 429a9–10; cf. III.3, 428a5; III.9, 432b26; III.12, 434b3.
15. Aristotle, *Metaphysics* I.1, 980a21; *De Anima* II.3, 414b18; III.3, 429a6–8.
16. Aristotle, *NE* VI.8, 1143a35–b5.
17. Aristotle, *NE* II.1, 1103a23–26.
18. Aristotle, *NE* I.7, 1097b22ff; I.13, 1102a18–26.

and live the good life. He seems to end up with an ambiguous view of human nature, which accounts for dispute amongst later commentators: is the human soul composite or rational?[19] The practical or political life indicates the former while the purely theoretical life indicates the latter as it involves that most divine part of man.[20] Whether or not Aristotle resolved this point is disputable.[21] In any case, the actualization of human potential depends upon what resources are available; human nature possesses certain natural abilities and capacities—the raw materials by which man can actualize and perfect himself. Human nature has certain essential capacities, the most distinct of which is rational capacity. Man's ultimate end will be in accordance with this.

The Human *Telos* (virtue and *theoria*) and Aristotle's *Theos*

Having characterized Aristotle's view on human nature, we are now in a position to talk about the human end(s). For Aristotle, if a particular thing has good, that good is specified by its *ergon* ("work") or characteristic activity or function.[22] Not all things have an *ergon*, as indeed some have no activity. The end goal, then, is to actualize human nature and the most characteristic aspect of human nature, in particular, to the fullest.

Aristotle's *NE* begins with a discussion of *eudaimonia*, which means "happiness" or "flourishing." He argues that every human agent acts for the sake of an end, happiness; the pursuit of which lies in an activity that perfects the highest faculty in man and is directed to the highest object. He concludes that human happiness lies primarily in contemplation—contemplation of the Divine. Human agents act for the sake of some end or some good, but those ends appear to differ in practice. Book I of his *NE* begins by discussing how we define the word *good*. He first looks at how people use the word, at what things they call good, and what is common to all of them. It turns out that *good*, broadly construed, is that which all things desire, the aim of all activity whether moral or not; and whether it is really good

---

19. See the following pieces on eudaimonia in Rorty, *Essays on Aristotle's Ethics*: Nagel, "Aristotle on *Eudaimonia*," 7–14; Ackrill, "Aristotle on *Eudaimonia*," 15–34; McDowell, "Role of *Eudamonia*," 359–77.

20. Aristotle, *NE* X.7, 1177b28–29, 1178a2–4; X.8, 1178a20.

21. Thomas Nagel concludes, "It is because he is not sure who we are that Aristotle finds it difficult to say unequivocally in what our *eudaimonia* consists" (Nagel, "Aristotle on *Eudaimonia*," 8).

22. Whiting, "Aristotle's Function Argument," 33–48.

or just an apparent good becomes a critical distinction. Desire is related to good like belief is related to truth. Not all beliefs are true and not all desires are good. Our desires and beliefs should be conformed to what is good and true, respectively, but the converse does not hold. Structured in this way, desire is not simply denoting a preference but something that is *per se* desirable. It is objective rather than subjective in nature in the same way truth is objective and is to be that which our beliefs map on to.

Some things are desired for the sake of other things (e.g., medicine for health), and some for their own sake (e.g., beauty and truth). It is the latter that is central to Aristotle's concern. And these two ways of accounting for desire mark out a distinction between means and ends. In the same way that Aristotle denies an infinite regress from effect to cause,[23] so he also claims that there must be some ultimate end that is worth desiring for its own sake that motivates us to desire all the means that lead to that end. If there is some end of the things we do, desired for its own sake, then this must be the chief end or chief good. This is because if we were to do x for the sake of y, and y for the sake of z, etc., we would never do anything. If there is some one good, then knowledge of it will have a profound influence on our lives. For him, "the human good turns out to be activity of the soul in accordance with virtue, and if there are multiple virtues, then in accordance with the best and most complete" (or perfect).[24] But what is that ultimate end for the sake of which all human actions are performed? This forms a very practical question for Aristotle: "Will not the knowledge of it have a great influence on life? Shall we not, like archers who have a mark to aim at, hit upon what is right?"[25] After filtering through select candidates for what this might be, Aristotle's contention is that the ultimate end for the sake of which all things are done in human activity is *eudaimonia* or happiness, at once the ultimate "ought" or "demand" or "aim" all men seek in the attainment of human perfection, the good life.[26]

However, one should not confuse Aristotle's understanding of happiness with happiness in the modern sense. The modern sense connotes something passive, something that happens to people like good luck. While luck or fortune may well play a role in Aristotle's ultimate understanding, it has comparatively little to do with it. Happiness in our modern conception has nothing to do with how good we are; it happens by chance and is

23. For instance, he affirms a First Cause or Prime Mover for the world that moves all other things in it (including ourselves) without itself moving (like a magnet whose power to move other objects is its attraction).
24. Aristotle, *NE* I.7, 1097b22–1098a20.
25. Aristotle, *NE* I.1094a18–25.
26. Aristotle, *NE* I.4, 1095a14–30; I.7, 1097a30b6.

somewhat of a temporary, fleeting accident. But for Aristotle, happiness is dependent on how good you are, is by choice rather than chance, and is lasting rather than temporary. *Eudiamonia* expresses an objectively good and lasting state of the soul. It would not make sense to a modern person to hear someone say to them, "You think you're happy, but you're not." But it would make sense to Aristotle. *Eudaimonia* is essentially the same for everyone. This is because it is the fulfillment of our deepest desires, which in turn comes from our essential nature, which is the same for every human *qua* human. Being good, being happy, and being a fully developed human are really three ways of saying the same thing.

Now, just as every occupation of man has an end, a purpose, and a function, as does every organ in the body, so man's proper end, his ultimate end, is *vita contemplativa*. The best life constituted by *eudaimonia* is one of contemplation. Reason is the highest part of man and that which makes us distinctively human. Living according to reason, then, is the human good, which includes moral and intellectual virtues. Moral and intellectual virtues are necessary preconditions to the highest end, at least initially. Indeed, Aristotle construes virtue as the most important means to the attainment of *eudaimonia*. Humans choose their virtues, and virtue is (generally) taken to be a mean between two opposing vices, one at each extremity.

But if the good for man is "activity of soul in accordance with virtue," and if there are several virtues, which if any is the most perfect? The best for man is happiness in accordance with the best amongst the virtues. In Book X, it turns out that the best is *sophia*, or understanding that perfect happiness is the activity of contemplation. Aristotle does not make this identification in Book II because no distinction has been made yet between moral and intellectual virtues or even among intellectual ones like practical wisdom (*phronesis*) and understanding. In Book I, he claims it is a characteristic of happiness that it should be *teleion* (translated either "perfect" or "complete"). Those holding an inclusive interpretation of *eudaimonia*—including all the virtues—favor "complete," while those favoring an exclusive interpretation (focusing on a select virtue) favor "perfect." It seems most plausible to opt for the latter which is the characterization adopted here.

Aristotle explains what it is for one good to be more perfect than another (1097a30–b6) and claims that happiness is the most perfect of all perfect ends. In X.7, he takes up the discussion of happiness where Book I left off. Having shown in the first book that happiness was the exercise of virtue, he now shows which virtue it is the exercise of. The best human virtue is the best part of a human being, the speculative intellect. Hence, it is the activity of speculative intellect together with its own proper virtue, *sophia*, which constitutes true perfect happiness. It is no wonder that for Aristotle the truly happy man is the philosopher, the lover of wisdom. The person devoted to the contemplation of truth and truth alone is the happiest; but happy in a secondary sense is the person who lives in accordance with the other virtue, namely *phronesis*, which is the guide of all the moral virtues.

Again, when considering just what kind of life constitutes the best life for man, his two top contenders as juxtaposed in *NE* are (1) the practical life (the life of moral virtue), and (2) the purely theoretical or contemplative life (the life that is by nature amoral and apolitical). It is not as though the contemplative person is no longer virtuous, but simply that such is no longer the purpose nor the desire given the ultimate happy life. It is a life whose desire is the activity of that most divine part in us, not the political life. The (penultimate) virtuous life provides the stable character as provisional for the (ultimate) contemplative life, the divine life.[27]

The practical reasoning involved in the moral life is not the same as theoretical reasoning in the contemplative life. Although we are not born ethically good (even if we are metaphysically good), we can become good over time given proper actions and practical reasoning. But pure theoretical reasoning is devoid of moral calculations as such (even if in morality there is required a minimum of external goods and internal stable character). The happiest life for Aristotle is *vita contemplativa* which is the life lived in accordance with the divine. Of course, Aristotle's conception of the divine, which we ought to imitate, is not what one might expect in traditional theism. It was the highest and most perfect object of knowledge but approximating a kind of narcissistic thinking machine whose activity might be described as thinking itself thinking, utterly unconcerned with human affairs. It is an impersonal yet conscious force, apolitical and amoral, functioning for humans as a sort of final cause.

To think Aristotle's divine as personal merely because of it involving thinking does not resonate with a personal God that thinks, intends, wills, etc. Aristotle's god does not act in any volitional sense that is usually associated with persons. If he acts at all, it is active thinking itself thinking. Now, there are traces in his later writing of a more traditional view of God as personal: "If the gods pay some attention to human beings, as they seem to ... it is reasonable for them to benefit most [those most like themselves]."[28] The contemplative, described near the end of the *NE*, places no premium on the performance of good deeds as the ultimate or best life given that happiness is a function solely of contemplation, a virtual life of *theoria*.[29]

---

27. Aristotle, *NE* X.7-8, 1177b26–1178a22.
28. Aristotle, *NE* X.8, 1179a25.
29. Aristotle, *NE* X.8, 1178a9.

Whatever one's conception of the divine is will determine to the best extent possible how a human ought to imitate it/Him.

Aristotle's *theoria* seems to require theology, an intellect or mind that is actively thinking primary substance which does nothing other than thinking itself thinking as the superlative state of actuality. This ultimate object of thought (and also of desire) moves others without itself being moved. There is a sense in which this God does move or change things, but not by taking any action *per se*; rather, the god moves everything "by being loved." John Hare uses the image of "God as a magnet" to summarize the role God plays in Aristotle's ethical theory.[30]

Desire in lesser objects provides the means whereby something else can cause motion without moving itself such that an object of desire need not itself move in order to cause the motion in those that desire it. Aristotle's god is unlike a theistic God. Jonathan Lear elaborates:

> Aristotle's god is not a directing general: he does not directly intervene in the world, or in any sense create it . . . nor is he a divine engineer. He has no purposes or intentions: so the teleological organization to be found in the world cannot be the expression of divine purpose. Nevertheless, the world manifests a rational order for which God is responsible, even though he did not plan the world. . . . God is the final cause. . . . God does not intervene in the world, but the world can be conceived as an expression of desire for God. . . . Form or primary substance at its highest-level actuality simply is God. And the desire which God inspires is none other than the desire of each organism to realize its form.[31]

Clearly, this description entails that he does not providentially intervene, create, engineer, or mentally intend anything, such that the human *telos* is not one of Divine Purpose quite like that understood of the Judeo-Christian God. Aristotle's god is the ultimate or final cause, and the order of the world bears some particular relation to god. All things desire self-actualization of their form. God's thinking is somewhat like ours, and it is desirable for us to imitate for "its life is such as the best which we enjoy, and enjoy but for a short time. For it is ever in this state *which we cannot be.*"[32]

Even if not traditionally conceived, God is not only frequently mentioned but does important philosophical work in Aristotle. The Greek

---

30. Aristotle, *Metaphysics* XII.6–10; esp. XII.7, 1072b3; Hare, *God and Morality*, 15.

31. Lear, *Aristotle*.

32. Aristotle, *Metaphysics* VII, 1072b13–30 (emphasis mine). This is Aristotle's claim that we cannot always be in the state of Aristotle's god.

words *theos* ("god") and *theios* ("divine" or "godlike") occur in *NE* roughly twice as often as the words *eudaimonia* ("happiness") and *eudaimon* ("happy"). This startling statistic is ironic when we stop to think that Aristotle considers happiness the goal of our lives. God's life is the best sort of life we can enjoy, and enjoy only episodically, given our natures. This is the contemplative life at the end of *NE*, according to which man contemplates primary substance. In man satisfying his desire to know, he realizes his own essence, and in fulfilling his nature comes to imitate God by engaging in the same activity as God: contemplation. We become like God or Godlike. His god is mind, which is thinkable as is any other object since mind is an object of thought. Understanding and the object are the same. God's activity is simply thinking itself thinking.[33]

Two potential problems emerge, however: (1) This concept of *theos* could pose a motivational problem, and (2) it is forever in a state that we cannot attain or, perhaps better, durably sustain.[34] Be that as it may, prior to actualizing our intellectual perfection toward an activity of *theoria*, certain preconditions must be met. One of these preconditions is that one must attain a certain level of moral virtue provisional for the ultimate happy life whose focus is contemplative rather than active. So the truly happy man is the philosopher, the one living the contemplative life. But to attain and to sustain this is not so easy, if it is possible at all.

Ethical Theory: The Possibility of Attaining One's *Telos*

Given the potential in human nature and the human *telos*, how does one go about actualizing this to the fullest? Aristotelian ethics is, in one sense, an attempt to answer the question, what is the good life for man, and how is it to be attained? In so doing, it offers a story of how one can make the transition from untutored man in the raw to man as he can be. Given that Aristotle's man is by nature a political animal, the attainment of the good life cannot be answered for an individual, at least initially, in abstraction from society, which provides much of the context and opportunity for the attainment of the good life.

But Aristotle's interest in the *NE* is no mere academic exercise. The aim of the *NE* is to provide one a reflective understanding of how one can achieve happiness, *eudaimonia*, flourishing, by living an ethical life within society. Reflective understanding is itself of practical value. Despite the

33. Kosman, "Divine Being," 165–88; "What Does the Maker Mind Make?," 343–58.
34. Aristotle, *Metaphysics* VII.7, 1072b13–30.

intense theoretical element, the *NE* is actually very practical in nature. Its purpose is to be studied for the sake of action and actually becoming virtuous, without which the good life is unattainable. Aristotle himself says in Book II that "the purpose of our examination is not to know what virtue is but to become good since otherwise the inquiry would be of no benefit to us."[35] The *NE* is a set of lectures about the human good whose ultimate goal was to make its audience members good. By way of audience analysis, we can see that the *NE* is geared toward those who are somewhat mature and already on the path to virtue; not those men who "lack experience of the actions in life" or him who "follows his feelings" rather than his reason, but rather those who have been properly trained and brought up in fine habits.[36] Only this group will truly benefit. So the audience is narrower than one might originally suspect.

But if the experienced, rational, and well-trained are already that, what point then is there in their listening to Aristotle's lectures? What is it that Aristotle surmises that they lack? The *NE* is an attempt to transition the ripened rather than the untutored from a merely behaviorist (i.e., not yet virtuous) framework to one of genuine virtue. Already he seems to be restricting the possibility of being virtuous to a limited class of people. The treatise is concerned with the state of the soul, with the whole person, not with just the action *per se*.

His audience possesses a starting point for theoretically entering the nature of the good, a prerequisite to adequately considering the subject, but they lack the reasons upon which the virtues are based and which they have come to learn and live. Thus, his audience is composed of people who are already immersed in the form of life regarding which Aristotle wants to add deeper reflection and real understanding. His hope is to provide an account of why what the student is doing and is becoming predisposed to is, in fact, the proper thing to do. To the predisposed, it provides the reflective ground whose understanding is itself partly constitutive of the good life such that "one's understanding of the ethical life reinforces one's motivation to live it."[37] So one's reasons and motivation for the good life are not simply precursors but partly constitutive of the good life.

Of the various sorts of knowledge, this is not simply propositional knowledge, nor is it knowledge by acquaintance. It is know-how; developed skill. In contemporary terms, and with regard to the ethical life, he is attempting to move his audience from simple seeing (knowledge by acquaintance

---

35. Aristotle, *NE* II.1, 1103b26–29.
36. Aristotle, *NE* I.3, 1095a3–4; X.9, 1179b20–35.
37. Lear, *Aristotle*, 159–60.

where one is directly aware of something; say, seeing an apple in front of me or an act of justice) to know-how (a reflectively acquired skill like knowing how to utilize things for certain purposes). And this is not *mere* know-how but *genuine* know-how, where one operates on knowledge and insight that is characteristic of skilled practitioners, rather than simply having the ability to engage in correct behavior with little or no knowledge of *why* one is performing it. Such understanding has a transformative impact on one's motivational structure, thus reinforcing and solidifying the direction one is already headed in. It is thus not for skeptics or bad people, *per se*.

The ethical life cannot adequately be understood from an external perspective. Acting virtuously is not a means to a distinct end of living a happy life. Acting virtuously constitutes, at least penultimately, a happy life. And without having a personal reflective understanding of this, one cannot be said to be in a state of *eudaimonia*. This cannot be adequately understood by a nonvirtuous person or a *merely* virtuous person. From the perspective of a vicious man, for instance, a virtuous act will appear onerous and a waste of time. For the immature, perhaps it may have some appeal, but the soul will be insufficiently formed for this to be the strongest desire, and he'll feel the tension of contrary desires and will not fully understand that acting virtuously is the way to be happy (which is why Aristotle did not want the young attending his lectures, whether young in years or in character).[38]

The argument for the good life in the *NE* is internal to the audience as the lectures are intended to reinforce reflectively the lives they are already inclined to lead. It is geared for those who are already on the path, the way, of the good life. One comes to understand (and thus fulfills the desire to understand) the nature of the good life and thus reinforces one's motivation to live it. The audience thus possesses both habituated actions in accordance with virtue and reliable beliefs about *eudaimonia*.

For Aristotle, the possession of virtues is a necessary precondition to *eudaimonia*. But what is a virtue? An ethical virtue is a condition that is intermediate (e.g., courage) between two other states, one involving excess (e.g., foolishness), and the other deficiency (e.g., cowardice).[39] He describes an ethical virtue as a *hexis* (a "state" or "disposition")—a tendency or disposition, brought on and induced by our habits—to have appropriate feelings.[40] Virtues are excellences (*arête*); they are states or dispositions of the soul which enable a person to live an excellent life, to fulfill one's *telos*. And not unimportant for living the good life, they are stable states that enable

---

38. Aristotle, *NE* I.3, 1095a2–11.
39. Aristotle, *NE* II.6, 1106a26–b28.
40. Aristotle, *NE* II.5, 1105b25–26.

one to make the right decision to act in the appropriate circumstances and that motivate one so to act.

Aristotle describes virtue as a state "which makes a man good and which makes him do his own work well."[41] This stability of character is a precondition to the contemplative life. It is the stability of soul that constitutes character because one's character has somewhat organized one's desire and thus motivates one to act via that properly ordered desire, a deliberative desire, sometimes translated as "desiring mind or thoughtful desire."[42] It is not, therefore, some mere emotional state. Desires, as understood by Aristotle, are impregnated with reason. The ethical virtues are not in us by nature, but are brought about by habit via repetitive action, where *actus* forms *habitus*. They are states acquired by doing the acts that one would do if one already had the state such that "states arise out of like activities." We become just by doing just acts, as it were. He says, "It makes no small difference, then, whether we form habits of one kind or of another from our very youth; it makes a very great difference, or rather all the difference."[43]

This explains why Aristotle's lectures were of little use to anyone not already brought up well; excellence arises from habit rather than from lectures. Given that ethics is not an exact science for Aristotle, and so there are not any rules for how a virtuous person should act,[44] we rely on habit as a mode of educating a person to virtue. Habits instill dispositions; more important, circumstantially sensitive dispositions. A person who is already courageous will have little need for rules as he'll be sensitively motivated. Habits organize the soul's desires well such that the virtuous life itself becomes desirable and pleasurable. For instance, a child who does not consider spinach to be good *to* her even though it is good *for* her must cultivate the taste so that what is good *for* her also becomes good *to* her. Aristotle says that "the man who does not rejoice in noble actions is not even good; since no one would call a man just who did not enjoy acting justly."[45] The virtuous person has a harmonious soul. The virtues are pleasant in themselves and become what we call "second nature" to this person. They are in themselves desirable, and the virtuous person organizes his desire so as to naturally desire that which is *genuinely* desirable, hence becoming the *genuinely* virtuous person. It is this reorganizing of our desire that constitutes the task of moral education

---

41. Aristotle, *NE* II.6, 1106a14–24.
42. Aristotle, *NE* VI.2, 1139b3; II.5, 1106a3. See also Lear, *Aristotle*, 165.
43. Aristotle, *NE* II.1, 1103b14–15.
44. Aristotle, *NE* I.3, 1094b11–27.
45. Aristotle, *NE* I.8, 1099a7–23.

by which we find the objectively good life *for* us to be subjectively good *to* us; living the good life becomes pleasant.

Importantly, for Aristotle, a man may act in accordance with a virtue without acting virtuously. That is, an act that *appears* virtuous on the surface is not *really* virtuous. This denotes the *mere* versus *genuine* distinction alluded to earlier. While it may appear objectionable at first glance, this two-tiered notion of virtue is very pronounced in Aristotle and will make a similar and significant appearance in both Maimonides and Aquinas. Someone may perform what we might call a merely virtuous act (which, to Aristotle, is not a virtuous act after all) rather than a genuinely virtuous act. A merely virtuous act will not consist in the things a fully or genuinely virtuous act will as performed by a fully or genuinely virtuous person. That is, it will lack or suffer the privation of certain necessary features for a genuinely virtuous act. To be a virtuous person is not simply to act in accord with a virtue or set of virtues. That is, it is not to be merely virtuous. Rather, it is to be genuinely or fully virtuous.[46] A comparison might help us understand the mere versus fully or genuine distinction.

Consider a stone. It possesses the requisite essential properties for being a physical object (e.g., spatiotemporal location, mass, etc.). Now consider a dog. It possesses all the essential properties for being a physical object as well. It is *fully* physical. But it is not *merely* physical because it has animate properties as well. The stone is *merely* physical as well as *fully* physical.

Then take a human being. While being fully physical, he is not merely physical as he also has organic and animate properties. So he is fully animate, but, unlike the dog, he is not merely animate given his rational, moral and aesthetic qualities, which mere organic entities lack. He is merely human as well as fully human. To be fully human means to fully exemplify human nature. To be merely human is not to exemplify a kind nature distinct from that of humanity. It is to exemplify humanity without also exemplifying a higher ontological kind of nature, such as divinity. It is this rationale some have used to claim the coherence of the idea that Jesus Christ of Nazareth was both fully (rather than merely) human and fully divine. Thomas Morris uses a similar distinction to explicate the two natures of Christ. Had he been *merely* human, he could not have also been *fully* divine. Those human properties logically incompatible with divine incarnation (e.g., coming into existence, contingency, etc.) would be at most essential to being *merely*

---

46. Julia Annas uses similar terminology to denote the fully virtuous person and the merely encratic person in Annas, *Morality of Happiness*, 369.

human, common to humans, but not essential to being *fully* human. The Christian claim is not that Christ is *merely* human.[47]

Now, instead of a stone, a dog, a mere human, and a fully human being, consider a human act, a proper human act, a merely virtuous human act, and a fully virtuous human act. For a human act consider blinking. It is an act done by a human, but is not properly so called because it is done involuntarily. It is a mere human act. A similar act known as winking is now a proper and fully human act because it is done voluntarily rather than involuntarily. But not all human acts are virtuous human acts (e.g., the act of simply looking at a tree is a fully human act but it lacks the property of virtuosity, that property exemplifying the nature of a virtue or multiple virtues). There are human acts that exemplify a virtue(s) and, as such, are virtuous acts. But they are not fully virtuous human acts. Rather, they are merely virtuous human acts; acts done, as Aristotle would say, "in accordance with virtue." Aristotle would not necessarily say that a person acting in accordance with justice is vicious, but neither would he necessarily say that such a person (or his attending act) was genuinely or fully virtuous. Merely virtuous acts are not identical to fully or genuinely virtuous acts. In order to be a fully or genuinely virtuous human act, it must be done by a genuinely or fully virtuous person for the right reasons and in the right circumstances. He is unified in motivation and deliberation.

As ethical beings, we begin with the potential to act or actualize some otherwise putatively virtuous act, but only upon fulfilling certain conditions over time can one's first acts bring one into a position of being in a second potential state so as to act genuinely virtuous and to fulfill one's second actuality. Aristotle affirms three conditions for acting genuinely or fully virtuous versus merely virtuous. For the former, the agent must have (1) practical knowledge (not just first actuality done in accordance with, say, justice) of what the right act would be in particular circumstances, (2) the act must be chosen and for its own sake (choose justice in these circumstances simply because it is the thing to do), and (3) the act, a case of second actuality, must flow from a firm or stable character (e.g., a character of justice). Now, these conditions are not isolated. Since ethics is not a precise science with rules governing action, the only way to determine how to act in a situation is to ask how the virtuous man would act, thus the importance for the role of modeling.

The practical knowledge found in the virtuous man is his *phronesis*. Aristotle is clear that philosophical wisdom (*sophia*), which is knowledge (*episteme*) plus comprehension (*nous*), is a higher form of knowledge than

---

47. Morris, *Logic of God Incarnate*, 55–56.

practical wisdom (*phronesis*).⁴⁸ Nonetheless, and of particular importance at this stage of moving toward human perfection, he considers *sophia* useless for human concerns and things about which it is possible to deliberate.⁴⁹ Thus, practical and philosophical wisdom seem to be two discrete types of life (*vita activa* and *vita contemplativa*), which may pose a problem for Aristotle later on. For now, practical mind is a motive force for humans, the highest state of which is *phronesis*. This is a developed ability to judge good and bad ends and to deliberately choose acts appropriate to securing those ends in particular circumstances.⁵⁰ But such acts themselves are not just means, but are partly constitutive of the good life.

The importance of *phronesis* is such that one cannot advance from the moral or political life to the contemplative or philosophical life without it. Aristotle distinguishes between intellectual and moral virtues. Man is at his best when he exercises to his best his most distinct feature, the mind (i.e., in knowing truth). The dispositions of the mind that enable one to know truth are called intellectual virtues which are contrasted with moral virtues, the dispositions of our emotions, which enable us to correctly respond to practical situations. The rational and emotional sides of us are different aspects of our nature, and their virtues do not overlap except in one case: *phronesis* (sometimes translated "prudence" or "practical wisdom"). It is the function of *phronesis* to help us know the correct way to behave. It is not itself a moral virtue but is closely connected.

Three of the intellectual virtues (knowledge, comprehension, and wisdom) concern facts about the world that we cannot change. The two others (*phronesis* and skill) concern things that we can change. Aristotle defines *phronesis* as "a state of grasping the truth, involving reason, and concerned with action about human goods," or as sometimes translated, "a true and reasoned state or capacity to act with regard to the things that are good or bad for man."⁵¹ It is the state of the fully developed virtuous person. It is the appreciation of what is good and bad for us at the highest level combined with a correct understanding of the facts of experience—the skill to draw correct inferences regarding how and when to apply our general moral knowledge to a particular situation quickly and reliably. If we possessed this quality, we would always act in the right ways, and we would have success. But since the virtues are those dispositions which, if possessed, make one do what is right, what is the point of having *phronesis*? It is so that we can avoid

48. For sorting out these various notions, see Reeve, *Practices of Reason*.
49. Aristotle, *NE* VI.7, 1141a20–b9.
50. Aristotle, *NE* VI.5.
51. Hutchinson, "Ethics," 205–8. See Aristotle, *NE* 1140a24–b21.

being morally clumsy. Although a virtue will provide us with the correct objective, without *phronesis* one still lacks the intellectual ability to know the correct steps to take in order to reach it. Aristotle holds that the virtues differ from each other because they involve different emotions. Also, if a man has one virtue, perhaps he has all of them. This is because if he has one fully developed virtue, then he will have practical wisdom. But if he has practical wisdom, then perhaps he has all of the virtues.

The *NE* thus provides the precise tools for the properly predisposed person to be fully or genuinely virtuous and to possess the master virtue, *phronesis*. The proper philosophical reflection thus serves the purposes of internally motivating and sustaining the good life at this stage. His is an ethical system based firmly in the study of human motivation since ethics was grounded in the study of human desire and the satisfaction of that desire. The point of *NE* is not to persuade us to be good or how to behave well, but is to give people who are already living a life in accordance with virtue a reasonable understanding and motivation to persist in living the kind of life they've come to understand, such that they move from being merely virtuous to genuinely or fully virtuous.

It is important to note, however, that the development of the virtues is similar to the development of the vices (the extremes of the virtues). Aristotle claims that (most of) the virtues are dispositions lying in a mean. While the capacity for virtue (as well as vice) is innate, the virtues (and vices) themselves must be acquired voluntarily, and their attainment is a precondition, though intrinsically valuable, to ultimate human perfection.[52]

Stability of character is ideal for Aristotle, such that one performs virtuous acts only when one knows the acts are virtuous, deliberately chooses them for themselves, and does so from a settled state.[53] Thus, we can say that for Aristotle, *an act is a genuinely virtuous act if and only if (1) one knowingly and deliberately chooses a virtuous act, (2) for its own sake, and (3) stemming from a settled state of virtue*. Vicious acts are similarly defined, except that the one performing such an act does not think they are doing vicious acts because they are mistaken. Obviously, it takes time to actualize the settled states. But this is important for perfectionism since the attainment of one's *telos* is normally self-sustaining as one finds her activity via "second nature" to be naturally pleasing and therefore worthy of continuing. The stability and duration of happiness depends on the stability of one's virtuous character (likewise for vicious character in terms of sustaining that mode of life).

---

52. Urmson, "Aristotle's Doctrine," 223–30.
53. Aristotle, *NE* II.4, 1105a30–33.

An agent's settled, sound conceptions of what is good are what enables her to see the practical world.

In *NE* VII, Aristotle lays out six moral states: superhuman virtue, virtue, continence, incontinence, vice, and brutishness.[54] These form contrasting pairs. From the states of virtue and vice come corresponding actions without internal conflict in the agent, except that the vicious person's view of the good is delusional. The continent and incontinent know the good as does the virtuous person, but, unlike the virtuous person, both struggle to do the good, consequentially being either successful (the continent person) or unsuccessful (the incontinent person) in their struggle with the passions. The virtuous person sizes up the particular situation, feels appropriately, and freely acts from a firm disposition. Both the brutish and superhuman are scarcely mentioned in the *NE*. The superhuman example seems to be a hyperbolic character briefly characterized by Aristotle as Homer's Hector, and the brute is found largely amongst non-Greeks, people who live by sensation alone.[55] The other four moral states (virtue, vice, continent, and incontinent) have similar starting points in that they are rational dispositions developed by rational agents. Even though vice is delusional about the good, the vicious person still has a view about the good. Not so the brute who lives by sensation alone like a beast and, by contrast, the superhuman who lives by reason alone.

Aristotle's moral realm seems virtually exhausted by the four positions. Yet near the end of the *NE* men are urged to transcend their nature by contemplating as much as possible. So here in Book VII divine heroic activity is the goal of practical excellence. So we are again asked to consider heroic virtue of a superhuman sort, which brings us back to *theos* ("god").

The Aristotelian *theos* functions as a magnet, drawing us toward the best human life which is also the life closest to the divine. Hence, the ultimate teleological connection in Aristotle is a theological connection. Aristotle says that God moves everything "by being loved."[56] His God is the prime mover, who moves other things (by being loved by them) but is without motion in the divine activity itself which consists in contemplation, which in turn is also how we most imitate God. While contemplation is central to the good life, Aristotle refers to theological premises in regard to ethical (as well as intellectual) virtues. He says that the good of an individual is a desirable thing, but the good of a city is greater and a more complete thing to obtain and preserve, because "what is good for a people

---

54. Wiggins, "Weakness of Will," 241–66.
55. Aristotle, *NE* VII.1, 1145a20–32; VII.5, 1149a10.
56. See Aristotle, *Metaphysics* XII.7, 1072b3.

or for cities is nobler and more godlike."[57] Interestingly, Aristotle ends the *Eudemian Ethics* (EE) by saying,

> For god is not an imperative ruler, but is the end with a view to which wisdom issues its commands . . . for god needs nothing. What choice, then, or possession of natural goods—whether bodily goods, wealth, friends, or other things—will most produce the contemplation of god, that choice or possession is best; this is the noblest standard. But any that through deficiency or excess hinders one from the contemplation and service of god is bad.[58]

So the penultimate life of stable, virtuous character is a prerequisite to the ultimate good life. While detailed analysis lies outside the scope of this book, it should be repeated that by the mere fact that notions like "God" and "divinity" are used in the Aristotelian corpus, we certainly should not assume that the same notions are in play as those found in the Abrahamic faiths, which will be important to consider in Maimonides's and Aquinas's treatment of the good life.[59] My point is that theological premises are significant in his system. The best life is in accordance with virtue, and this means being as much like God or the gods as possible (i.e., acting divinely in keeping with the divine element in us). Aristotle says:

> But we must not follow those who advise us, being men, to think of human things, and, being mortal, of mortal things, but must, so far as we can, make ourselves immortal, and strain every nerve to live in accordance with the best thing in us . . . that which is proper to each thing is by nature best and most pleasant for each thing; for man, therefore, the life according to intellect is best and pleasantest, since intellect more than anything else is man. This life therefore is also the happiest.[60]

If we omitted the theological premises in this system, we would be missing the power within our lives of an attraction toward a kind of life that is not merely human (i.e., the divine element). And we would be missing the divine life toward which we are attracted on the first picture, a life that is foundational to the way the whole universe is ordered, so that when we live in a way consistent with this attraction we are mirroring in our own lives the order of the cosmos. Without the theological component in

---

57. Aristotle, *NE* I.2, 1094b10.
58. Aristotle, *EE* 1249b13–20.
59. Wolfson, "Knowability and Describability of God," 98–114.
60. Aristotle, *NE* X.8, 1177b30–1178a1.

Aristotle (an essential element in his teleology and psychology), we will lose this harmony.

So to sum up, we can say that man, according to his nature, has a high *telos*; indeed, it is to imitate God or the gods like only man can do given his nature and capacities. But one must first become *genuinely* virtuous, possessing *phronesis*, before living the contemplative life. But how realistic this is becomes a serious question or problem to which we now turn.

Problems in Attaining the Prize

We are now at the point where we can discuss the *aporia(s)* or problems in Aristotle's system. The impasse emerges between what seems to be the good life attainable and yet not so attainable on the Aristotelian account. There are those who fail along the way to attain the end for the sake of which their natures are otherwise inclined. Man has a particular *telos* grounded in his nature. It is the *telos* of man, *qua* man, that determines which human qualities are virtues. Virtues are required for the attainment of moral perfection, a prerequisite for intellectual perfection. In Aristotle's system, his *theos* is both the source of the moral (and metaphysical) "demand" (the divine kind of life according to which we ought to strive) and, in some respects, the enabler to reach that goal as the supreme object of desire. All people are naturally inclined according to their human nature toward the good life, the sort of life lived by the gods. Yet for most (if not all) it seems to be a sham. While we are designed or naturally inclined according to our natures toward a certain *telos*, actualizing such an end seems constantly, if not perpetually, elusive. While the potentialities present in human nature seem to suggest that we can be all we can be, *qua* man, something required for this to transpire seems to be missing. It seems that our natural capacities in and of themselves are inadequate to bridge the gap between them and the teleological demand such that the good life is perhaps beyond our grasp. Our natures incline us but do not adequately supply us for such a high aspiration. The teleological demand is simply too high for the good life such that most will never and can never obtain it. At the outset, the gap makes the good life elusive for most. This is so for both internal and external reasons.

Externally, most are not even in the range of qualification for candidacy simply on account of their lacking certain external goods. Aristotle's distinction between the elite and the masses alludes to this in some respect, giving the impression that the end of man is only seriously possible for a member of the elite Aristocratic class. For example, according to Aristotle, slaves can never possess reason but can only apprehend it as in participating in that which is owned by another, inasmuch as a slave is owned by a master and can participate in that which belongs to the master. Curiously, slaves are what they are by "nature." In other words, slavery is suited to the nature of certain men.[61]

More generally, few people seem to be internally (let alone externally) endowed for the effective transition from man as he is by nature, to man as he could become if he realized or actualized his *telos*. There is a minimal requirement one must have without which it spells "the end" for the *end* (*telos*). Below we will observe with more detail the external and internal reasons for why this large class of people is precluded from the good life.

Internal Disqualifications

The ultimate good life is contemplation of the divine, which requires theoretical virtues. Yet not all meet the conditions of moral perfection, a prerequisite for intellectual perfection. Recall that along the spectrum of the most common types of people are the virtuous, the continent, the incontinent, and the vicious (hero and brute are uncommon). The continent person has sound conceptions of the good, but he experiences internal struggles with his passions, which make it difficult to consistently satisfy those conceptions. Similarly, the incontinent man has sound conceptions, and he too struggles, but he often fails. The vicious person, by contrast, has unsound conceptions but often does not know it. If this should be revealed, given the fixity of character, it is difficult or even impossible for such an individual to extricate himself and so reform. Aristotle admits that some agents become "ethically disabled,"[62] as it were, but are nonetheless still culpable for their disability given the role voluntariness plays in becoming a settled agent. For the most part, Aristotle held that people are responsible for their actions and have substantial responsibility for their character. But we do not have fine-grained control over the precise ways in which our actions affect our dispositions. We do not know, for instance, how many lies it takes to become a liar. We do not know how many times one must act a certain way before developing a good or bad habit and formed character, and thus establish a virtue or vice. In the case of vice, at some point it also corrupts our judgment and our perception of good. Aristotle says,

---

61. Aristotle, *Politics* 1254b20–36; Brunt, "Aristotle and Slavery."
62. Jacobs, "Aristotle and Maimonides," 145–64; "Taking Ethical Disability Seriously," 141–58.

Actions and states, however, are not voluntary in the same way. For we are in control of our actions from the beginning to the end, when we know the particulars. With states, however, we are in control of the beginning, but do not know, any more than with sicknesses, what the cumulative effect of particular actions will be. Nonetheless, since it was up to us to exercise a capacity this way or another way, states are voluntary.[63]

In this regard, Jonathan Jacobs argues that, although it is voluntary, given Aristotelian character formation and corresponding modification of judgment, vicious agents can get to a point where, like virtuous agents, character is fixed, stable, and unchanging. Thus, a significant number of rationally responsible agents will become far too ethically disabled to extricate themselves from their situation and respond appropriately to what is ethically required or demanded in order to satisfy genuine virtue (e.g., to genuinely do justice). Not all ethical considerations available are necessarily accessible as live options for agents.[64]

Ethical requirements are objective in Aristotle, but are not always or equally accessible given certain character states. Aristotle says of what is genuinely good that it "is apparent only to the good person; for vice perverts us and produces false views about the origins of actions," and "in all such cases what is really so is what appears so to the excellent person."[65] This is not some sort of ethical relativism; rather it underscores that there is an objective perspective, but also that very few are so privileged to occupy it. Only Aristotle's *phronimos*, the individual possessing practical wisdom, has the know-how, like a wine connoisseur who has acquired or developed the ability to detect genuinely good wine. It is the master ethical virtue *phronesis* that supplies direction to the virtues of character, a precondition to ultimate human perfection. It is *phronesis* that unites the virtues since they need to be informed by a true grasp of what is good in order to be genuine virtues of character.[66] *Phronesis* is allegedly that which makes ethical requirements, or the demands of normative activity, truly accessible. Pre-rational habituation by repetitive action modeled on moral exemplars serves to modify character.

While not knowing where along the spectrum of repeated activity that habit or settled character becomes established, it nonetheless makes a causal difference *that* it becomes established. As self-moved movers, we control voluntary actions that make a difference to our settled states of character,

---

63. Aristotle, *NE* III.5, 1114b30–1115a3.
64. Jacobs, *Law, Reason, and Morality*, 45–46; "Some Tensions," 221–44.
65. Aristotle, *NE* VI.12, 1144a35; X.5, 1176a16–19.
66. Aristotle, *NE* VI.13, 1144b25–1145a5.

even when we may not intend to bring about particular states. Without necessarily intending it, one can come voluntarily to lead an unhappy life. As character develops and matures, it typically becomes fixed and difficult (or impossible) to change. Even if the vicious man were somehow to be motivated to aspire toward virtue, it is not clear in Aristotle that he would even know how to do so unaided, or even aided, given that particular actions guiding considerations become framed with respect to one's maturing character, shaping one's ability or disability to *see* what is really good. If the Aristotelian conception of virtue theory is correct, and a naturalistic conception of anthropology is adopted, then it may be true that unaided humans are susceptible to ethical disability. The natural resources of human reason and volition do not seem to make plausible provision for moving one from a vicious state to a virtuous state on their own. This opens the door to consider a theistic conception (including revelation and a concomitant conception of human willpower in repentance) for the possibility of ethically significant modification of character. Hence, the importance of a Maimonidean or Thomistic overhaul of the Aristotelian schema.

Jonathan Jacobs makes this suggestion: If something like Aristotelian naturalism is the correct view of unaided human agency, then it may be true that without grace, either in the form of revealed law (and the human capacity to repent effectively) or in the form of infused virtue (for example, in the Thomistic view) human beings are susceptible to ethical disability. It would be unreasonable to expect those whose cognitive and motivational alienation from ethical requirements is quite fixed to change or be changed in the direction of virtue.[67]

The more robust theistic meta-ethical requirement makes provision for human volition to respond effectively by faith and repentance in light of God's gift of aid or grace, without which the horizon of human perfection may, for most if not all, be hopelessly beyond reach. Given our nature and our *telos*, the story of achieving the *telos* is significantly hampered for many based on Aristotelian fixity of mature character. The possibility for ethical perfection seems a long shot for most on this account. One needs to be virtuous, rather than continent, incontinent, or vicious. Further, the elusiveness of the good life for most on Aristotle's account applied well before considerations of ethical disability (a resulting fixity of vicious character consequent on past action). This is because the majority of humans are constrained by matters beyond their control (e.g., slaves, women, children, and barbarians, etc.), making the good life a gentlemen's club for the elite as we will see next.

---

67. Jacobs, "Aristotle and Maimonides," 145–64.

External Disqualifications

Aside from virtue or vice, not all qualify for the prize given contingency, accident, circumstances, or "moral luck."[68] For Aristotle, external goods are required for the good life. Even a "well-endowed slave," assuming there was such in Aristotle, may be out of luck despite his potential. Aristotle says that "happiness evidently also needs external goods to be added, as we said, since we cannot, or cannot easily, do fine actions if we lack the resources."[69] Some external goods enable the excellent political life (e.g., good birth, good children, beauty, or other good fortune). Without such external goods, the aim of moral perfection is virtually eliminated. According to Aristotle, certain virtues are available *only* to those of great riches and high social status (i.e., the aristocratic gentleman); there are virtues which are unavailable to the slave, which in Aristotle's day constituted a significant portion of the population. Worse yet, even if he is not a slave, there are still some virtues unavailable to the poor man. And those are, on Aristotle's view, centrally important virtues to human life (e.g., magnanimity and munificence).[70]

Many actions we perform require, for example, friendship, wealth, and political power as instruments. And any deprivation of things like good birth, good children or beauty, detracts from our happiness. Being born in an impoverished state or childless or in a lacking social state, all of which are often products of circumstance, often render the good life off-limits or nearly so. Fate plays a role here in Greek thought. Aristotle is forced to ask whether happiness is the result of some divine fate, fortune, or luck.[71] He admits that if the gods give any gift at all to human beings, it is reasonable for them to give us happiness more than any other human good insofar as it is the best of human goods. Happiness is "one of the most divine things." We need a certain amount (an amount Aristotle never defines) of fortune or external goods, in order for happiness to obtain. Because happiness cannot obtain without obtaining moral perfection, and the latter cannot obtain without prerequisite external goods—the things most people in Aristotle's world would then be lacking—happiness at the outset is scarcely attainable by the majority. Its seems, then, that happiness relies a bit on a matter of luck or chance circumstance, things that are out of one's control.[72]

---

68. Williams, *Moral Luck*, 20–39; Nussbaum, *Fragility of Goodness*, 1–8, 322–30.

69. Aristotle, *NE* I.8, 1099a30–b10; Cooper, "Aristotle on the Goods of Fortune," 173–96.

70. Horner, "What It Takes to Be Great," 415–44.

71. Aristotle, *NE* I.9, 1099b11.

72. Ten Elshof, "Problem of Moral Luck," 139–52.

The thought that while certain things seem obligatory for all (e.g., moral goodness), their attainment might be possible only for the few favored by fortune, is strikingly scandalous by measures of contemporary sentiment.[73] For that which is universally obligatory seems to require that it be within our power to do. It should not be so dependent on contingency or, as someone has said, available only to "those with special skills, or kindly feelings, or exceptional intelligence, or luck in other ways."[74] If nature determines normativity, and if most humans are precluded, do we negate their humanity? It therefore seems that some features relative to normativity are lacking in Aristotle. As a normative theory, this creates potentially systemic problems.

Each being has its natural *telos*, its own perfection. For Aristotle, what ought to be the case—normatively speaking—is grounded on the natural tendency and potentiality to flourish. As humans, we naturally desire our *telos,* and fulfillment of it rewards us with happiness. For humans who do not attain the good life, given their great potential, this amounts either to tragedy (someone with greatness who experiences an event or entire life that ends in despair due to some character flaw or limiting circumstance or fate) or is due to the fact that they never had the potential in the first place. Such are, perhaps, a good number of people (women, slaves, poor) in Aristotle's system.

But if they cannot live the virtuous life, are we to believe that they are incapable of justice, wisdom, courage, and temperance? Can we find them ethically culpable since they, the masses perhaps, can only be all that they can be and what that precludes is being virtuous? Alas, in the nonhuman world, tadpoles have a certain *telos* to become fully developed frogs and yet not all become frogs. But we do not blame them in the same way we would blame a human for being unjust since we assume some ability exists that comes along with the demand of humans acting justly. We need to be careful not to import deontology into Aristotle's teleology, but it does seem that there is within his normative ethical system, where nature determines normativity, some measure of "obligation," even if it is not the same as that in typical deontological ethics. This is what John Hare refers to as the moral gap.[75]

Furthermore, as Aristotle makes clear, ultimate happiness requires both complete virtue and a complete life. That is to say, even assuming the requisite external goods and that one has obtained the moral excellences, such a good

---

73. Equally scandalous, perhaps, might be considerations about the lack of universal availability of Torah in Maimonides and views of total depravity or certain views of election in Aquinas.

74. Casey, *Pagan Virtue*, 202.

75. Hare, *Moral Gap*; *Why Bother Being Good*; *God and Morality*.

is fragile and susceptible to being lost. Even though many events happen by chance, small things do not weigh in favor or disfavor much, but a multitude of them could make life good or bad, making happiness vulnerable. The virtuous person's happiness is unstable (despite his otherwise stable character) and vulnerable to circumstance of misfortune throughout his life (e.g., the tragedy of King Priam of Troy), such that if one experiences misfortune to a certain degree, no one calls that person happy. Even beyond death, one's status as a happy person is disputable if his legacy is to a certain extent out of his control given what sorts of lives his posterity live and whether this brings honor or dishonor on the dead and otherwise virtuous man. Nonetheless, virtuous activity, activity in one's control, is the best possible means of securing what is ultimately not securable, happiness. This constitutes part of the tragic nature of Aristotle's theory on the good life.

So moral virtue is vulnerable to circumstance or accident in Aristotle. Yet, it seems intuitively plausible to most of us that from a human perspective we should not judge a person morally for what lies beyond his control. If he fails to do right because of unavoidable ignorance, or external constraint, or because of unforeseeable events that produce disaster, we do not normally assign culpability to him as a bad man. We might go so far as to say that someone's lack of intelligence, right feelings, or imagination cannot be relevant to the moral worth of his actions or to him as an agent. Since morality is obligatory on all, the demand of normative activity, it would be a kind of scandal if only some were sufficiently lucky. But this egalitarian principle that moral goodness is accessible to all and is invulnerable to circumstances outside our control is not agreeable with Aristotle. For him, such a moral demand, while obligatory on all, is not really accessible to all. It seems to be misguided on the Aristotelian account to talk of the good life for man, when it is really only appropriately geared for the *aristocratic* man.

There is an evident inadequacy in Aristotle's account to bridge for the masses the potential in human nature with the human *telos*. For not all are favored by fortune, and even if they are there is no guarantee of retaining it even when one has done her moral and epistemic best. So for human perfection in Aristotle (i.e., the good life); to obtain, one must possess a minimum of external goods, be a virtuous person, and somehow retain all of this after death. This is not very good news for the prospect of obtaining the good life.

Recall Aristotle canvassing the candidates for what might constitute *eudaimonia* (pleasure, honor, esteem, wealth, and moral virtue itself). Variously, all of these are too base, too instrumental, or too dependent on an external source to be viable. Aristotle claims each of these plays a role, but by itself none is sufficient to guarantee it. Each is necessary, to the point that he says happiness requires external goods such as wealth, good birth, physical beauty, without which the final goal is impossible to attain and one is rendered an outcast. Aristotle's position forces him into a dilemma. Either happiness is something within our control (like moral virtue) and not easily lost, or it is outside of our control and at least partially dependent upon luck and fortune. For the former, external goods and moral luck play little or no role, but for the latter it seems quite dependent upon luck and good fortune. So either the good life is attainable and sustainable purely by our own efforts or it is not (e.g., King Priam of Troy). Human life is ultimately tragic for Aristotle because of the interwoven contingency, even for the best of men. For him, happiness requires external goods and is consequent upon good fortune, rendering happiness; on the one hand, within our control and, on the other hand, greatly beyond our control. Contingency is woven into happiness to the extent that misfortune and moral luck are ever present, making the good life tragically fragile indeed.[76] The seemingly ineliminable element of tragedy in Aristotle's account seems unmatched in Maimonides and Aquinas.

A Way through for the Virtuous: "The Few, the Proud"

In the United States Armed Forces, the elite fighting force is the Marines. As opposed to the slogan of the United States Army—"Be all you can be"—the Marines have as a slogan, "The Few, the Proud, the Marines." For Aristotle, who can "be all you can be"? Who can attain a durably good life? Given the multifaceted problem that the good life is off limits to most, even though it seems strongly tied to the nature of things, there does seem to be a narrow way through for "the Few, the Proud."

In Aristotle's *NE*, he describes the *megalopsychos*, the "proud man." There are those to whom honor is due, those who have run the race with pride. Aristotle affirms the virtue of pride (*megalopsychia*, "great-souledness") as a mean between two vices or errors—vanity and humility.[77] The *megalopsychos*, according to Aristotle, deems himself worthy of great things and is so. Thus, he is justly deserving of honor by others. While the vain man deems himself worthy, he is not. And the humble man, while worthy, sadly does not deem himself such. Thus, he is both ignorant and unjust to himself (since he fails to claim his rightful due), which is why he is in error. So honor is the prize, not the goal, of virtue, such that pride is the "crown" of

76. Nussbaum, *Fragility of Goodness*, 318–42.
77. Aristotle, *NE* IV, 1125a19.

the virtues. It is a second-order virtue supervening, as it were, upon a fully virtuous person. Attaining this is not easy and is impossible without nobility and goodness of character.[78]

The proud man disdains some men. Take, for example, the merely wealthy men who base their honor on their wealth rather than on virtue, and commoners who because of lack of wealth cannot partake of virtuous action. Of them, Aristotle says that one ought "to be dignified toward people who enjoy high position and good fortune, but unassuming toward those of the middle class; for it is a difficult and lofty thing to be superior to the former, but easy to be so to the latter."[79] It is not surprising, then, that it is a cardinal sin for the proud aristocrat—the *megalopsychos*, the *phronimos* man upon whom Aristotle's ethical theory is based, the paradigm of the virtuous man—to show dignity to the commoner. To be sure, it is not that he is necessarily pompous, but that he is simply claiming his due, according to Aristotle. If the proud man is the mean, then at the extremes are the vain man and the humble man. Aristotle holds that the just prize of virtue is honor, and he should be honored. If pride were of little importance, then humility would not be a vice.[80] Not only does Aristotle's proud man seem scandalous to common sentiment, but one wonders how such a cold, self-sufficient, self-regarding deliberator can be ethically good, let alone provide an ideal for others. And, of course, it is not one of the common but the uncommon who attains this. But even if such a person were admirable, he would still be a notable example of moral luck whose final estate rests in part on that good fortune to be able to act in a grandiose scale worthy of honor.

As heirs of a western, Augustinian, tradition where pride, egotistically understood, is near the center of everything deplorable, we should understand both that Aristotle's notion of a proud man and our contemporary notion of it are not identical and yet there is still a basis for finding objectionable elements (some to be discussed later in relation to both Maimonides and Aquinas). Even Aquinas has an innocent, nonpejorative, notion of pride that he discusses. In commenting on two kinds of pride, Aquinas says, "Hence a gloss of Jerome on the same passage (Isa 61:6) says that 'there is a good and an evil pride'; or 'a sinful pride which God resists, and a pride that denotes the glory which He bestows.'"[81]

While Aquinas says that humility is not necessarily opposed to magnanimity, under right reason, it would be questionable whether Aristotle's

78. Aristotle, *NE* IV, 1124a1–10.
79. Aristotle, *NE* IV, 1124b19–21.
80. Frank, "Humility as a Virtue," 89–99.
81. Aquinas, *ST* II-II.162.1.

notion functions in such a manner as right reason. Aquinas says, "But humility, considered as a special virtue, regards chiefly the subjection of man to God, for Whose sake he humbles himself by subjecting himself to others." Aristotle's *phronimos* does not seem to be one to subject himself to all others in humility. The honor that is seemingly right and due to the *phronimos* is misplaced from a Maimonidean and Thomistic perspective, as we will see when it comes to the virtues of faith and humility.

Let us take stock one last time. We found that happiness is an activity in accordance with excellence or virtue, with the highest excellence or virtue, which will be the best things in us. Aristotle says, "Whether it be itself also divine or only the most divine element in us, the activity of this in accordance with its proper excellence will be complete happiness."[82] Clearly, for Aristotle, that activity is contemplative. For he says, "This activity is the best (since not only is intellect the best thing in us, but the objects of intellect are the best of knowable objects). And secondly, it is the most continuous, since we can contemplate truth more continuously than we can do anything."[83] As well, self-sufficiency belongs most to the contemplative activity. While a wise man and a just man and all others require the necessities of life, when sufficiently equipped with such the just man needs people with whom he can act justly. But the wise man, even when solitary, can contemplate truth. Happiness is also thought to depend upon leisure, but the political life seems unleisurely. The activity of intellect, which is contemplative, seems to be superior in worth and aims at no end beyond itself, and its pleasure is proper to itself. This contemplative life is "the complete happiness of man, if it is to be allowed a complete life."[84] Of course, Aristotle then turns around and says that "in a secondary degree the life in accordance with the other kind of excellence is happy; for the activities in accordance with this befit our human estate."[85]

Practical wisdom is linked to virtuous character, which is also connected to the passions, indicating that such moral virtues belong to our composite nature. The excellences of the composite nature are human, and so are the life and happiness to which these correspond. So, it seems that we have the composite and the noncomposite good lives. While the active political life with all its deeds is necessary for such a life, the man of contemplation needs no such deeds with respect to his activity, and they may even be said to hinder such activity. Aristotle argues in favor of the contemplative life as the best life

---

82. Aristotle, *NE* X.7, 1177a16.
83. Aristotle, *NE* X.7, 1177a20–23.
84. Aristotle, *NE* X.7, 1177b25.
85. Aristotle, *NE* X.7–8, 1178a9–10.

for man on the grounds that the gods above all other beings are considered happy, and the sort of actions we assign the gods/God, the best activity, is contemplation. Once again, however, Aristotle seems to be dragged down by the fact that *qua* man one will also need external prosperity. For he says, "our nature is not self-sufficient for the purpose of contemplation, but our body also must be healthy and must have food and other attention."[86] For him, the truth of practical matters is discerned from the facts of life which are the decisive factor. He says that when we test our understanding of happiness against these facts and they harmonize, great. If not, then we must suppose our understanding to be a mere theory about the ideal.

To wrap up, in Book I Aristotle says three kinds of lives are thought to be especially attractive: pleasure, politics, and knowledge.[87] In X.6-9, he returns to these, exploring them more fully than in Book I. Dismissing pleasure, he turns in X.7-8 to the two remaining alternatives, politics and philosophy, and presents a series of arguments to show that the philosophical life, a life devoted to *theoria* (contemplation), is best. *Theoria* is not the process of learning leading to understanding since that would be a means to an end and not the end itself. For him, *theoria* is the activity of someone who already attained theoretical wisdom. The happiest life is the life lived by one who has a complete understanding of the fundamental causal principles governing the operation of the universe, and who also possesses adequate resources for living the life devoted to the exercise of such understanding. Such a life he compares to the life of a god. God thinks without interruption and endlessly. Likewise, the truly happy man, the philosopher, enjoys something similar for a limited, episodic duration, or at least ideally so.

It is perhaps odd that he ends the *NE* this way such as to leave ethics behind. Perhaps instead X.7-8 is to be continuous and consistent with the other themes in the *Ethics*. Perhaps we should understand him to be assuming that one needs to possess the ethical virtues in order to live the life of a philosopher, like a god, even if such exercise of the ethical virtues is not the philosopher's ultimate end but his penultimate end. One needs to be adequately equipped for the philosophic life by having practical wisdom, justice, and the other ethical virtues. That is to say, the political life is not useless, but it is only a necessary precondition as the penultimate life to living the ultimate life, the life of *theoria*, which is true *eudaimonia*. But whichever of the two ways of life one interprets Aristotle, yet still the good life is precluded for the vast majority and is even admitted to being limited or perhaps even only an ideal for the best and most fortunate of men.

86. Aristotle, *NE* X.8, 1178b33-35.
87. Aristotle, *NE* I.4, 1095b17-19.

Perhaps the most salient revelation of the defects of the political life is that it is in a sense not such a leisurely life.[88] Aristotle insinuates that ethical activities are remedial. That is to say, they are required when things go wrong. For example, courage is exercised in war, which is a remedy to some evil and not something sought. And so on for the other ethical virtues. The just person living in the real world must experience a certain degree of dissatisfaction. Normally, the pleasures of ethical activity are mixed with pain. Unalloyed pleasure is only attainable for us when we are not involved in the mundane world and can contemplate the rational order of the cosmos. The exemplars of human happiness are those who are lucky enough to devote their time to the study of such a world far more orderly than the real world we live in, a world that does not so much require the continual exercise of the practical life. Hence, the good life seems to be somewhat idealistic rather than real, even for the best of men.

Interestingly, in X.9, the final chapter of the *Ethics*, Aristotle reveals that his task is not yet complete because humans can only become good or bad when they are existing in a certain political community. We are precluded from attaining happiness, or even something that approximates it, unless and until we live in communities that foster good habits and provide the basic equipment of a well-lived life. Thus, the best life for man is not found in the political life. Yet the very possibility of anyone attaining the good life requires the willingness of some to lead the second best life, the political life, so that someone else may eventually live the best life, the ultimate end, the life of contemplation (*theoria*), the divine life.

So, even for Aristotle, the possibilities are bleak. Either the good life is simply an ideal, or there is a way out if only for episodic durations. While it appears to be a very pessimistic outlook in terms of anyone actually attaining and sustaining the good life for both external and internal reasons, perhaps a better description is tragedy.[89] The tragedy of contingency plagues most during life and even the best of men after we die.

Given the tight connection between (1) man's nature and (2) man's *telos*, the story of how one moves from (1) to (2) reveals some tragic inadequacy, something lacking in man's capacities or the high demand to reach the good life. His view creates a systemic gulf between man as he is and as he could be, rendering the prospects of the good life as not very good.

---

88. Aristotle, *NE* X.7, 1177b4–15
89. Jones, *On Aristotle and Greek Tragedy*.

The Medieval "Aristotelian" Turn

Given the Aristotelian tragedy, both Maimonides and Aquinas have proposals for addressing the issues that do not require straining to either increase the human capacity or lessen the demand in order for man to live the good life. Maimonides and Aquinas, though differing in perspective, note something lacking, even lacking in a greater way than that which Aristotle let on, in terms of our human condition and capacities to reach the apex on our own.

Chapters 2 and 3 of this book focus on Maimonides's and Aquinas's respective departures from Aristotle by exploiting the Aristotelian picture's insufficiencies for attaining the good life, while exploring their differing views of man's fallen condition and human perfectibility. All three thinkers believe that the highest end for man involves some account of theoretical contemplation, the knowledge of God. If the knowledge of God constitutes human perfection, then human *imperfection* is somehow constituted by a lack of the knowledge of God. Not only are there substantive differences in their accounts compared to Aristotle's relative to the *summum bonum*, but even leading up to that end certain key features lacking in Aristotle's account are areas for which their own views make provision (either with respect to their conceptions of endowed human nature and its capacities, or with respect to some form of divine providence by which those capacities are extended in order for man to reach the *summum bonum*).

Unsurprisingly, faith is not a virtue in Aristotle. And while the knowledge of God in Maimonides and Aquinas is the highest end of man as it is for Aristotle, there are semantic differences. Both claim—in the *Guide of the Perplexed* and the *Summa Theologica*, respectively—that faith is a virtue. As a virtue, there is some excellence that this provides. The role of faith as a virtue in both of them makes a substantive difference over Aristotle in theoretical and practical ways, extending (1) our knowledge and (2) our motivation in actualizing the *summum bonum*. While Aquinas talks about faith much more than Maimonides, nonetheless both take faith as an important virtue that does philosophical work in each of their systems; faith (or its lack) plays a role in, and can be used to exploit their accounts of, the human fall or lapse, moral perfection, and ultimate human perfection.

Maimonides and Aquinas, in accordance with their theistic traditions, provide a philosophical account of the nature and extent of the fallen human condition. While differing from one another in their own assessments, both accounts reveal a clearer picture than Aristotle's as to why man fails to obtain the good life. By examining their views of the original state of integrity and what constitutes or constituted the ultimate failure, bringing about the distorted human condition, we can best see what is missing and what ontological resources are available to help man resolve those limiting conditions such that the good life can be attained.

The accounts of the *summum bonum* in all three thinkers involve some account of intellectual perfection, accounts which are markedly different given their understanding of the object of intellectual contemplation (i.e., the deity). This difference also *makes* a difference in terms of the broadly shared structure of human nature, the human *telos,* and the transition to the actualization or fulfillment of one's *telos*. All agree that the *summum bonum* involves imitating God. But what this means, given the respective ontology each holds, makes a difference, where Maimonides's and Aquinas's accounts provide resources for a more robust, universally accessible, and durably sustainable account of human flourishing, in ways that Aristotle's account does not. Their accounts, because of man's limitations and or fallenness, required some form of Divine providence and appropriate human response. Aristotle's account, to be sure, provides motivation to live the good life, but not nearly as robust as the accounts of his medieval counterparts. An account of worship of a worshipful being or person provides a richer motivational base than merely imitating a principle thinking itself thinking whose *summum bonum* may be more motivationally deflating than appealing.

Although certain conditions are required for attaining the good life, notions construed as some form of divine providence as well as faith are present in their own ways in Maimonides and are emphatic in Aquinas, especially given the gravity of Original Sin in the latter as accounted for in our exploration of the fall. Given this, Aristotle's *phronimos* (the virtuous person) is less than virtuous or simply less virtuous than otherwise thought, as there are certain virtues of the *phronimos* (e.g., pride) that run in opposition to virtue as understood by the medievalists (e.g., humility), rendering the Aristotelian vision as falling short of even moral perfection according to their respective accounts.[90] This is in part because of one's understanding of oneself in light of one's understanding of the ultimate object of contemplation (the deity). Given the requisite, but relatively applied, notions of what might be called *grace* or *gift* and *faith*, all other things being equal, the Maimonidean and Thomistic man will always be in a superior position (NB: not superior nature) relative to the good life over their Aristotelian counterpart at any corresponding level (in the same way as an Aristotelian gentleman would be over a slave or poor man

---

90. More will be said later to clarify that Aristotle's notion is not as opposed as it might appear, but is still problematic in Maimonides's and Aquinas's view.

lacking certain resources relative to satisfying conditions for the good life to obtain). The best life is that of the philosopher-prophet/saint, not the philosopher-sage.

2

Maimonides and the Good Life

As the saying goes, "From Moses to Moses there was none like Moses." Moses Maimonides's (1135/38–1204) impact is far-reaching. While it is clear that Maimonides influenced many later thinkers both within and without Judaism, he was also informed by others in his own intellectual development, an important factor one needs to consider in trying to understand his thinking.[1]

In this chapter, I will show how Maimonides's view on the good life enhances Aristotle's view in several ways, most of which connect with a feature absent in Aristotle; namely, the virtue of faith; a virtue not often discussed in Maimonidean scholarship but clearly one of significance for him.[2] First, I will examine Maimonides's notion of faith, which not only avoids being fideistic in nature, but which, to use Aristotelian vernacular, quite substantially fills in the form where Aristotle's view is lacking.[3] This necessary condition for the good life—the faith factor—can be shown to operate along the spectrum from the fall to human perfectibility (i.e., the presence of faith or its lack plays a crucial role in accounting for the fall and man's rise to human perfection). Second, I will show the essential role Maimonides's faith plays in explaining his interpretation of the fall and human

---

1. Harvey, "Islamic Philosophy and Jewish Philosophy," 349–69; D'Anconca, "Greek into Arabic," 10–31; Burnett, "Arabic into Latin," 371–404.

2. Given that the nature of this exploration when it comes to textual work is closer to a work in systematic theology than biblical theology, relevant data is drawn broadly from a number of Maimonidean works—the major legal works being the *Commentary on the Mishnah* and the *Mishneh Torah*, and the major philosophical work being *The Guide of the Perplexed*.

3. This refers to Aristotle's hylomorphism, his form/matter composites. In Aristotelian vernacular, when some object, for example, O, is lacking a particular form it ought to otherwise have, then O's lack is taken as a privation (e.g., a wall has the absence of sight, where a blind man has the "lack" of sight. It is only in the case of the blind man, but not the wall, that we have a case of privation). In this case, the virtue of faith is something of substance one ought to possess if one is to live the good life. To live without it is to live in privation, to live in lack.

lapse in general. In the last two portions of the chapter, I will examime his faith's role in recovering both the practical as well as the theoretical life of man such that without faith the best life is not obtainable, not even by one so great in the mind of Maimonides such as Aristotle.

Maimonides shares a great many similarities with Aristotle in much of his thinking, so it is fair to say that his philosophy is quite Aristotelian. Indeed, "Maimonides without Aristotle is unthinkable."[4] This is the case on a number of issues, but most important for our purposes at this juncture is that they both affirm the same fundamental structure of the good life (including human nature, the human *telos*, and the general transitional story from the former to the latter). Of course, there are important distinctions in every one of these points (e.g., the image of God, and what it means to imitate God in the *summum bonum*, to name a few), but the basic framework is nonetheless present for comparison and contrast.

Now, as is well noted within Maimonidean scholarship relative to the good life, like Aristotle before him, "there is nothing Maimonides values more than knowledge, especially knowledge of . . . divine science."[5] But the content of this knowledge and the means by which it is obtained will, at times, mark a significant difference that *makes* a difference. Maimonides is dissimilar from Aristotle, especially on substantive issues, not the least of which is owing to his meta-context of what might be called his "faith tradition." This should not be contrasted with a knowledge tradition. It could, however, be misleading to use this term if one is not careful, since Maimonides comes across as intellectualist, and this term may seem to express a form of fideism. But what is meant here is that he is part of a tradition, Judaism, which possesses not only philosophical prowess of its own but also an additional source of knowledge that aids in promoting human perfection—the Torah, which means "instruction" given by God.

Like other faith traditions (including the major Abrahamic traditions: Christianity and Islam), one's conception of God and of the nature of man will determine, in part, what it means to imitate God and how that is done best. Both thinkers believe that the highest end for man involves some account of theoretical contemplation, the knowledge of God. But if the knowledge of God constitutes human perfection, then it follows that human *imperfection* is constituted by a *lack* of the knowledge of God in some way. Before we diagnose what constitutes this imperfection in the human soul and consider Maimonides's prescription for it, we will explore one important but often neglected feature found in Maimonidean philosophy

---

4. Frank, "Introduction," 3.
5. Stern, "Maimonides's Epistemology," 105.

that will appear all along the path to human perfection, a feature that radically distinguishes his view from Aristotle's. While initially consonant with Aquinas, it ultimately marks out a distinction there as well.

Maimonides on Faith

Unsurprisingly, faith is not a virtue for Aristotle. While it may come as a surprise to some, faith is, in fact, a virtue for Maimonides. While the knowledge of God in Maimonides is the highest end, the role of faith as a virtue makes a substantive difference in theoretical and practical ways over Aristotle's view. It would be a grave mistake to apply a conception of the nature of faith in Maimonides that opposes it to reason or knowledge. The account of faith found in Maimonides is not the sort of thing one might expect from some contemporary adherents of fideism who seem to delight in the act of closing their eyes and plunging with confidence into the absurd, as it were. (Whatever the level of accuracy this has in representing Soren Kierkegaard's particular notion of fideism, it is often what is meant by fideism and sometimes attributed, even if falsely, to Kierkegaard.)[6]

But rather, the essence of faith—biblical or perhaps otherwise—is confidence or trust in a worthy object. One can have faith in a thing (e.g., a chair or even a practice like daily prayer) or a person (e.g., a parent, a king, or God), and one can have faith in the truth of a proposition, such as confidence that the following propositions are true: "Aspirins help alleviate the pain from a headache," "Mutual Fund X is a good investment," or "God exists." When faith as trust is directed toward a person/thing, it is called "faith-in"; when faith is directed toward the truth of a proposition, it is called "faith-that." Contemporary philosophical vernacular uses "belief-in" and "belief-that." In many cases, belief-in or faith-in reduces to belief-that or faith-that (e.g., "I believe in spirits" reduces to "I believe that spirits exist"), but such a reduction is not always the case.[7] That is, belief-in may presuppose belief-that, but is not reducible to it.

Appropriate faith is grounded in knowledge and is as good as its object. Take a chair, for example. On the basis of my knowledge about the chair, I am able to exhibit confidence and a disposition to act (e.g., sit in the chair) as if some proposition about the chair is true (the durability of the chair is such that it can hold my weight). Faith is rooted in knowledge, including misplaced faith where one might root that faith in what one takes oneself to know, perhaps mistakenly. So, given that the object

---

6. Kierkegaard, *Fear and Trembling*, 44.
7. Price, "Belief 'In' and Belief 'That,'" 5–28.

of consideration in Maimonides is ultimately God, we could well do what Menachem Kellner, following Abraham Joseph Heschel, has done, and that is to see the distinction between faith-that and faith-in as the distinction between "theology and depth theology."[8]

Let us consider a model or exemplar of faith within historic Judaism. Although there were things he did not understand concerning his faith, the highly revered patriarch of Western religion, Abraham, placed his faith in God; a faith that was grounded in a minimal set of things he knew about God and was not at all a case of blind faith akin to fideism.

Further, his faith *in* God was not reducible to faith *that* God exists. As with all of the Abrahamic faiths, Abraham is highly regarded in Judaism and, in particular, by Maimonides. Maimonides was not alone among well-known Jewish philosophers in commenting on Abraham's faith. From the early Jewish philosopher Philo, we see an apparent reference to faith as a virtue in the context of Abrahamic righteousness before God (Gen 15:6). In fact, for Philo not only is faith a virtue, but it is taken to be the "queen of virtues." This is not of course to say that all forms of fideism are without cognitive content. But the account of faith given here certainly is not fideistic wherein religious beliefs are ungrounded, not being subject to rational assessment. Of course, religious beliefs may be directly grounded in religious experience without inference to other beliefs and thus rationally warranted akin to how perceptual beliefs are grounded in perceptual experience. But this is not ungrounded faith we are dealing with here in Maimonides, the one who is responsible for the greatest systematic work on Jewish law (i.e., *Mishneh Torah*). In this work he sought to show that every piece of Jewish law actually serves a rational purpose.[9]

In Harry Wolfson's account, Philo takes faith to have two aspects: cognitive and non-cognitive.[10] Surely, Abraham believed certain propositions about God to be true (e.g., those propositions pertaining to God's unity, providence, and existence). And Abraham also trusted God with human life, including his own posterity, no less.

Like Abraham, Maimonides affirmed certain propositions about God and believed that others should as well. In fact, in his *Commentary on the Mishnah*,[11] specifically in his discussion concerning the world to

---

8. Kellner, "Heresy and the Nature of Faith," 299–318. See also Heschel, *God in Search of Man*, 7.

9. Philo, *On Abraham* 6.1333 (270).

10. Wolfson, *Structure and Growth*, 216–18. It includes both assent to propositions and trust in God.

11. This early commentary is to be distinguished from his greatest legal work, the *Mishneh Torah*.

come and how all Israel has a share in it, Maimonides lists thirteen principles (the closest one comes to credal dogma in Judaism) that he considers binding on every Jew.[12] So it seems that there are certain propositions Maimonides thinks every Jew needs to believe are true. Some may consider this somewhat surprising in light of the emphasis in Judaism on actions rather than beliefs, and also in light of the contemporary variegated viewpoints in Judaism. One author, for example, claims that "it is difficult to imagine Jewish identity without a belief in God. Yet, for many Jews today, belief in God is a major stumbling block in relating to Judaism."[13] The contemporary Jewish lens might be shaded by a post-Enlightenment viewpoint that is non-theistic. But for Maimonides, subscribing to doctrine was not a problem; it was a virtue. For, unlike other popular Jews of academic report, such as Karl Marx, Sigmund Freud, and Peter Singer, he was not an atheist; and unlike Spinoza and Einstein, he was not a pantheist. Granted, some dispute whether Einstein was a theist or pantheist, but it is immaterial here. Maimonides was, like Moses before him, a theist.[14] He affirmed, and thought others should affirm, certain doctrines to be true, even if tempered by the *via negativa*.

But can Maimonides, an intellectualist of sorts, make room for faith? Indeed, he does. In Arabic, he says faith (*al-iman*) is a virtue (*fadilah*) saying, "I refer to the *virtue of faith*."[15] His Hebrew equivalent is *emunah*. After we have unpacked it, this notion will prove useful in situating his understanding of ethics, the transition from raw human nature to the human *telos*. The context of this claim near the end of his philosophical *magnum opus, The Guide of the Perplexed*, is in the discussion of three substantial terms: *hesed* ("loving-kindness"), *mishpat* ("judgment"), and *zedaqah* ("righteousness"). With respect to the last of these he says:

> The word *zedaqah* is derived from *zedeq*, which means justice; justice being the granting to everyone who has a right to something that which he has a right to and giving to every being that which corresponds to its merits. . . . For when you walk in the way of the moral virtues, you do justice unto your rational soul, giving her the due that is her right. And because every moral virtue is called *zedaqah*, it says: "And he believed in the Lord,

---

12. For the "Thirteen Principles," see Maimonides's commentary on Sanhedrin 10, in Maimonides's *Commentary on the Mishnah* (Maimonides, *Maimonides Reader*, 401–423).

13. Ariel, *What Do Jews Believe?*, 88–90.

14. Jammer, *Einstein and Religion*.

15. Unless otherwise stated, references to Maimonides's *Guide* refer to Shlomo Pines's translation and page numbers. See Maimonides, *Guide* III.53 (631).

and it was accounted to him as *zedaqah*" (Gen 15:6). I refer to the virtue of faith.[16]

To digress for a moment, it is not simply that Abraham, to whom Maimonides here refers, had a high regard for God, but rather that he recognized God's authority, and Abraham could be counted on to obey God in light of this understanding. His faith was characteristic of him like a common virtue. The Hebrew term *emunah* is sometimes translated "faith," and at other times "faithfulness." Kenneth Seeskin claims that from the standpoint of traditional Judaism, there is no difference because the man of faith is reliable; he is loyal. It is no surprise, then, that the Jewish concept of faith is found in the expression of a covenant whereby one's faith in God is committed to keeping God's commandments.[17] In Exodus 24:7, the Israelites responded in the covenant made with God, not with "we believe" but "we will do." Given that the object of faith is a moral agent—God—faith can be seen as reciprocated where *emunah* is ascribed to God's relationship to Israel. This is not propositional nor even some blind faith God has in Israel (i.e., neither purely cognitive nor fideistic), but is an expression of God's faithfulness or righteousness to Israel to whom He has made a covenantal promise. So there is a sense in which faith-in is an expression of trust or loyalty to another moral agent that is irreducible to faith-that.

Both the cognitive and non-cognitive elements can be found in Judaism in general and in Maimonides in particular, and there is interplay between the two. For example, while Seeskin claims faith-that (an expression where one is convinced that something is the case, e.g., "God will keep his promise") presupposes faith-in, where we must trust the person (i.e., God) who vouches for it, implying our loyalty. I suggest it often works the other way around as well. To trust the person, one must know something about the person (e.g., that they are trustworthy). One cannot love, believe in, or obey God in ignorance. In the end, having faith in God implies remaining true to God (i.e., faithful) as an object worthy of one's endeavor, which explains why *emunah* is often translated alternately as either "faith" or "faithful."

Returning to the passage above, not only does Maimonides understand justice here as giving each his due, but he goes beyond this to hold that even when we act morally (e.g., curing the hurts of those whom one has not even injured), we do justice to our own rational soul. For Maimonides, intellectual perfection cannot be attained without the prerequisite moral perfection.[18] He refers to moral virtues as *zedaqah*. As noted, his example

16. Maimonides, *Guide* III.53 (631).
17. Seeskin, "Judaism and the Linguistic Interpretation," 227.
18. He says that "the moral virtues are a preparation for the rational virtues" (Maimonides, *Guide* I.34).

is of Abrahamic faith: "And he believed in the Lord and it was accounted to him as *zedaqah*" (Gen 15:6).[19] He explicitly states what he means by this, saying, "I refer to the virtue of faith." Therefore, I suggest that faith *qua* virtue in the Hebrew understanding of it is neither blind nor mere intellectual assent but involves consent; it is not primarily propositional but morally dispositional.[20] As has been shown, it is closer to the concept of *faithfulness*, that which is borne out in action, given one's confidence, devotion, loyalty, and trust in the object of one's faith. This is borne out in the Bible and in the Talmud with which Maimonides was obviously quite familiar, having written an extensive commentary on it, establishing him as the greatest legal scholar of his day.[21]

Not only is faith a virtue for Maimonides, it is perhaps initially surprising that it is not an intellectual virtue, but is instead a moral virtue. One might initially think it otherwise given some things Maimonides says about "belief," namely, that belief is not "what is said but rather what is thought when a thing is affirmed."[22] Further on in the same section he says, "We cannot believe unless we think, for belief is the affirmation that what is outside the mind is as it is thought to be within the mind." So here, belief does not seem to be found as a relational quality or disposition with respect to other persons. Instead, it has particular cognitive content such that the proposition held is either true or false. Indeed, in contrast to some of the Talmudic statements, Maimonides does seem to require some cognitive belief in individuals who may convert to Judaism; that is, cognitive elements required in religious beliefs (e.g., oneness of God and prohibition of idolatry).[23]

So it seems that we have here evidence of the nature of religious faith being primarily a dispositional attitude of the believer, but also one of propositional content with specific propositions to be affirmed or denied. Maimonides opens his commentary containing the "Thirteen Principles" this way: "I have seen fit to speak here about many principles concerning very important doctrines [*al-itiqadat*]," and concludes that "when all these foundations are perfectly understood and believed in [*itiqaduhu*] by a person he enters into the community of Israel."[24]

---

19. Maimonides, *Guide* III.53 (631).

20. When applied to our relationship to God it carries with it not merely a tendency but also a moral component.

21. Kellner, "Heresy," 299–318.

22. See Maimonides, *Guide* I.50.

23. Kellner, "Heresy," 117.

24. For Maimonides's comments in his "Thirteen Principles," see his discussion in Kellner, "Heresy and the Nature of Faith."

He insists that Torah commands affirmation of certain beliefs, some of which he takes to be philosophically demonstrable (e.g., belief in the unity of God and belief in God's existence).[25] So belief is, for Maimonides, a matter of the intellect in some contexts. But in others, it is also a matter of the non-rational or appetitive part of the soul. He subordinates the moral to the intellectual, the moral being instrumental and preparatory for the intellectual. And he uses both *al-iman* (*emunah* in Hebrew) and *al-itiqad* (*da'at* in Hebrew) for our notions of faith or belief, consistently distinguishing them. *Iman* is trust or consent, and *itiqad* is confidence or (intellectual) assent. This coheres with the distinction in contemporary philosophy of belief-in and belief-that.

Someone might claim, for example, that a statement such as "I believe in ghosts" constitutes a legitimate objection because it would imply something like "I trust the ghosts" or "I trust that there are ghosts." However, when people utter the statement "I believe in ghosts," what they ordinarily mean is that "I believe that ghosts exist." That is, in keeping with the distinction, they are denoting "belief-that" rather than "belief-in," where the latter connotes trust or a pro-attitude.[26]

His intellectualist definition of belief is *itiqad*, and the term used of faith as a virtue is *iman* (*emunah*). So the faith he denotes as a virtue is a moral virtue and notably involves characteristics of trust, loyalty, devotion, and commitment to God.

Like Aristotle, Maimonides makes a distinction between intellectual and moral virtues and does this early on in his career in the *Treatise on the Art of Logic* where he says that "moral habits are settled states which form in the soul in such a way that they become fixed dispositions from which actions stem" and are termed "virtue and vice." Likewise, he speaks of "rational virtues and rational vices" when speaking of reason.[27] Thus, moral virtues can become fixed in the soul through exercise such that they become a habit. So faith, like other moral virtues, matures with time and practice. Trust is something that develops in relationships with agents and is borne out in action when one comes to rely on the trustworthiness of the thing or person in question, whereas the affirmation or denial of a proposition may have little or no effect on one's behavior. On the other hand, intellectual virtues are such as to have excellence in reasoning about propositions.

Elsewhere, when he distinguishes between moral and intellectual virtues, for example in "Eight Chapters," he claims that justice is a moral

25. Kellner, "Virtue of Faith," 197.
26. Seeskin, "Judaism and the Linguistic Interpretation," 71–81.
27. Maimonides, "Treatise on the Art of Logic," 160.

virtue and resides in the appetitive part of the soul where man desires or is repulsed, and where fear and love reside. A person who trains and controls the appetitive part of her soul is said to possess moral virtues; the appetitive should be guided by the rational part, since it "distinguishes between base and noble actions."[28]

So faith construed as a virtue would be a moral virtue for Maimonides, residing in the appetitive part of the soul whose vices would likely be viewed as excessive or deficient faith (a state of affairs wherein one does not believe where one ought to or believes where one ought not to). If faith is *iman* (in Arabic) or *emunah* (in Hebrew), then clearly it would be good to possess proper trust in God. In fact, if moral perfection is a prerequisite for human perfection, and faith is a moral virtue for Maimonides as we have shown, then one can hardly be morally perfect (a prerequisite to human perfection) without faith. This virtue is central to a Jewish theocentric ethic with God as the object of faith and the author of the commands which carry with them divine authority. This inspires enhanced moral motivation, much more than, say, in Aristotle whose portrait of the divine is thought thinking itself thinking, which may be motivationally deflating by comparison.

So in short, faith (*emunah*) is a moral virtue. This serves to dispel the hyper-intellectualist view often portrayed of Maimonides. Given the context of Abrahamic faith where this is discussed, although not an intellectual virtue, it is still a prized moral virtue, and since moral perfection is a prerequisite to authentic intellectual perfection, it is indispensable for human perfection. Significantly and unsurprisingly, there is no evidence in Aristotle's writings that faith, much less faith in God, is a virtue. All of this is not to say that Maimonides would prefer simple faith to knowledge of God; not at all. But rather, genuine knowledge of God will entail faith (as in trust). Knowledge and this kind of faith are not mutually exclusive. As Seeskin states, "If the purpose of reason is to search for truth, the purpose of faith is to insure the integrity of behavior."[29] Faith is a serious motivational factor. It is the knowledge of God, as we will see, that brings about the love of God and trust (as Abraham surely trusted God based on some knowledge he had of God). We will see eventually that the virtue of faith plays a significant role in explaining the fall, human perfection, and the transition between the two—a major distinction from Maimonides's philosophical predecessor's vision of the good life, with whom he shares the basic teleological structure. Without faith, the good life is neither attainable nor sustainable.

---

28. Maimonides, "Eight Chapters," 61–63.
29. Seeskin, "Judaism and the Linguistic Interpretation," 231.

The Fall and Ethics

In addition to arriving at a philosophical account of human nature in order to understand that in which human perfection consists, Maimonides also has a religious text, the Torah, whose instruction informs his moral theory via divine commands and whose text provides certain key insights into the human condition. Relative to faith and its relation to the good life is man's lapse from the ideal state. In *The Guide of the Perplexed*, he discusses the fall of man in chapter 2 of the first part, where he applies a philosophical line of interpretation to Genesis.

Within Judaism, interpretation is a fundamental category of its intellectual history. There are several modes of interpretation as well as schools of thought given in rabbinic literature that Maimonides certainly understood (e.g., *pesher, derash, remez, sod, midrash*, etc.) These range from literal, mystical, ethical, to philosophic. Thus, to get to the account of the fall in Genesis, we are interpreting a text through an interpreter whose interpretation is of a philosophical sort as found in the *Guide*.[30]

At the outset, human perfection for Maimonides turns out to be rational contemplation (although, as we will see, this is richer than Aristotle's notion of *theoria*), as intellectual perfection is the highest achievement of man.

He discusses the four perfections of man in this ascending order of perfection: (1) wealth, (2) health, (3) ethical virtues, and (4) true human perfection (i.e., attainment of rational virtues leading to correct opinions on matters of metaphysics or divine science). Maimonides says that only (4) true human perfection, "brings man eternal life and by it man is man." All the others, including ethical virtues, are of instrumental value to this end.[31] Knowledge of God—metaphysics, or divine science—is of the highest importance to Maimonides.[32]

The *Mishneh Torah* begins with the basic metaphysical truths everyone is obligated to know and ends with the world being engaged exclusively in the pursuit of knowledge. The *Guide* also opens and closes with two parables depicting true human perfection, not as the moral, but with the acquisition of rational virtues conjoined with true opinions about divine things. We will find that intellectual and moral perfection in Maimonides are richly interwoven.

---

30. Rawidowicz, "On Interpretation," 45–80.

31. Maimonides, *Guide* III.54.

32. Maimonides, *Guide* III.51 (621): Even the greatest of religious commands, to love God, is often construed as knowing God; *Guide* I.36: The worst form of idolatry is construed as cognitive error about God.

In the *Guide*'s dealing with Adam in the Garden of Eden, the straightforward reading might suggest that Adam gains something that he did not possess before—namely, knowledge of good and evil. Thus, Adam started as a mere animal or beast, and his action of partaking of the fruit gave him a new "moral sense." But, in fact, Maimonides reverses this and claims instead that Adam became a beast consequent to the disobedience. This is why it is considered the doctrine of the fall. He never really gained anything; indeed, he lost something or came to *lack* something (a case of Aristotelian privation). Maimonides holds with Aristotle that ethical and political matters pertain to "generally accepted" things or opinions,[33] but that "generally accepted" things are not something accessible to the intellect but to the imagination. And the imagination is not constitutive of human perfection *per se*. More will be said on this later as Moses, the paradigmatic person in the Bible and Jewish religion is believed by Maimonides to utilize his imagination, a faculty that seems problematic in the account of the fall.

Now, Maimonides does hold that one of the functions of the rational faculty is to rule cities,[34] so perhaps we might be inclined to think that the intellect may know good and evil (or is at least poised for such). Once the imagination knows good or evil, then it can employ the intellect to discern between them.

Genesis 3:5 says, "And you shall be as gods (Heb., *elohim*), knowing good and evil." It should be pointed out that the term *elohim* is not the specific covenantal name of God as expressed in the tetragrammaton, *YHWH*; rather, it is generic. As Maimonides points out, it has multiple meanings given in various contexts: deity, angels, judges or rulers over cities or states, strong ones, etc. He takes *elohim* here to mean rulers governing cities. (Maimonides does not mention Genesis 3:22 here, "And the Lord God said, 'The man has now become like one of us, knowing good and evil.'" This poses a potential problem since it seems to contradict his interpretation of '*elohim*.')

Notably, Maimonides is in part fulfilling one of the dual purposes of the *Guide* as mentioned in his introduction, namely, providing a basic lexicon that assists in explaining various meanings that biblical terms may have. So, according to Maimonides, it is not the case that man was an irrational animal before the fall; he was the epitome of rational man, a philosopher, in that he was exclusively concerned with truth and falsehood, theoretical perfection, which just is human perfection. Among the powers of the human soul, two are noteworthy here: the rational and the imaginative. The latter, while sometimes useful, can also be perilous.

---

33. Maimonides, *Guide* II.33.
34. Maimonides, *Guide* I.53.

The imagination is basically the power to both "store the impressions of sensibly perceived objects" when not currently being perceived and to combine and separate these things into things yet perceived.[35] On the one hand, it provides input for the intellect and allows the prophet to translate abstract philosophical truths into figurative representations that can then be grasped by the community.[36] On the other hand, the imagination's interference with reason is suspect according to Maimonides, since its representations are always of composite particulars rather than universals on which demonstrations are based. Further, the imagination misrepresents immaterial things for material ones since it is a bodily faculty representing things as bodies, which could be perilous in divine science. Thus, he attacks the *Kalam* for its reliance on imagination and failure to distinguish between it and the intellect.[37]

Genesis 3:6 says that the tree of knowledge of good and evil was "good for food and pleasing to the eye." Man partook of the fruit of this tree in disobedience and turned toward the lusts of the imagination and the sensual pleasures, and was thus deprived of intellectual perfection. He acquired the sense for the generally agreed or accepted. It is in the fallen condition, as it were, from the realm of contemplative thought to the material world that man is concerned with ruling in ethical and political matters.

Maimonides supports his interpretation of *elohim* to refer to rulers governing cities by appealing to two factors. First, he alludes to the *imago Dei*, the fact that man is made in God's image, which, according to the previous chapter of the *Guide*, implies that there is some similarity between the intellect of man and of God, understood as pure intellect. This will, of course, have to be understood in light of his negative theology, not that we have something in common with God's essence, but with his attributes of action, *imitatio Dei*.

Second, man is given a commandment that reveals his possessing both practical (at least in latent form until necessary for utilization) and theoretical intellect.

So on one level, the fall consists in a change of priorities from a life of the mind to a life of the body, from intellectual contemplation of truth(s) to being ruled by one's passions, a move from intellect to imagination. It is taking one's intellectual "eyes off the ball," as it were, where Adam subordinated a higher good for a lower good(s). Man was no longer concerned exclusively with truth and falsehood but with good and evil, with the

---

35. Maimonides, *Guide* II.36 (370).
36. Maimonides, *Guide* II.36 (369–70).
37. Maimonides, *Guide* I.73 (206–212).

"generally accepted." Recall that Aristotle distinguishes between demonstrative syllogisms grounded on true premises and dialectical reasoning grounded on generally accepted opinions, leading only to probable conclusions.[38] Maimonides reapplies this distinction to the realm of theoretical truth and the realm of moral action. This is also consistent with Aristotle's holding that ethics is not an exact science like the theoretical sciences and is related to the distinction between nature and law emphasized by the sophists.[39] For Aristotle, generally accepted opinions are those accepted as known by the wise and are the basis of dialectical arguments.[40] Thus, instead of being solely concerned with matters of the intellect as he was prior to the fall, man is now concerned with matters pertaining to the imagination, with political ruling. This tension between the ideal theoretical life for human happiness and the political life in the cities runs throughout the *Guide*.

According to Maimonides, we find in the Torah that the theoretical life was again made possible by people like Abraham, who prepared the philosophical groundwork for the teaching of Moses to take root and be promulgated. The Torah, then, is intended to train the beastly man to be obedient to theoretical and practical intellect, idolatry being fundamentally subjected to the deliverances of man's imagination. Maimonides's interpretation of *elohim* as connoting rulers indicates that he takes this story as a philosophical allegory. And Maimonides here is accomplishing a second purpose of the *Guide* in this narrative, namely, explaining obscure parabolic works of the prophets which are not explicitly identified as such. That is, it is to be taken in its hidden rather than apparent sense. Maimonides then seeks to solidify his allegorical interpretation by noting that the term *open* need not be taken in its literal sense either in Genesis 3:7. The passage says, "Then the eyes of both of them [Adam and Eve] were opened, and they knew that they were naked," which according to Maimonides means, "They then became alert to the fact that being naked was to be considered an evil matter." Whatever it was that seemed to them to be desirable to make them wise either was not itself desirable (only desired) or else was inordinately desired in light of other priorities (e.g., being captured by lesser goods instead of greater good[s], like failing to subject oneself to the authority of God's command in order to obtain something else).

Finally, he looks for other biblical passages to confirm his view. He says that he will give the significance and meaning of a particular verse in Job,

---

38. See his *Posterior Analytics* and *Topics* for his treatment of demonstration and dialectic reasoning.

39. Aristotle, *NE* I.3, 1094b13–1095a14.

40. Aristotle, *Topics* I.1, 100b21.

and then he reapplies that meaning in Genesis. The verse from Job 14:20, which the *Guide* states as "He changes his face and Thou sendest him forth," denotes man's directional stance in disobedience to his true nature, and as a punishment he was expelled from his blissful state.

How could Adam have moved from a state of blissful intellectual contemplation, the things of the soul, to things of the body, imagination, ethics, and politics? While Maimonides does not mention Eve or the serpent in the story, he gives hints elsewhere in the *Guide*.[41] She appears to represent matter (resting on a platonic tradition of identifying woman with matter). Man's flaw is his composition of matter and form. It is the matter that prevents him from being a disembodied intelligence, unconcerned with material things. The serpent seems to be imagination uncontrolled by reason.[42] So man's fall is a consequence of being distracted with matter or material goods and imagination.[43]

Maimonides's prelapsarian Adam represents man's ideal state wherein no excessive or evil desires are present. Hence, rather than man beginning as a mere animal, disobeying and then becoming moral, which is his highest calling; because his true nature is philosophical and contemplative, his disobedience causes him to lose sight of his true priorities and become controlled by his passions, like an irrational animal. He became in his corruption less than man, failing to imitate God as the best or optimal state of man.

Given what we have said about the notion of *emunah*, we can now see that what came to be a fundamental lack in Adam was the loss of trust, loyalty, and commitment to God as expressed in God's authoritative command not to eat the forbidden fruit. Upon seeing that its appearance was desirable and acquiescing to temptation, man was deceived by such a prospect, which revealed a compromise that took hold in man's soul relative to his commitment to God. *Emunah* was broken. Adam's disobedience revealed his disloyalty and lack of commitment to God in favor of that which is not God. Consequently, the way things ought to be in *shalom* was lost.

This raises some questions. To begin, why assume that the philosophical rather than the literal interpretation is the intent of the narrative? First, Maimonides, like other medievalists both inside and outside of Judaism, affirms

---

41. Berman, "Maimonides on the Fall of Man," 1–15; Klein-Braslavy, "Bible Commentary," 245–72.

42. This was Kellner's understanding per personal communication with the author (January 30, 2009). He thinks we should differentiate between an imagination controlled by reason (cf. Moses) and an imagination uncontrolled by reason, or rather, an imagination that controls reason. For more, see the extensive discussion of Maimonides on imagination in Faur, *Homo Mysticus*.

43. Maimonides, *Guide* I.6 (17); II.30 (355–57).

what we might call the Unity of Truth thesis: Truth is one and cannot consist in contradictory interpretations. Maimonides, a disciple of the Muslim philosopher Al-Farabi, on the relationship of philosophy and religion holds that philosophical truth temporally precedes religions.[44] Hence, unchanging philosophical truths about the world precede and set the rational framework for the acceptance of true religious claims. In ethics, for example, nature is to history what natural law is to divine law. Specific Mosaic commandments are rooted in a true moral philosophy, as evidenced by the Noahide Laws that are binding to Jew and Gentile alike. Take the story of Cain and Abel, for example, which shows that Cain was held accountable for murdering his brother Abel. Given that he had no explicit command concerning murder, it implies that it was known via nature.[45]

So the interpretation of a religious text must cohere with what is true philosophically about the world. Now, since what sets man apart from other species is rationality, the contemplative life is the ultimate goal of human perfection. So any interpretation of a fall would presumably diminish this aspect of man in some way. And, of course, one can affirm this and also be committed to the view that *emunah* was broken at the same instant.

Second, following Al-Farabi, religious texts are of a certain genre, a genre of communicating truth to the masses in a way appropriate to their understanding (i.e., via imagination). True religion, truth for the masses, cannot contradict philosophic truth, truth for the elite. Like Al-Farabi and Aristotle, Maimonides distinguishes between the masses and the elite. Maimonides naturally takes the prophets as philosopher-statesmen, since the philosophic worldview informs the religious. In the case of Judaism in particular, philosophic meaning is present in the text because the Torah represents in popular form for the masses the truth of philosophy, and it was composed by a philosopher, Moses. This was also, according to Maimonides, previously prepared by philosophic groundwork via Abraham.

Maimonides thinks that the philosophic tradition by Abraham was present for a time but was later, for various reasons, lost (mainly during the Egyptian captivity). Likewise, Adam's philosophic knowledge, whose knowledge was the most perfect metaphysical knowledge one can achieve prior to expulsion from the Garden was also lost and had to be rediscovered by Abraham and again by Moses.[46]

---

44. Berman, "Maimonides, the Disciple of Al-Farabi," 164, 167; Mahdi, "Al-Farabi on Philosophy and Religion," 5–25.

45. See Novak, *Natural Law in Judaism*; *Image of the Non-Jew in Judaism*.

46. Maimonides, *Guide* I.2; III.29; *Mishneh Torah*, s.v. "Idolatry" I.1–2.

For Maimonides, the highest human achievement is doubtless the perfection of the intellect,[47] an impossible feat without the ability to pursue truth, an ability shared by all humans albeit on a varying scale. The Tanakh, as a sacred document, is a source of truth for Maimonides. Such truths contained therein may not always be apparent, but we know that they are there if one were to dig sufficiently deep. It follows that any interpretation of the Bible that is demonstrably false (e.g., "God is corporeal because the Bible uses anthropomorphic language about God") must be a false interpretation regardless of how straightforward it may seem. Biblical interpretation must accord with philosophical truth given the Unity of Truth thesis. In accounting for Adam's total lapse due to disobedience (entailing a morally vicious lapse), it would be impossible for Maimonides to provide such an account without also affirming a necessary lack of *emunah*. Adam was motivated ultimately by lesser goods than by remaining true or faithful to the ultimate good because he was somehow captured by perhaps what were, in fact, goods, but goods found in disordered priority.

As pointed out earlier, Maimonides takes faith to be an important virtue that is philosophically important in his system, a virtue often neglected in Maimonidean scholarly discussions. Faith (or its lack) plays a role in and can be used to exploit his understanding of the human fall or lapse, moral perfection, and ultimate human perfection. In accordance with his theistic tradition, he provides a philosophical account of the nature and extent of the fallen human condition that, without mentioning it, indirectly supports a lack of faith in God as at least a partial explanation of human lapse, making faith a necessary condition to ultimate human perfection. Maimonides affirms that Adam was a philosopher-prophet. Kenneth Seeskin points out that early in the *Guide*, Maimonides depicts Adam as having the most perfect metaphysical knowledge one can achieve prior to his expulsion from the Garden (including belief in a timeless, changeless, immaterial God).[48] Even if the biblical text is silent about Adam's theology, Maimonides thinks no one could be this close to God and have fundamental misunderstanding.[49] Unfortunately, per Maimonides, Adam's knowledge was lost during the time of Enosh and was picked up again by Abraham.[50] Again, even though the biblical text is silent, Maimonides

---

47. Maimonides, *Guide* III.27.
48. Maimonides, *Guide* I.2.
49. Maimonides, *Mishneh Torah*, s.v. "Kings and Wars" IX.1.
50. Maimonides, *Guide* III.29; Maimonides, *Mishneh Torah*, s.v. "Idolatry" I.1–2.

thinks he is justified in claiming that Abraham had proofs for God's existence, a God who is neither a body nor a force in a body.[51]

Maimonides's view on the matter of divine providence via prophecy is such that whoever is fit and also prepared for prophecy will invariably become a prophet as God will never withhold prophecy from anyone deserving it. It is not that God cannot, but that God will not. He claims that "according to the foundations of the Law, of the Torah, [God] has never willed to do it, nor shall He ever will it."[52] Adam's prelapsarian gaze was devoutly focused on divine truth. For Maimonides, divine providence never ceases while one is so gazing. This human gaze or contemplation of the knowledge of God and divine providence would have obtained in the original state of integrity.

Like Aristotle, Maimonides provides an account of the highest end for man, which involves theoretical contemplation, the knowledge of God. If the knowledge of God constitutes human perfection, then human imperfection is constituted by a lack of the knowledge of God. But, as per our earlier discussion on the nature of Jewish faith, we have no reason to assume that Adam suddenly changed his theistic propositional faith from affirmation to denial, hence becoming an atheist. No, what seems explanatory is that he came to lack in *emunah* (faithfulness, loyalty, or commitment).[53]

So what is the fall after all if not ultimately a revelation of some *lack of knowledge of God*? Trust, devotion, and loyalty to God as the ultimate good and to whom we should give our obedience was compromised in a failure to acquire some lesser good(s) as though it were superior, which came to explain the fallen human condition. Now, if faith be a moral virtue as we have come to understand it in Maimonides, and if concern for good and evil were supposedly relegated entirely to the postlapsarian human condition, how could such faith exist in a prelapsarian state? We must keep in mind first that for Maimonides the Adamic story is allegory rather than literal history, and so any prelapsarian state is an abstraction; but secondly that faith has both cognitive and non-cognitive elements. The non-cognitive may lie dormant during contemplative states. It depends, in part, on what one's focus is on.

Maimonides portrays the story of the fall in Eden as part of an account of the fundamental nature of human reality, not a historical account of an individual. But nothing significant for our purposes hangs on whether Maimonides actually believed the Adamic story to be historical. Even if he

---

51. Seeskin, "Maimonides."

52. Maimonides, *Guide* III (529).

53. Material things are not evil for Maimonides; he was not Plotinus, after all. But on the hierarchy of good, they do not compare to God.

did, it is not clear, and his interpretation is nonetheless completely allegorized throughout (e.g., Adam represents intellect, Eve represents matter, the serpent represents one's appetitive faculty, etc.) If it is not allegory, the interpretation is certainly allegorical. In his entry on Maimonides in the *Internet Encyclopedia of Philosophy*, professor Jonathan Jacobs writes, "In his treatment of Adam and Eve, Maimonides is presenting key elements of his anthropology rather than exploring details of a particular episode of human history. His primary concern is to explicate basic features of human nature and the human condition and to make fundamental points about human intellectual capacities and the aspects of human nature as the basis of an ethical life."[54]

Following Shlomo Pines's interpretation of Maimonides here,[55] Maimonides said that while in his perfect and excellent state, Adam was endowed with "the intellect that God made overflow unto Adam" through which he distinguished between truth and falsehood. Fine and bad (or good and evil) belong, for Maimonides, to the *endoxa* (generally accepted opinions), not those things cognized by the theoretical intellect. Prior to his disobedience, man "had no faculty that was engaged in any way in the consideration of generally accepted things" or moral judgments.[56] But when he disobeyed and was inclined towards the desires of his imagination and pleasure of corporeal senses, he was punished and deprived of intellectual apprehension and became absorbed with judging things good and bad. Hence, "And you shall be like *elohim* knowing good and evil."

It seems apparent that if God gave a command prior to the fall, then even if Adam had never in fact engaged a faculty prior to this moment useful for considering and obeying a command, he was nonetheless at once capable of doing so upon receiving a command. Since the practical intellect comes into being concomitantly with the theoretical intellect given that man is composite, then, as Aristotle remarks, the theoretical and the practical intellect differ only with respect to their *telos*, the *telos* of the theoretical being the apprehension of truth, and the *telos* of the practical being the good.[57] When the intellect reaches towards higher things, its activity is theoretical; when towards lower things, its activity is practical. Both exist even if the latter is only in latent form owing to the existence of the intellect but whose practice depends upon the *telos* at hand. The two intellects seem to be identical as to their *upokeimenon* and differ only in respect to their *logos*

54. Jacobs, "Maimonides."
55. Pines, "Adam's Disobedience," 105–125.
56. Maimonides, *Guide* I.2.
57. Aristotle, *De Anima* II.10 (433).

(i.e., what they are considering). The practical intellect is what it is because of its relation to the body and bodily things. This concentration on material things has become our concern now in this fallen condition rather than being ultimately concerned with and committed to divine truth. Having seen that Maimonides views faith to be an indispensable moral virtue and how it plays a role in accounting for the fall and ethics, we can now examine how he moves out of lapse and towards the good life.

Morality and the Path to Attaining Human Perfection

Aristotle's problems were multiple. Most men could not obtain the good life and fulfill their natural *telos* for various reasons which were out of their control. First, the Aristotelian man who had developed a fixed vicious character could not extract himself from it. Second, whether slave or free, one is consigned to the interwoven contingency of external goods of fortune and luck, even after death. At best the life of happiness is found to be rare and unsustainable, and at worst only an unattainable ideal. These things, however, are not beyond remedy for Maimonides, as we will see in the next few sections. Holding a robust view of free will, he invokes the notion of repentance, given that knowledge of the deity via Torah creates greater motivation, and his treatment of Job shows contingency to be unproblematic. And, of course, we have the significance of the virtue of faith.

The Dispensability of Fortune

As noted, the path to intellectual perfection requires moral perfection, but that path is vulnerable to some things; for example, one's vulnerability to misfortune could bring about a disqualification for the prize, at least according to Aristotle. Recall that for Aristotle, tragedy is interwoven in the human condition. The contingency of happiness based upon forces outside of one's control threatens the attainability and durability of human happiness, the good life. But Maimonides does not consider the vagaries of fortune as being indispensably tragic.

He uses the parable of Job to illustrate his own view of divine providence (which simply is divine knowledge in human affairs). Maimonides's discourse on the parable is rooted in Aristotelian thought and grounded in Aristotle's discourse on moral virtue and its ultimate insufficiency to procure sustainable happiness. Job is to some extent Maimonides's analogue to Aristotle's *phronimos* with his portrayal of the passage construed as an implied critique of Aristotle. His view of Job is that Job is ultimately good but ignorant, and so not wise. Maimonides notes that, although righteousness is attributed to Job in the story, wisdom and knowledge are not.[58] Job's tragedy is not brought about on account of his moral virtue or lack thereof but on account of ignorance. Dan Frank interprets Job as someone who "suffers on account of his innocence, i.e., lack of wisdom."[59] Else, why would Job be perplexed about his situation given his relative goodness? He suffers from the common delusion that moral virtue procures happiness, often reckoned to be constituted by such entities as material wealth, health, and family. Adopting this, Job is presumptuous and has no true understanding of that which is of most value; he has no grasp ultimately on why what is happening to him is happening.

Like Aristotle, Maimonides sees misfortune as being compatible with moral virtue, and thus that moral virtue is not ultimately what procures or secures happiness.[60] One could be morally virtuous and suffer misfortune and thus lose happiness. All the candidates that are considered by Aristotle (e.g., wealth, health, virtue, etc.) to be necessary are not by themselves sufficient conditions. The question persists whether happiness is in our control and to what extent. As Frank puts it, "Aristotle's position drives him to the following dilemma . . . either happiness (like moral virtue) is something in our control . . . in which case external goods and moral luck play no role, or happiness is, at least in part, outside our control."[61] It is no wonder there was unresolved tension in Aristotle regarding stability and fragility in happiness. Misfortune and moral luck consign us to tragedy. King Priam of Troy is a prime example of someone who had it and lost it, and this is true given the contingency of happiness whose attainability and sustainability lie outside ourselves, whether in this life or thereafter.

But differing here from Aristotle, Job's "misfortune" according to Maimonides, is ignorance. If there is tragedy in Maimonides, it is that not all can be philosophers.[62] For him, the antidote to human suffering (as with everything else) is knowledge of God. Job misunderstood this until the end when he realized that his assumption about the role of moral virtue or external goods in securing happiness was insufficient. Only knowledge

---

58. Maimonides, *Guide* III.22 (487).
59. Frank, "Prophecy and Invulnerability," 80.
60. Aristotle, *NE* I.5, 1096a1–2.
61. Frank, "Prophecy and Invulnerability," 81.
62. Not all can be philosophers on Aristotle's view either. Aquinas's views in later chapters may provide some remedy for this relative to the availability of the good life.

of God guarantees that one possesses a sense of the relative value of things. Such knowledge brings with it invulnerability to fortune. Without it, we suffer concern for lower things.

Thus, for Maimonides in contradistinction from Aristotle, misfortune is not an ineliminable part of the world because it is often a function of ignorance which is soluble. Such ignorance—at least of what is of ultimate rather than even penultimate importance in life—reflects an imperfection. Misfortunes of the type revealed in Job would not be misfortunes if one had genuine wisdom and knowledge of God.[63] And Maimonides held that Job had "no true knowledge and knew the deity only because of his acceptance of authority, just as the multitude adhering to a law know it."[64] Job is portrayed to be like those later in the *Guide* who merely consider traditional authority but do not engage in speculative thinking in religion.[65] Such people are merely folks of unreflective common sense and are captured by contingency. Not so those who engage in philosophical understanding of the human good, which entails that prophecy is the highest good and, of course, the prophet (especially Moses) is the human ideal. Divine providential care is no less than a function of intellectual apprehension of the divine. Here's what Maimonides says about providence:

> Providence watches over everyone endowed with intellect proportionately to the measure of his intellect.... Providence always watches over an individual endowed with perfect apprehension, whose intellect never ceases from being occupied with God. On the other hand, an individual endowed with perfect apprehension, whose thought sometimes for a certain time is emptied of God, is watched over by providence only during the time when he thinks of God; providence withdraws from him during the time when he is occupied with something else... and becomes in consequence of this a target for every evil that may happen to befall him.[66]

For Maimonides, then, the human condition is not ineliminably tragic given its tie to contingency because we are far more in control of our destiny than Aristotle held. Not until the end when Job encountered the divine did he come to his wits in humility and understand that happiness is not dependent upon things in the contingent realm, which are now viewed as "dust and ashes." Further, the Maimonidean man is at an advantage over the

---

63. Maimonides, *Guide* III.23 (492–93).
64. Maimonides, *Guide* III.23 (492).
65. Maimonides, *Guide* III.51 (619). See chapter 4 for further discussion.
66. Maimonides, *Guide* III.51 (624–25).

Aristotelian man given both divine aid and motivation towards the divine, having a more robust conception of the divine and man being made in that image. The bridge between human nature grounded in the *imago Dei* and the human *telos* given the divine aid of the Torah is closer for many than Aristotle imagined. Man need not be a cosmic orphan. As Frank points out, "though prophecy, the *summum bonum*, is for Maimonides not wholly a natural occurrence, the first step is very much in our power."[67] The dispensability of fortune, then, is such because the knowledge of God eclipses all other fortunes by comparison.

Habituation, the Fixity of Character, and Moral Motivation

Beyond the issue of external goods of fortune serving to disqualify many, in Aristotle's schema, from attaining the good life, there is another issue weighing against the Aristotelian vision, namely, the hardness of moral character itself. Maimonides adopts and adapts Aristotelian vernacular for his own ends. He finds company at many points, for example, the nature and acquisition of the virtues via voluntary activity towards habituated character. Human capacity and voluntariness seem more elastic for Maimonides in order to meet ethical demands that are brought into reach for us by divine aid in a more proximate sense than for Aristotle. The relation between human capacity for, and accessibility to, the good life is thus increased on Maimonides's account.

Virtue ethics generally speaking tells a story about the transformation of character through a habitual process something like this agricultural metaphor: "Sow a thought, reap an action; sow an action, reap a habit; sow a habit, reap a character; sow a character, reap a destiny." Aristotle's virtue theory entails a certain level of fixity of character, an ideal for him because it provides a measure of self-sustaining happiness. Having settled dispositions comes with advantages because it stabilizes character and leads to destiny. Having a virtuous character enables one to move to the ultimate contemplative good such that fixity is a good thing in terms of creating a potentially durable happiness. The achievement of one's *telos* is itself said to be somehow self-sustaining.

But what if one possesses vicious character? It cuts both ways in terms of virtue and vice. The positive for some becomes a death knell for others given this fixity of mature character. While Maimonides shares with Aristotle that most of the virtues are dispositions lying in the mean which we

---

67. Frank, "Prophecy and Invulnerability," 83.

are naturally capable of acquiring via our own volition, he has substantial differences with Aristotle. The naturalistic Aristotelian view entails that a person who acquires vices to a certain degree may wind up with such a fixed character as to render him utterly incapable of ever extracting himself out of it and rendering the good life forever beyond reach.

Pre-philosophical moral thinking and the structure shared by Aristotle and Maimonides (i.e., human nature in *potentia*, human *telos*, and the transition of actualizing one's natural potential) may seem to imply some notion of "ought implies can," where certain ethical demands or considerations can somehow be satisfied by the obliged agent. But the obligation imposed upon the Aristotelian perhaps entails a demand that cannot be met by natural human capacity alone. Given the stability of character, the developed character of a bad agent seems to preclude his extracting himself from a state of developed vicious character in the same way that it fosters stability for the happy life in the good character. While the continent and incontinent man have proper conceptions of what is good, and struggle (successfully or not, respectively) to satisfy them, the vicious man's conceptions become corrupt and perverse such that he does not even know that what he is doing is not good. In this way, character informs cognition. Even if he were to discover or be shown his vices, his character now seems to preclude him from doing anything about it. Though the agent is culpable for getting there, she is virtually incapable of getting out of there. Ethical considerations, while objective, and possibly even ordinarily accessible, cannot be satisfied.

However, available on Maimonides's account is the notion of repentance, entailing *emunah*, which greatly enhances Maimonides's notion of voluntariness over Aristotle's such that one can through repentance always extract oneself. Furthermore, the Aristotelian *phronimos*, while not vicious, does suffer on Maimonides's account from some epistemic and ethical dysfunction or defect and may not be aware of it. He is, on the Maimonidean account, lacking in some crucial sense. And by Aristotle's own lights, the answer to the question, how should one live? is grasped from the inside out, from the standpoint of the virtuous person.[68] But whereas *phronesis* functions for Aristotle as the master virtue informing the other virtues, Torah functions for Maimonides in a similar way. Thus, in another sense the answer to the question may be grasped from outside help. The Torah brings with it potential for restoration. As Jonathan Jacobs notes pertaining to *phronesis*, "The role that practical wisdom fulfills for Aristotle, in making ethical requirements accessible is, in Maimonides's view, performed by the Law,

---

68. Jacobs, "Aristotle and Maimonides," 149.

the revealed will of God."[69] This is the case even for those generally accepted opinions known by the many or the wise and which are rationally defensible and discernible even if not demonstrable, since they are ultimately "justified and sanctioned by their being part of revealed law."[70]

Jacobs is correct in affirming that revelation guarantees the ethical demands authoritativeness in a way unparalleled in Aristotle. But it seems that Jacobs is incorrect in believing that it guarantees its equal accessibility, unless one means all are capable of receiving prophecy, or in comparison with an Aristotelian need for a properly endowed community to foster good laws and upbringing such that the Maimonidean has that necessary communal element. But clearly, the Maimonidean man, a man with revelation, potentially achieves ethical understanding via the gift of Torah and the knowledge of God. Maimonides claims that the commandments "discipline the powers of the soul" in the sense that they are capable of making a transformative difference in the agent rather than merely changing behavior.[71] They are graciously given by God as instructional but can become transformational in character by obedience. The Torah then sets a demand which we are capable (via repentance) of satisfying by our capacities (see Deut 30:11–14). Revealed law is a difference that makes a difference in terms of its availability or accessibility. In light of Torah, repentance, entailing *emunah*, is a powerful motive force.

A fundamental difference is scope of voluntariness or freedom, given the ability to extract oneself from a vicious state via repentance. True, habituation to settled character initially requires robust freedom, and our actions do make a causal difference, but Aristotle's view seems to allow self-determination to determine oneself right out of any further self-determination, whereas Maimonides's conception of freedom is always an open question given the nature of the covenant between man and God. In his *Commentary on the Mishnah*, where he is dealing with free will and punishment, he says, "to sum up the matter . . . just as God wishes man to be erect in stature . . . so, too, he wishes him to move or be at rest of his own accord and to perform actions voluntarily. He does not force him." And in reference to the fall (e.g., Gen 3:22) when man rebelled, Maimonides says that Adam

> has become unique in the world, i.e., a species having no similar species with which he shares this quality he has attained. What is this quality? It is that he himself, of his own accord, knows the good and the bad things, does whatever he wishes, and is not

---

69. Jacobs, "Aristotle and Maimonides," 151.
70. Jacobs, "Aristotle and Maimonides," 151. See also Jacobs, *Law, Reason*, 39–106.
71. Maimonides, "Eight Chapters," 72.

> prevented from doing them. . . . All of this is just. It is necessary for him to accustom his soul to good actions until he acquires the virtues, and . . . should not say he has already attained a condition that cannot possibly change, since every condition can change from good to bad and from bad to good; the choice is his.[72]

Maimonides says that "whoever is bad is so by his own choice. If he wishes to be virtuous, he can be so; there is nothing preventing him."[73] For Aristotle, mature character, in whatever state it is in, typically becomes fixed and then hard if not impossible to alter. Even if not impossible, this is where the motive force is greatly enhanced by *emunah*, a moral virtue directed to a person, not to a principle. For the Aristotelian virtuous or vicious agent, certain ethical considerations do not even figure into the matrix in decision making since they become tone deaf to either vicious (if a virtuous person) or virtuous (if a vicious person) actions as they've become conditioned otherwise. For Maimonides, repentance (and lapse) is always possible.[74] Repentance is an activity that has a transformative effect if one does it from a knowledge and love of the law and, ultimately, of the Law Maker. For Torah not only makes one wise but "restores the soul." Its guidance and potential action-guiding response (faith) provides a wider scope of voluntariness than does *phronesis*.

To some extent, as nature is to history, so natural law is to revealed law. Not only are moral principles rationally discernible, generally speaking, but they and other moral injunctions are authoritatively codified and sanctioned in the Torah, providing the commoner and not just the philosopher with necessary authoritative tools. So the ethical demands known generally through rational discernment are sanctioned by Torah, which guarantees authoritativeness and, in principle, broader accessibility amongst the masses. Such generally accepted ethical demands (e.g., murder, theft, etc.) are "laws about which the sages said 'If they were not written down, they would deserve to be written down.' Some of our modern wise men who suffer from the sickness of the dialectical theologians call them rational laws."[75]

But Maimonides believes that the reason to follow the law is not mere legalistic obedience but to perfect the soul, saying, "Great is repentance, for it brings men near to the Divine Presence (Hosea 14:2)."[76] The repentant

---

72. Maimonides, "Eight Chapters," 88. See also Shatz, "Freedom, Repentance," 51–57.
73. Maimonides, "Eight Chapters," 89.
74. Maimonides, "Eight Chapters," 84.
75. Maimonides, "Eight Chapters," 79–80.
76. Maimonides, *Mishneh Torah*, s.v. "Laws of Repentance" VII.6.

individual is said to undergo transformation of character.[77] The authoritative definiteness of certain moral injunctions for Maimonides is available for the vicious in a way that is not so on Aristotle's schema. Jacobs says concerning Maimonidean meta-ethics:

> If something like Aristotelian naturalism is the correct view of unaided human agency, then it may be true that without grace, either in the form of revealed law (and the human capacity to repent effectively) or in the form of infused virtue (for example, in the Thomistic view) human beings are susceptible to ethical disability. It would be unreasonable to expect those whose cognitive and motivational alienation from ethical requirements is quite fixed to change or be changed in the direction of virtue.[78]

This brings us to an important point. Goodness without God may not be good enough. Grace of sorts enables capacity to satisfy the demand for humans to be all that they can be and attain the good life.[79] But given the additive facets in Maimonidean resources over the Aristotelian situation (e.g., divine aid of Torah and the extended scope of volition allowing one the seeming perpetual possibility to express *emunah* and repent), the bad person can truly be restored such that one is left without excuse for continuing outside of virtue and the good life. So factors that contribute to the problems of the contingency of fortune and fixity of character do not seem to plague Maimonides like they do Aristotle in ordinary situations.

Sagacity, Saintliness, and Moral Motivation

While anyone can achieve this moral perfection, in principle, perhaps it is practically unachievable outside of Judaism. Recall that Aristotle's *NE* was geared to a particular audience, an audience already prepared, in part, for his lectures. They were already inclined towards the good life (having been brought up in fine habits and externally endowed with sufficient fortune), but Aristotle has something to offer which they lacked: a reflective grounding for the basis and motivational reinforcement to continue living the good life to the fullest extent. He wanted to move them from unreflective behaviors in accordance with virtue to an actually virtuous life. One's understanding reinforces one's motivation to live it. The *NE* provides those with habituated

77. Maimonides, *Mishneh Torah*, s.v. "Laws of Repentance" II.4.
78. Jacobs, "Aristotle and Maimonides," 160n37. See also Jacobs, "Taking Ethical Disability Seriously," 141–58.
79. For more on this issue, see Garcia and King, *Is Goodness without God Good Enough?*

virtue what they need so as to be fully virtuous, possessing *phronesis*. Now, Maimonides similarly has something he is offering the audience of the *Guide*, a reflective grounding and motivational reinforcement to continue in the good life over and against merely going through the actions.

Interestingly, as we will see, he is committed to the view that the Aristotelian man, indeed the *phronimos* himself, is by comparison merely living in accordance with the virtues, but not actually living the virtuous life. Like the lectures of the *NE*, the *Guide* provides its audience, the virtuously predisposed, the necessary reflective grounding to continue the lives they are inclined to live. The *Guide* is a dialectical work that starts from *endoxa*, beliefs of the many or wise, and siphons out the truth from them. The addressee is one for whom the validity of the Law has both become established in her soul and actual in her belief. He is trying to reconcile *halakhic* (the body of Jewish religious law) faith with philosophic wisdom. So it is an audience who has thus far lived a life consonant with Jewish virtue but now wants philosophical edification to motivate and sustain such a life.

Like Aristotle, Maimonides thinks that an account of human nature and its *telos* is necessary to understand what it means for a human person to flourish. It is this natural teleology from which the morality of happiness, the good life or flourishing, emerges.[80] But unlike Aristotle, Maimonides gives an account of human nature with an importantly distinct facet grounded in the image of God (Heb., *tzelem*; Ltn., *imago Dei*) and human fallenness relative to his understanding of Torah, an additional and authoritative epistemological light accessible to the Maimonidean man. Given human nature's fallen or lapsed condition, man has an acute problem that needs resolution if human perfection is to be obtained.

Now, Maimonides does not affirm the fallen condition with such gravity as does the Christian world, which is given to the doctrine of original sin. He says that man does not possess either virtue or vice at the beginning of his life.[81] It does not seem plausible to attribute to Maimonides the view that man has a sinful nature or inclination. Recall that Maimonides's philosophical interpretation of the fall is allegorical. But it still points to a problem that is a reality of our current estate even if not understood to be inherited by the rest of humanity directly from Adam. We suffer from a lack of knowledge of God, the ultimate human perfection. One reason that moral perfection cannot be the highest form of human perfection is that moral perfection is "an instrument for someone else" and thus involves others besides the person seeking

---

80. Aristotle, *NE* I.8, 1099a20.
81. Maimonides, "Eight Chapters," 68.

such perfection rather than the solitary individual.[82] Another reason is that moral claims, unlike scientific or metaphysical ones, are non-demonstrable. They are not deducible from self-evident premises. A yet third reason is that the prerequisite to moral judgment relies on the pitiful fact that we are beings of passion, possessed with acquisitive lusts consequent to our being composed of matter and form (intellect).

Despite its secondary position in order of human perfection, morality plays a crucial role in Maimonides's thinking. For we must quell the impulses of matter that distract from intellectual pursuits en route to true human perfection, whose quelling is associated with "holiness."[83] Now, even though there is a certain kind of morality that *precedes* and is instrumental to the life of contemplation, Maimonides also affirms a kind of morality that *proceeds* from and is a consequence of the life of contemplation, representing an overflow from the intellectual perfection. Relative to the point of intellectual perfection, let us call the former *anterior morality* (AM) and the latter *posterior morality* (PM).[84]

Maimonides claims that "the improvement of moral habits is the same as the cure of the soul and its powers" such that the proper cure for the soul via moral habituation makes knowledge of God possible (to the extent that man can know God) and may even bring about prophecy, whereas vices function as veils inflicting the soul and preventing prophecy. In improving the soul via AM, a process that occurs over time and with proper actions forming habits of character, Maimonides largely concurs with Aristotle's doctrine of the mean between two extremes, both of which are vices (either excess or deficiency).

Interestingly, along with Aristotle, Maimonides holds that some extremes are further from the mean than their opposites. For example, cowardice is more opposed to bravery (or courage) than bravery is to rashness (or fool-heartedness). So for him, acquiring a virtuous character trait may require performing acts deviant from the mean for purposes that are either corrective (bringing his characteristics toward the mean), or preventive (sustaining someone on the mean).

Aristotle did allow deviation at times with respect to some emotions (e.g., shamefulness and envy) and actions (adultery and murder), where it is not the excess or deficiency which is bad, but the emotion or act itself. Maimonides claims that with respect to some traits, we ought to move to

---

82. Maimonides, *Guide* III.54.

83. Maimonides, *Guide* III.8, 33.

84. The key texts in discussing AM and PM are Maimonides, "Eight Chapters"; "Laws Concerning Character Traits"; *Guide* I.54; III.54.

the extreme and not land on the mean. Take as examples humility (a vice for Aristotle, but a virtue for Maimonides), and anger (a vice). Maimonides cannot follow Aristotle in taking pride as a (crowning) virtue here as it would imply man take interest in worldly honor via pride and thus to forget God as though God did not exist.[85]

If someone is inclined toward cowardice, he should act with great boldness in the direction of fool-heartedness such that he corrects the extreme and ends up on courage. Then he can continue to perform only courageous acts so as to sustain the mean. This deviant stance for corrective or preventive purposes is what justifies ascetic behavior (e.g., the Nazarite), apart from which purposes such behavior would be a vice.

While he invokes the mean almost as an ideal, Maimonides often displays inclinations towards asceticism, particularly for those who are living the life of the intellect (including prophets). There is the "wise man" or sage who acts according to the mean, and next to him the "pious man" or prophet who, in practicing preventive therapy, intentionally leans toward one of the extremes. Maimonides alternates in praise between the two, citing Solomon and the philosophers in favor of the wise man (the virtuous person whose desires are in accord with his actions), and the rabbis in favor of the pious man (similar at this stage to the continent man who is duty bound and succeeds despite his desires to obey the laws). These are, in his eyes, eventually reconciled as they are denoting two different aspects (traits considered with respect to generally accepted opinions on murder, lying, etc., on the one hand, and obedience to mitzvot traditional laws like wearing two kinds of clothing, on the other).[86] Both Aristotle and Maimonides agree that the ultimate good life entails the imitation of God, whose activity is superhuman. But they disagree specifically regarding the nature of the *imago Dei*, the deity, and the involvement of the moral component.

A stark contrast between Aristotle and Maimonides on at least one of the virtues each prizes concerns the virtues of pride and humility.[87] For Aristotle, the proud man (*megalopsychos*) is his highest achieving specimen en route to the life of contemplation. It is his *phronimos*, or man of practical wisdom, whom Aristotle believes is entitled honor from others. Honor is the prize (*to athlon*) for the morally virtuous individual, keeping in mind that not all qualify for the prize. Those who because of fixed vicious character

---

85. Aristotle, *NE* II.6, 1107a8–15.

86. Maimonides, *Guide* III.53–54; "Eight Chapters," 6; *Mishneh Torah*, s.v. "Laws Concerning Character Traits" I.4–5; "Laws of Kings" VIII.11.

87. Frank, "Humility as a Virtue," 89–100.

cannot extricate themselves, and those who don't have the resources due to a lack of external goods or misfortune cannot attain.

Aristotle demands honor, whereas Maimonides disdains it. The proud man's crown of virtue is like a second order virtue that supervenes upon its subvenient virtuous base. While wealth and good birth are not what is awarded, neither are they irrelevant, for one cannot exercise virtues such as liberality without money to do so. And the crown cannot be had without the virtues.[88] This proud man is the great-souled man or *phronimos* upon whom the Aristotelian ethical theory is based. In opposition to this, Aristotle thinks the humble man is somehow lacking. This would be anathema for Maimonides. For him, given what the Torah says, one is forbidden to pursue the disposition of pride or approach it as to some sort of mean.[89]

But Aristotle thinks that the extremes of the proud man—vanity and humility (or undue humility)—are vices. Humility does not give the honorable person his due. Indeed, the humble man suffers from both self-injustice and ignorance (moral and epistemic deficiencies). So the Maimonidean man who is supposed to be humble is, for Aristotle, lacking in some important aspect of virtue, either moral or epistemic. While the vain man claims more than his due, it is the humble (and not just extremely humble) man who is ignorant of his due because he is ignorant of himself, a failure of the maxim to "know thyself."[90] Putting Aristotle's proud man in perspective may not resolve the differences.[91] What is mainly at issue here is how an agent sees himself and his actions in reference to God. For Maimonides, at least in reference to God, there is a profound humility: "He will be filled with fear and trembling, as he becomes conscious of his own lowly condition, poverty, and insignificance. . . . He will then realize that he is a vessel full of shame, dishonor, and reproach, empty and deficient."[92]

The partial disagreement actually serves to shed light on Maimonides's and Aristotle's different conceptions of human nature in reference to God. For Maimonides, humility will be seen as the crown, as shown in *Hilkhot De'ot*.[93] For him, the sage or wise man (*hakham*) is the one whose character traits generally lie in the mean. But the saint-prophet

---

88. Aristotle, *NE* IV.1–3.

89. Maimonides, "Laws Concerning Character Traits" II.3.

90. Aristotle, *NE* III, 1125a22.

91. Hardie, "Magnanimity"; Curzer, "Great Philosopher's Not So Great Account"; "Aristotle's Much Maligned *Megalopsychos*."

92. Maimonides, *Maimonides Reader*, 48.

93. Maimonides, *Mishneh Torah*, s.v. "Laws Concerning Character Traits" I.4–5; 2.3. *Hilkhot De'ot* is also known as "Laws Concerning Character Traits" (part of the *Mishneh Torah*).

or pious man (*hasid*) transcends the *hakham* due to the fact that his ways do not all lie in the mean: "Whoever is exceedingly scrupulous with himself and moves a little toward one side or the other, away from the mean, is a pious man." And further, "Whoever moves away from haughtiness to the opposite extreme so that he is exceedingly humble is called a pious man." For Maimonides, the paradigm of virtue was the pious man, Moses, who was "very humble" (Num 12:3) rather than merely humble, which is what the wise men are commanded to be in *Avot*.[94]

It may seem that Maimonides parallels Aristotle here in that Aristotle has both the *phronimos* and the scarcely mentioned hero of super human virtue while Maimonides has both the *hackham* and the *hasid*.[95] Surprisingly, Frank takes the *hakham* (wise man) to be Maimonides's equivalent to Aristotle's *phronimos*. But this cannot be correct. For while many of the same moral virtues may reside in them, they come to be opposed in at least one crucially significant way—the *hakham* is humble, and the *phronimos* is proud. What Aristotle takes here to be a virtue, Maimonides takes to be a vice, and vice versa. If Maimonides is right about pride, given the Torah, then the *phronimos* cannot be a *hakham* virtuous person, much less can he be deserving of honor. And even more significant is *emunah*, that without which moral perfection is lacking. Thus, from Maimonides's perspective here, Aristotle could not have achieved the prerequisite penultimate goal, the morally virtuous person, so he could not have attained the ultimate goal, *theoria*. Frank's analysis here is therefore incorrect.

To make matters worse, the *hakham* is merely humble. The *hasid* is extremely humble. So it is not just the *hakham* that is opposed to the *phronimos* but also the *hasid*. And given the difference at the penultimate level, the difference at the ultimate level is, *a fortiori*, greater. A humble Aristotle is simply anti-Aristotelian, but an extremely humble Aristotle (a pious man) is not even close to hitting the mark, for this is an extreme case of ignorance according to Aristotle. Interestingly, if Aristotle's *phronimos* were a proud wise man, as is his description, then according to Maimonides, anyone who makes his heart haughty actually denies God's existence.

Deuteronomy 8 says, "Beware lest you *forget* the Lord your God *by not keeping His commandments* . . . then your *heart becomes proud, and you forget* the Lord your God who brought you out from the land of Egypt. . . . But *you shall remember the Lord* your God, for it is He" (Deut 8:11, 14, 18). Implied here is that to forget is effectively to deny God; to remember

---

94. Maimonides, *Maimonides Reader*, 396–97; *Mishneh Torah*, s.v. "Laws Concerning Character Traits" I.5.

95. Frank, "End of the Guide," 489.

is to obey God. Aristotle's *phronimos*, as a proud man, would fall under the first category.[96]

Frank claims no awareness that, like Maimonides, Aristotle makes a distinction between two different levels of morality (*hakham* and *hasid*), but surely Aristotle does, as he distinguishes between a nominally or merely virtuous act and a fully or genuinely virtuous act. Now, if that is not two levels, and ultimately this is to be interpreted as nonvirtuous versus virtuous (rather than merely versus fully virtuous), then the same bifurcation will be implied in Maimonides's view about Aristotle—namely, that the Aristotelian man does not simply commit *merely* virtuous acts, but *non*virtuous acts in the same way that without *phronesis* the other so-called virtues are not real virtues. A similar situation obtains without *emunah*. Either way, the distinction is profound and is a difference that *makes* a difference. Now, given the *emunah* factor and humility of *hakham* (and certainly *hasid*), the bifurcation demonstrated in Maimonides and Aristotle is clearly explained, given the virtue of faith, which actually underwrites the humility and also serves as an enhanced motivator to living the good life.

What is it, after all, that brings about humility as a virtue? What alerts Maimonides to the fact that humility and not pride, à la Aristotle, is a virtue? It is seeing oneself more accurately in light of the cosmic drama and a greater understanding of who God is via instruction given in Torah. Reminiscent of Isaiah 6, Maimonides draws attention to our sense of awe in reference to the divine: "When a man reflects on these things, studies all these created beings, from the angels and spheres down to human beings and so on, and realizes the Divine Wisdom manifested in them, his love for God will increase, his soul will thirst, his very flesh will yearn to love God. He will be filled with fear and trembling, as he becomes conscious of his own lowly condition."[97] It is the virtue of faith that underwrites one's moving to humility (on any scale, extreme or moderate). Whereas most virtues for Maimonides are defined by the mean, this virtue is not one simply found in the mean, but grows in virtue toward the extreme as knowledge of God grows. Maimonides does not expressly say it, but he is committed to it.

Yes, Moses was ostensibly the paradigmatic person of utter humility,[98] but the highly regarded Abraham was an example of faith, and it was evident through his life that he grew in it. Thus, if faith be a moral virtue, and a seriously motivating virtue, then *emunah* would be something that explains, in

---

96. Maimonides, *Maimonides Reader*, 396–97.
97. Maimonides, *Maimonides Reader*, 48.
98. As cited in Numbers 12:3 in Maimonides, "Laws Concerning Character Traits" II.3.

part, the humility, but is also a key to understanding a bifurcation between Jew and non-Jew. A proud virtuous man (*phronimos*) would not be identical to a humble virtuous man (*hakham*), much less an extremely humble one, and one with *emunah*. Maimonides is implicitly committed here to doing what Aristotle does in *NE* II.4,[99] where for Maimonides the *phronimos* is a virtuous man in name only because he lacks the virtues of *emunah* and humility like Aristotle's hypothetical person who acts virtuously only homonymously because he lacks *phronesis*.

Aristotle's pride of place is not with the moral but with the contemplative, which is amoral/apolitical like unto his deity. For Maimonides, the pride of place is given to the contemplative, but that is positively moral/political, the *hasid* (e.g., Moses) above the plane of *hakham*. But again, note that since *hakham* might not be PM morality, it is still AM morality and on a higher plane than the *phronimos* which is lacking, and indeed opposed to, the Maimonidean man of humility and *emunah*. If an example of *hasid* is Moses, then, of course, *hasid* has actually reached moral and intellectual perfection and is now in PM morality, fulfilling the *imitatio Dei* at its best. Humility disregards other humans' assessment, utter humility far more. Frank observes:

> For the *Hasid*—and this point is obvious but nonetheless important—the ultimate ground for morality is God. "Anyone who makes his heart haughty denies the existence of God," said the rabbis of *Avot*, thinking of Deut 8:14, a passage which we have seen Maimonides quoting with approval. To take interest in worldly honor is to forget God, to live and to act as if God did not exist.[100]

So the *hasid* existing without the virtue of faith cannot be, but this is also true of the *hakham*. The *hakham* is therefore not equivalent to the *phronimos*. Obviously, this all makes for an utterly different ethical perspective. As Steven Schwarzschild says, as a general rule, "look for the evaluations of honor and humility, and you will find the fundamental rift between Greek and Jewish ethics down through the ages."[101]

Frank admits that with respect to Maimonidean humility, it "manifests nothing less than his anti-Aristotelian theocentric morality," and that Moses is the paradigm of what man may achieve in this life; that "for him, God, not man, is the author of the moral law, and as a *result* of this ethical theocentrism

---

99. See Aristotle, *NE* II.4, 1105b5–9.
100. Frank, "Humility as a Virtue," 97.
101. Schwarzschild, "Moral Radicalism and 'Middlingness,'" 64–95.

the Mosaic stance toward God was one of extreme humility."[102] Frank points out that "In the case of Moses, the paradigmatic *hasid*, extreme humility and disdain for worldly honor necessarily follows from the knowledge that God is the author of the moral law and that man's ultimate felicity depends on obedience to this (divine) law, and to nothing else."[103]

Implications often go unnoticed. It is thus surprising that Frank has not been more aware of the role of the virtue of faith within Maimonides. Perhaps this is the intellectualist interpretation often construed of Maimonides, or perhaps it is a sensitivity toward the Christian emphasis on belief versus the Jewish emphasis on action. In either case, Maimonides speaks for himself when so allowed.

Extreme humility was brought about and is explained by Moses's understanding of the source of the moral law and the authority it carries. This is, of course, why I say again that the virtue of faith is important, and further that it serves as the greater rift through the ages between Jew and pagan.

For Maimonides, then, disdain for worldly honor is compatible with a proper self-concept, especially in light of a theocentric ethic motivated by the virtue of faith. One's value is not determined by what others think but by the One in whose image we are made. Humility, for Aristotle, points to ignorance of self (an epistemic deficiency) and lack of self-worth as shown by man's robbing himself of the honor due himself.[104] Being humble as a result of faith is a matter of self-injustice, the opposite of the Maimonidean virtue of faith which is doing justice to one's own soul. Humility may be, as Frank suggests, *the* virtue becoming a pious man, a man of God, but I suggest that the virtue of faith is the prerequisite for becoming a genuine *hasid* (as well as *hakham*), without which we have a virtuous person who is virtuous in name only, *phronimos*, one who in a Maimonidean sense denies God.

Finally, consider Aristotle's *theoria* where his interpretation of *imitatio Dei* reflects the activity of God as thinking itself thinking. He divorces godlike happiness from the practical life, being engaged in wholly theoretical ways (even if only for a short while). By contrast, Maimonides claims that the ultimate human good entails a life devoted to deeds of justice, righteousness, and lovingkindness. Why? Because one's deeds need to be informed by a sense of awareness that such are the sort which God himself does. Maimonides says that all affection is evil, entailing for him that moral activities at their highest level are done dispassionately, just as God does them. One cannot invoke virtuous dispositions here since virtue has to do with

---

102. Frank, "Humility as a Virtue," 98 (emphasis mine).
103. Frank, "Humility as a Virtue," 98.
104. Aristotle, *NE* IV.3, 1125a19–23.

affections and actions per Aristotle. For Aristotle, one's virtuous acts are to be accompanied by appropriate feelings.[105] Thus, the theistic foundation serves as a supreme motivator such that merely doing actions without the awareness of the divine foundation is insufficient.

Aristotle's *phronimos* lacks such a sufficient foundation. Indeed, given his theology, "the gods will appear ridiculous" if they engage in such practical lives.[106] For Aristotle, the foundation for the morally virtuous person was the *phronimos*; for Maimonides, it is God. This could not be for Aristotle because he has no such concept of a moral divinity in his ontology. Aristotle's *theos* is utterly unconcerned with human affairs in the moral sphere. Perhaps his man of superhuman virtue (the hero) mentioned briefly in the *NE* could be a comparative candidate, but not so in the end because Aristotle's divinity is incorporeal, and moral virtue requires corporeality, entailing capacity for affection. He says, "as animals cannot possess badness or excellence, so neither can a god."[107] It's as though he wants to make room for a superhuman moral agent, but cannot.

In addition, the faith factor directed toward a substantially thicker version of the deity is a substantial motivator for the Maimonidean over the Aristotelian. While Aristotle clearly has a place for wonder in his worldview, it does not compare with what is available to Maimonides because the divine cannot ground morality for Aristotle as the divine does for Maimonides. For one, moral motivation surrounding *imitatio Dei* in Aristotle is incomparable with Maimonides given the providential care and authoritativeness that comes along with divine command theory in Maimonides. As Frank's explication points out, for Aristotle, the divine evinces unconcern for the material world, while Maimonides's divine (displayed paradigmatically via Mosaic prophecy), reveals God's providential care for creation.[108] As noted by Jonathan Jacobs, "The gift of Torah is what enables human beings to be close to God by being like God, and that essentially involves exercising judgment, righteousness, and lovingkindness." If moral requirements are commanded by God, regardless of whether some are discernable by human reason, then there is the question of whether responding to them is essential to proper motivation.[109]

In the end, whereas Frank claims that the penultimate human good as the virtuous life or moral perfection is one and the same for Maimonides

---

105. Maimonides, *Guide* I.54.
106. Aristotle, *NE* X.8, 1178b11.
107. Aristotle, *NE* VI, 1145a25–26.
108. Frank, "Maimonides and Medieval Jewish Aristotelianism," 136–56.
109. Jacobs, *Law, Reason, and Morality*, 139.

and Aristotle, differing substantially only on the fourth level of perfection, intellectual perfection, his analysis is shortsighted. It seems clear that even AM morality at the third level differs given the fact that without *emunah* the *phronimos* is a virtuous person in name only.[110] We are now in a position to see what PM morality might look like after attaining the highest perfection, intellectual perfection.

"Morality" upon the Attainment of Perfection

As previously noted, the knowledge of God is of the highest importance to Maimonides. Human perfection turns out to be a matter of rational contemplation where intellectual perfection is the highest achievement of man. But the question was also raised about moral theory in relation to human perfection. Is it only of instrumental value on our way up, as it were, such that only AM exists? Considering the fact that Maimonides does not believe that we can know God in his essence (what God is), but only in his effects (that God is), it follows that knowledge of God is knowledge of God's effects. The nature of the object known and loved will determine the understanding of the ultimate end, the imitation of that object. Given Maimonides's via negativa, the best we can know are God's ways which are perceived by us as the actions done by God. This is why Moses asks God to show him His ways so that Moses could know God (known via his actions). To know God's ways is the route by which God can be known. Interestingly, Aristotle once referred to God as "a way of life" (diagoge) in Metaphysics XII.7. This notion of "the way" figures prominently in Christianity as Jesus ascribed the title to himself and then the early Christian church took upon itself that same name.[111] To follow God in this way is to imitate God in his "actional attributes" (hence, the imitatio Dei mentioned earlier).

This is where PM comes into play in relation to the perfection of the intellect. Maimonides says that "the end of the universe is . . . a seeking to be like unto His perfection as far as in its capacity."[112] Human intellection may be a mode of *imitatio Dei*. But given his negative theology, it is not open to Maimonides to imitate God outside of God's ways, and certainly not understood à la Aristotle's *theoria* where God is "thought thinking itself thinking."[113] God talk (or thought) is equivocal for Maimonides; in other words, there is no comparison between our thoughts and God's thoughts.

110. Frank, "End of the Guide," 489.
111. Aristotle, *Metaphysics* XII.7, 1072b14.
112. Maimonides, *Guide* I.69.
113. Seeskin, "Sanctity and Silence," 7–24.

The best we can do is to imitate God's actions or effects; in other words, his actional attributes. The contemplative life does issue in a sort of conduct, however, which is what constitutes *imitatio Dei*. The AM morality has been informed and therefore transformed into PM morality.

Another contrast that is tied into the understanding of the object of one's ultimate contemplation is that in which the state itself consists. If Aristotle's view of God is right, then it is no wonder that Aristotle adopts (on an exclusivist view of the human good) an account of an amoral/apolitical *theoria* as the way of imitating the divine. Moral virtue is not depicted in this section for Aristotle as the *summum bonum*. For both thinkers, the true self is the immortal and divine part of 'ourselves,' and correlative to this metaphysical claim, we can understand their choice of philosophical understanding as the *summum bonum*. For Aristotle it is the philosopher, for Maimonides it takes the shape of the philosopher-prophet.[114]

This vision of the summum bonum, the life of happiness, is at best rare or episodic and at worst only an unachievable ideal, elusive for most. But for Maimonides, however, it is an obtainable reality, a life that can be lived in light of divine providence. He adopts a moral/political aspect of the contemplative life. His paradigm is the prophet-philosopher-statesman, Moses, who parallels the platonic philosopher-king. He is the halakhic contemplative. But unlike Plato's philosopher ascending from the cave, enamored by the intelligible world of forms (and, like Aristotle, preferring to stay in that state), he is compelled to return and teach the masses; Moses descends from conviction and emunah.[115]

So we have two discrete visions of the *summum bonum,* active versus contemplative, grounded in what human nature and knowledge of God consist, in accordance with the notions of the *imago Dei* and *imitatio Dei*. Frank has argued that Maimonides moves from one kind of virtue theory early on in the "Eight Chapters" (in his *Commentary on the Mishnah*) and "Laws Concerning Character Traits" (in his *Mishneh Torah*) to a view near the end of the *Guide* where his mature philosophical views are expressed in his conception of *imitatio Dei* as "walking in God's ways."[116] The paradigm case of prophecy is in the giving of Torah by Moses and is rooted in divine science to the extent possible for a human being, which is not a completely natural phenomenon. Prophecy itself may be natural, but the proclamation of it is not, nor is the foretelling of future events which flows from the perfected imaginative faculty of the prophet. There neither was

---

114. Aristotle, *NE* X.7–8.
115. Plato, *Republic* 520a8.
116. Frank, "Development of Maimonides's Moral Psychology," 89–105.

nor will there be another prophet like Moses any more than there was or will be another Torah. Frank offers an interpretation of Maimonides's Mosaic experience of the *summum bonum*, referring it as "somnambulism," akin to a mode of sleepwalking, where the prophet is in a contemplative state while simultaneously acting dispassionately in the world. Moses is the ultimate multitasker, able to walk in God's ways while simultaneously in a state of blissful divine contemplation.[117]

Knowledge of the divine discovered in creation is the foundation for prophecy whose human limitations are accounted for both in terms of man's finitude and fallenness, both of which can be aided by instruction from the Torah (which is a display of God's gift to us). It is from such knowledge that we gain *amor Dei* (love of God), manifested as a desire to imitate God's ways (e.g., lovingkindness, justice, and righteousness), not to imitate his dispositions which we are precluded from positing in accordance with his *via negativa*. Just as our knowledge of God is of His ways and not His character traits, so we are to imitate in a like manner, dispassionately.[118]

So the best life is one that is reflectively dispassionate, and a regimen for its attainment is given for those who have attained or are on the path to attaining knowledge of God. Along these lines there is a bifurcation between *sacred* and *secular*, but a bifurcation which collapses in the prophetic lives (especially those of Moses and the Patriarchs like Abraham). Maimonides says, "It is thinkable that a man should achieve such a degree of perfection ... and happiness ... that he is able to talk to people ... while at the same time his intellect is turned towards God."[119] Maimonides claims that this way of life, a wholly sacred life of divine providence, obtains so long as one's gaze is upon God. It is as though the immortal, rational self, without emotional expression, is somehow in a state of detached divine legislation. That is, he is somehow detached from the world in divine contemplation whilst simultaneously attached and functioning as a living medium or conduit, providing divinely revealed legislation.[120]

At the end of the *Guide*, following his description of the four perfections of man (wealth, health, morality, and theoretical levels), he goes on to talk about the subsequent imitation of God, *imitatio Dei*, which is shown by nature to include a moral/political component such that the life of action is esteemed. Only the last in the order of these four perfections is

---

117. Maimonides, *Guide* III.51. Maimonides describes this as walking in God's ways with limbs only.
118. Maimonides, *Guide* I.54.
119. Maimonides, *Guide* III.51.
120. Dobbs-Weinstein, *Maimonides and St. Thomas*, 155–71.

the proper end, all others being means to the proper end. Yet near the end of the *Guide*, after one has achieved the exalted state of apprehending God (in His ways), in conjunction with Jeremiah 9:23–24 he says, "The way of life of such an individual, after he has achieved this apprehension, will always have in view lovingkindness, righteousness and judgment, through assimilation to His actions."[121]

In the Jeremiah passage, as Maimonides points out, God *performs* actions of loving-kindness, righteousness and judgment, and these things are to be done by the one in the fourth level of perfection as *imitatio Dei*. For Maimonides, the passage reflects how an individual, transformed by an enlightened encounter with God, should imitate God. Maimonides's man is impelled (by transformation) to descend back into the cave, as it were, on account of what he's learned about imitating God, driven by a love for God; *amor Dei*. On the love of God, which every Jew is commanded (Deut 6:5), Maimonides seems to hold that love of God and knowledge of God are identical. But it does not follow that they are. Textually, while some passages seem to equate them, others imply that loving God is a consequence of knowing God. Arguably, the textual evidence implies that the more one knows, the more one loves, such that there is a corresponding increase.[122]

Hence, the role of morality in human perfection is shown once intellectual perfection has been achieved as PM, distinct from AM. The final result, seeming to be of a moral/political end, however, provokes reaction. Does Maimonides intend that intellectual perfection really is not the highest perfection and may simply be an ideal as opposed to the real life of action?[123] Maimonides gave an argument against the highest perfection being practical since it requires the involvement of other people. Shatz seeks resolution here in virtue of the fact that the way of life following the highest perfection is not itself the perfection per se but an overflow of the perfection itself.[124] Support comes from the *Guide*: "Know that in the case of every being that causes a certain good thing to overflow . . . and the end of the being conferring the benefits . . . the end is nobler than the things that subsist for the sake of the end."[125]

In any case, in relation to intellectual perfection, the crucial role of morality is present in accordance with both AM and PM, instrumental

121. Maimonides, *Guide* III.54.
122. Maimonides, *Mishneh Torah*, s.v. "Laws of the Foundations" II.1, 35; "Laws of Repentance" X.6, 92b. For more, see Kellner, "Is Maimonides's Ideal Person Austerely Rationalist?," 140–42; Benor, *Worship of the Heart*.
123. Pines, "Limitations of Human Knowledge," 100.
124. Shatz, "Maimonides's Moral Theory," 186.
125. Maimonides, *Guide* II.11.

and consequential. In AM, the focus was on psychological, dispositional traits and stabilizing character, whereas in a robust *imitatio Dei*, man will share no emotions or passions in the matter (which are evil when taken in reference to a prophet-ruler's decision-making) since neither does God. So the difference between Maimonides's legal writings (and the traits exhibited) and the *Guide* (where the truly virtuous person is on display) shows a development in Maimonides of the AM/PM distinction between the former and the latter.[126]

What is important about this distinction for Maimonides emerges from the following description of two different kinds of perfect individuals. The first kind is able to be perfected on his own; the second kind is not only perfect in his own right, but is also able to significantly help others perfect themselves in a way not otherwise possible. For Maimonides, both the philosopher and the prophet receive the truth in their intellects through conjunction with the active intellect,[127] but only the prophet with his imagination governed by reason (the reversal of the fall and the negative role of imagination) is able to use those truths to help other people (viz., the masses—those who cannot on their own receive truths from active intellect) live in accordance with truth. This further ability on the part of the prophet is precisely tied to his having a strong imaginative faculty, one that is ruled by reason as opposed to one that rules reason (à la our fallen condition).

The Active Intellect was greatly discussed in medieval philosophy, but first mentioned in Aristotle's *De Anima*.[128] I will not attempt to settle the disputes here. Roughly, though, the human intellect goes from its original state of not thinking to an actual or acquired intellect. The passive intellect receives intelligible forms, but the active makes the potential knowledge into actual in a way that light makes actual colors from potential ones. In his *Metaphysics*, Aristotle seems to identify the active intellect with the unmoved mover, external to the human mind.[129] But Maimonides, shaped here a bit more by a neo-Platonist impetus, held that Active Intellect was the lowest of the ten emanations and cites it in his definition of prophecy as an emanation flowing from God by means of the Active Intellect first upon the rational faculty and then upon the imaginative faculty

We have seen Maimonides's departure from Aristotle at several points, but a notable point is with respect to becoming a prophet. Maimonides defines prophecy as an "overflow overflowing from God" via active intellect

---

126. Kellner, *Maimonides on Human Perfection*.
127. Maimonides, *Guide* III.36 (225).
128. Aristotle, *De Anima* III.5, 430a10–25.
129. Aristotle, *Metaphysics* XII.7–10.

toward the rational faculty in the first place and thereafter toward the imaginative faculty. This is the highest degree of man. ... This is something that cannot by any means exist in every man. And it is not something that can be attained solely through perfection in the speculative sciences and through improvement of moral habits, even if all of them have become as fine and good as can be. There is still need in addition to the highest possible degree of perfection of the imaginative faculty in respect of its original natural disposition.[130]

So beyond moral and intellectual perfection, there must be a reasonably developed imagination. One virtue of this faculty is that it distorts reality and enables communication of divine truths to the masses. It retains sense perceptible objects in the mind, combines them, and imitates them. "A certain overflow overflows to this faculty according to its disposition ... and is the cause of prophecy. There is only difference in degree, not in kind."[131] Thus, human perfection is more than simply perfection in abstract knowledge. It is not wholly natural, even though it enters into what is natural, as "it is our fundamental principle that there must be training and perfection, whereupon the possibility arises to which the power of the deity becomes attached."[132] There are natural constraints. It is not possible for God, for example, to make an ignorant or vulgar person into a prophet.[133] For Maimonides, a person both fit for prophecy and prepared for it will invariably, though not necessarily, be a prophet (allowing, of course, for God's free providence in the withholding of prophecy).

He points out that "with regard to everything that can be known by demonstration, the status of the prophet and that of everyone else who knows it are equal; there is no superiority of one over the other."[134] So the content is the same for (the Jewish) philosopher and prophet. But, of course, Aristotle, given the lack of certain virtues like faith and humility, could not even reach moral perfection to get there. The philosopher or man of science (for contemporary purposes these are to be synonymous) becomes a prophet on account of the imagination, a divine overflow. (Most unusual, though, is that Moses prophesied without imagination. Of course, Moses was not a normal prophet and cannot be taken as the ideal to be emulated.)

130. Maimonides, *Guide* II.36 (372).
131. Maimonides, *Guide* II.36 (370).
132. Maimonides, *Guide* II.32 (362).
133. Maimonides, *Guide* II.34. See also Kaplan, "Maimonides on the Miraculous Element," 233–56.
134. Maimonides, *Guide* II.33 (364).

Typically, there are two kinds of prophets: those who prophesy for themselves (i.e., reach a high level of personal perfection), and those who prophesy for others. It makes sense to interpret him to mean that a perfected imagination is only necessary for the second kind of prophet; but, in point of fact, he does not say that and indeed distinguishes scientist/philosophers from prophets by saying that the latter have perfected imaginations and the former do not. One might want to differentiate between an imagination controlled by reason and one which controls reason.[135]

For Maimonides, knowledge is transformative, and intellectual perfection is the true human good. Yet without initially arriving at and sustaining moral perfection, one cannot achieve any significant intellectual perfection.[136] And, of course, intellectual perfection is a prerequisite to becoming a prophet. According to Kellner, Maimonides thinks that most non-Jews (and many Jews) are unlikely to attain intellectual perfection, and it is clearly harder without the Torah, showing Maimonides pointing to clear advantages for those in possession of the Torah.[137] But I think Maimonides stakes out more radical territory than what Kellner grants.

While Maimonides may not always be so explicit about it, it seems that he is committed to the view that the non-Jew who is without faith, a moral virtue, can never in this life reach the highest human good, the good life. Perhaps it is less likely without divine aid via Torah, as Kellner posits. But even with Torah, if one is without *emunah*, then one cannot achieve moral perfection. And, of course, Aristotle does not take faith to be a virtue, a significant moral virtue for Maimonides and his notion of moral perfection.

One cannot achieve significant intellectual perfection without antecedent moral perfection, given the product of tranquility and quiet that moral perfection brings; and, of course, obedience to Torah *mitzvah* is the very best tool available for this. Thus, it is easy to see why it follows that few non-Jews if any will make it. Divine providential care accords with the degree of one's intellectual perfection. Indeed, as Maimonides says, "the moral virtues are a preparation for the rational virtues, it being *impossible* to achieve true, rational acts—I mean perfect rationality—unless it be by a man thoroughly trained in his morals and endowed with the qualities of tranquility and quiet."[138]

---

135. I owe this to my personal correspondence with Menachem Kellner (January 30, 2009). See also Kellner, "Is Maimonides's Ideal Person Austerely Rationalist?," 138–39; Maimonides, *Guide* II.37; Faur, *Homo Mysticus*, 73.

136. Maimonides, *Guide* III.48 (599–600), 54 (635).

137. Kellner, "Is Maimonides's Ideal Person Austerely Rationalist?," 128n15.

138. Maimonides, *Guide* I.34 (76–77) (emphasis mine). See also Maimonides, *Guide* II.32 (361), 36 (369–72); III.27 (510), 54 (635).

While Maimonides affirms the theoretical possibility that non-Jews could prophesy, he thought that practically speaking it was impossible for them to achieve this since moral perfection is a prerequisite, and as we have seen, a Gentile cannot be morally perfect in this life since he lacks at least, the virtue of faith. This entails that not even Aristotle achieved prophecy.[139] Some of Maimonides's interpreters read him as though he held that Aristotle reached the highest human level of intellectual perfection available without prophecy. But as we have shown, this fourth level perfection does not seem possible without the third level antecedent perfection, which is not possible without *emunah*. For this reason, and in light of Maimonides's perspective, Oliver Leaman says that, given "Aristotle's lack of religious commitment, he is insufficiently cognizant of the role of humility," a virtue produced by another virtue, *emunah*.[140] If not Aristotle, as highly as Maimonides regarded him, then the possibility that other non-Jews could is bleak.

Aristotle may well have been a religious man in terms of his own culture, but not in accordance with Maimonides's perspective regarding the particular virtues of humility and *emunah*, both of which are related in some sense to man's relation to or knowledge of God. Aristotle simply did not consider humility or faith as virtues and so would have lacked the kind of religious commitment Leaman is referring to.

As said at the beginning, Maimonides adopts various Aristotelian viewpoints and strategies, and (with substantive disagreement) adapts them for his own philosophical purposes. We have seen some advantages that the Maimonidean may have over the Aristotelian. Yet in the process of our discussion, questions have been raised as we have also seen that Maimonides's viewpoints are also quite exclusionary in their own right, and one wonders whether he can be acquitted or perhaps there is a better way.

In chapter 3, Aquinas's viewpoint on the good life will be considered as was Maimonides's in this chapter, and then in chapter 4 the two medievalists will be compared side by side more directly where implications will be drawn one for another and a further development of Aquinas's position considered in light of modern discussions in neuro and social sciences.

---

139. Kellner, *Maimonides on Human Perfection*, 35–50.
140. Leaman, "Ideals, Simplicity, and Ethics," 111.

3

Aquinas and the Good Life

Thomas Aquinas, once known as the "Dumb Ox," became the most prolific writer of the Middle Ages. His theory on the good life is greatly influenced by the one he commonly refers to in the *Summa Theologica* (*ST*) as "the philosopher," who is none other than Aristotle. In particular, Aquinas's moral theory seems to adopt and adapt for his purposes Aristotle's *Nicomachean Ethics* (*NE*), which drew substantial criticism and was at the heart of the argument for the Protestant Reformation.[1] But Aquinas's moral theory and the *summum bonum* more generally are also shaped by his theology, primarily the biblical and Augustinian portrait, so that his system is sometimes looked on as an attempt to synthesize Aristotelian philosophy and Augustinian theology, both of which share a teleological and eudaimonistic framework.

In this chapter, I will provide an account of the good life as explored through Aquinas's doctrines of the fall and human perfectibility. In the first section, I will exploit the Aristotelian background to set up and illuminate the similarity with and significant departure from Aristotle. Like Maimonides, Aquinas shares with Aristotle the same fundamental structure of the good life (including human nature, the human *telos*, and the general transitory story from the former to the latter); the caveat is that there are important distinctions at every point (e.g., the image of God and what it means to be god-like in the *summum bonum*, and the significant features of grace and living faith making this possible, to name a few). I will not be overly concerned with the good life beyond the here and now (i.e., the beatific vision) except insofar as one's view of it may or may not affect one's appropriation of the good life in the here and now.

In the second section, where I consider the prelapsarian state of human flourishing, I will lay out the relevant information for understanding the nature and extent of the fall by considering Aquinas's meta-ethical background, human moral psychology, and human action relevant to the fall and

1. Martin Luther cited in Oberman, *Luther*, 121.

human perfectibility. In the third section, I will provide a Thomistic account of sin, primal sin, and the consequences for human perfectibility relevant to original sin. Given the nature and extent of the lapse, in the fourth section, I will put forth what I take to be some necessary conditions for the transition to and attainment of the good life in light of what at first glance appears to be a more pessimistic state than either Aristotle or Maimonides imagined. Finally, in the fifth section, I will show how Aquinas's position responds to many of the problems saddling Aristotle's position in light of these necessary conditions, even with the intense gravity of human lapse.

The Aristotelian Synthesis

Aquinas's corpus is replete with explicit Aristotelian influence. Some claim that "without Aristotle, Thomas would not be."[2] Indeed, aside from the Apostle Paul and St. Augustine, it seems that no one is cited more by Aquinas than Aristotle.[3] Yet while comparisons run deep, Aquinas is far from a mere apprentice of Aristotle. For it is also believed that without Thomas, Aristotle would be silent![4] With respect to the good life, Aquinas explores and exploits Aristotle's thought for his own purposes in a number of different contexts.

One might think that it simply reduces to this: The moral life and the overall good life must fall under the rubric of Christian revelation; and since Aristotle (a pagan philosopher) fails at this, then Aquinas's views are correct and Aristotle's incorrect; end of story. But Aquinas does not take that road. He does not reject outright Aristotle's notion of an ultimate end, but distinguishes between such an end and that in which such a notion is realized. He takes Aristotle's view to be that the notion of an ultimate end could not be realized by humans. Aristotle spoke as though such a state was durable and permanent, but then claimed that humans could never attain that ideal since human happiness amounts to an imperfect realization of the ultimate end (bringing about the charge in chapter 1 that Aristotle's view renders man a "cosmic orphan"). For Aquinas, moral theology purports not to be a total alternative to natural knowledge about the human good but to be complementary (as well as necessary). To use Aristotelian vernacular, Aquinas's view provides

---

2. McInerny, *Thomas Aquinas*, 34.
3. Jordan, *Ordering Wisdom*.
4. Owens, "Aristotle and Aquinas," 38–59; Jaffa, *Thomism and Aristotelianism*; Kenny, "Aquinas on Aristotelian Happiness," 15–27; MacDonald, "Ultimate Ends in Practical Reasoning," 31–65; MacIntyre, *Whose Justice?*

the form to the lack or privation found in Aristotle's view on the matter. His consideration of Aristotle is, however, significant.

First, consider Aquinas's commentary on Aristotle's *NE*, where he simply seeks to explicate what he takes to be Aristotle's view.[5] While it's debatable whether Aristotle's final view of the good life is inclusive (i.e., includes all of the virtues) or exclusive (i.e., contemplative activity alone as posited in Book X of the *NE*), Aquinas thinks Aristotle's understanding of happiness is along the lines of the exclusively contemplative life.[6] As in the case of Maimonides, there are certain virtues Aquinas affirms, like humility, and others he negates, like those he thinks makes a fundamental difference to the virtuous life (e.g., pride). Thus, Aristotle, had he held to an inclusive view, would have been seen by Aquinas as falling short of the life of the virtuous person, without some modification of particular virtues in order to ensure that he possessed them all, given that pride precludes humility and vice versa. Given this, while the inclusive view would shut Aristotle out of the best life, so would Aristotle's exclusive view, the one Aquinas thinks Aristotle actually held, because the intellect is not fully optimized without the virtue of living faith. Aristotle says that the good for man is "activity of soul in accordance with virtue, and if there are several virtues, in accordance with the best and most perfect."

Second, *qua* Christian, with some significant agreement he attempts to reconcile Aristotle's doctrine of happiness with the beatitudes expressed in the biblical Sermon on the Mount. Anthony Kenny comments on the irony: "The Christian texts are distorted to fit the Aristotelian context rather than the other way around."[7]

Third, as a faithful Catholic, Aquinas also provides application and extension of Aristotelian happiness to the Christian doctrine of the ultimate goal being union with God. He understood church doctrine to teach that the ultimate goal of human beings was happiness, Augustinian theology having certainly contributed to this end, which ultimately consisted in heavenly union with God. But it is not entirely clear (and even unlikely) in *NE* that any part of the human being could experience post-mortem life. In locating happiness, they both deny many candidates. But whereas Aristotle affirms that it is a good activity of the soul, Aquinas claims (with Augustine) that, while it is good, it cannot be obtained via a finite or created good.[8] Thus, while it is in

---

5. Aquinas, *Commentary on the "Nicomachean Ethics"*; Kenny, "Aquinas on Aristotelian Happiness," 15–27.

6. Nagel, "Aristotle on *Eudaimonia*," 7–14; Ackrill, "Aristotle on *Eudaimonia*," 15–34; Kenny, *Aristotle on the Perfect Life*.

7. Kenny, "Aquinas on Aristotelian Happiness," 20–21; Aquinas, *ST* I-II.69.4.

8. Aristotle, *NE* 1098b13–20; Aquinas, *ST* I-II.2.1–8.

the uncreated, namely God, that happiness is ultimately found for Aquinas, it is in man's soul that it is ultimately experienced. In agreement with the arguments of Book X, Aquinas claims with Aristotle that happiness is an activity in accordance with perfect virtue and within the intellect, as intellectual activity rather than appetitive, but a sharp difference in nuance will be unpacked once we understand Aquinas's notion of living faith.

Aquinas's development may be seen as an attempt to resolve the ambiguity found largely in Book X of the *NE*.[9] Humanity's deepest aspirations cannot be satisfied in the purely natural and limiting activities of a rational animal. Perfect happiness requires sharing in the superhuman activities of the divine, which requires the supernatural assistance of grace. This is, in part, why Frederick Copleston claims that "Aristotle's truly happy man is the philosopher, not the saint" clearly distinguishing the ordinary philosopher-sage from the philosopher-saint.[10] He also claims that a form of imperfect happiness can in this life be attained by purely natural means just as the virtues can.[11] One may inquire if this rejects the whole Aristotelian doctrine of nature and natural teleology by invoking such assistance. His reply would be that nature provides what is necessary. In the same way that man has not been given fur and claws but instead reason and hands to make a living, so also nature has not given man a natural capacity for perfect happiness; rather, he has been given free will according to which man can turn to God who can then make man happy.[12] Thus, the normative demand found in the ethical theory is not greater than the capacity we have in our limited human natures, *assuming* we take advantage of those capacities and everything available to them, including divine aid. Aquinas develops an enhanced Aristotelian position for this life, not just for the life to come.

Fourth, not only was Aquinas an Aristotelian Christian under the authority of the church, but he was of a particular order, the Dominican order. He uses Aristotelian happiness as part of his own justification of a religious life devoted to teaching and preaching, giving a defense for his own Dominican order as a way of life on the path to perfection or *eudaimonia*. His view was that the *Nicomachean* contemplative ideal is ultimately realized only in the afterlife. But the contemplation and practice of god-likeness is for Aquinas accessible here and now as he tries to make clear the value found within the Dominican order of teaching and preaching the fruits of

---

9. Aristotle, *NE* X, 1177a26–1178b23.
10. Copleston, *Medieval Philosophy*, 398.
11. Aquinas, *ST* I-II.5.5.
12. Aquinas, *ST* I-II.5.1.

contemplation, in that it is better to ignite the light in others than simply be enlightened in isolated solitude.

In this sense, one might think of the platonic philosopher come back to the Cave to enlighten others rather than remain in isolation, the Buddhist Bodhisattva returned from Nirvana to teach others, or Moses from a mountaintop experience with God come back with a code of ethics for life. While the contemplative must possess the moral virtues (to prevent such contemplation from being disrupted by passions), they are not an essential part of the contemplative life itself. Aquinas claims that even though contemplative life is supreme, along with Aristotle, the callings of all religious orders are for the sake of charity, and charity includes love of neighbor, but primarily, love of God, out of which comes an overflow of love of neighbor.[13]

Given two types of active lives—one being a sort of care for the poor, the other being teaching—Aquinas sides with the latter. In authentic and effective teaching and preaching, the religious person is drawing on the fruits of previous contemplation, passing on to others the truths thus grasped. Even though the purely contemplative life is in one sense to be preferred, the best life of all includes the teaching and preaching of the religious life since it is better to share the fruits of one's contemplation with others than to contemplate alone.[14]

It is clear upon analysis that Aquinas shares a common thread with Aristotle at several points, points drawn out in commentary and in comparison with his Christian, Catholic, and Dominican points of view. He greatly admires Aristotle, seeking to "baptize" him where appropriate, even stretching matters at times, but also divorcing himself where he sees Aristotelian shortcomings vis-à-vis his own considered viewpoints, because he does not see Aristotle's viewpoint as a completely successful system. The charge of "cosmic orphan" remains. However, if Aristotle's gap between human nature, human *telos*, and the story seeking to draw them together failed, can Aquinas's view possibly stand, given that his view of the human condition is much more dismal than Aristotle's? After all, given the reality of sin and his view of the human *telos* which is much more enhanced on the thicker expression of his theology and *summum bonum* (e.g., man being made in the image of God, God being personal rather than impersonal, etc.), both contributing to a potentially wider gap between the human capacity and its *telos*, does this not bring about a diminished chance of man actually satisfying the conditions for the attainment of the good life?

---

13. Aquinas, *ST* II-II.180.2, 188.2.
14. Aquinas, *ST* II-II.188.6; Kenny, "Aquinas on Aristotelian Happiness," 27n16.

Prelapsarianism and Human Rectitude

In order to address this question, I will explicate Aquinas's account of the prelapsarian state of human flourishing in juxtaposition to another state denoted as postlapsarian as well as his account of human lapse more generally. Here I will lay out the relevant background material for understanding the nature and extent of the fall from the original prelapsarian state, and consider both how it was possible given this background and the consequences of lapse with respect to human perfectibility.

The Meta-Ethics of Goodness

Aquinas's entire project, of course, takes place within a worldview such that one can hardly talk about his views on human nature and action without recognizing the context in which they exist, namely, a teleological framework of goodness. "Good" is taken as a basic concept both in his ethics and metaphysics in that they share a fundamental relationship.[15]

The Aristotelian claim that "good has rightly been declared to be that which all things desire,"[16] the context for which human action is discussed in Aquinas, is not a psychological description but a normative statement. This is because every art, action, decision, and thought aims at some good, such that good is that which all things desire. Something is not good merely because it is desired; rather, it is desired because it is good. Good is that which is desirable. Its desirability is indicative of its causal nature, being that of a final cause.

We often think of "good" as an exclusively ethical notion. But for Aquinas, it is most fundamentally a metaphysical notion such that good is actually convertible with being.[17] Good is said by him to be among the "firsts" (*prima*) of conceptions of the human intellect.[18] The good each thing desires is in accordance with its nature. While being and goodness are convertible, they are not identical. To be a human being is good but is non-identical to being a good human being (i.e., the good life for a human). What is primary being (e.g., substance) is only initially good, not ultimately, or finally, fully good. This distinction between being and good apply to every finite thing, since for each thing to be and to act are non-identical. The first act of a thing

---

15. Stump and Kretzmann, "Being and Goodness," 98–128.
16. Aristotle, *NE* I.1, 1094a1–3.
17. Aquinas, *Commentary on the "Nicomachean Ethics"* I.1.9.

18. Elsewhere he lists four of these: one, being, true, and good. They are said to transcend the Aristotelian categories and are thus called *transcendentia*.

is its form or substantial being, whereas the second act is its operation. By its first act, it has being absolutely; by its second act, it has good absolutely. Each thing's good differs according to the nature of the species in that a good human being is one who acts in accordance with his nature, whose nature is fundamentally a rational nature.

Aquinas ties metaphysics with ethics by drawing an analogy between theoretical and practical reason by virtue of their first principles: respectively, being and goodness. The transcendental nature of good, then, is the key for Aquinas in understanding his relation of metaphysics and ethics. As a transcendental, "good" is common to the various kinds of goodness, including both metaphysical and moral. Good grounds the first principle of practical reason in the same way that being grounds the first principle of theoretical reason. Sharing the same formal structure, the two aspects of reasoning differ only in their ends (e.g., knowledge of the truth versus extending or directing truth to action as its end in the operation). When we consider good theoretically, we consider it under the aspect of the true. When we consider good practically, we consider it insofar as it is the end of an action. Good is thus the link between the theoretical and practical lives whereby theoretical reason becomes practical by extension.[19]

Human Moral Psychology and Human Action

There is a connection between human psychology and ethics. Ethical eudaimonism, under which Aquinas's moral theory falls, entails the proper functioning of the individual in question in accordance with its natural kind. The goodness of a thing depends upon the thing's nature, in this case human nature, in that nature determines normativity. In human actions, good and evil are essentially related to reason, since "the good of man is to be in accordance with reason."[20] This is the case because of the sort of being man is, a rational being. Aquinas offers a complicated but elaborate and dynamic interrelationship between the various faculties of the soul, all of which adhere to a general teleology and proper function to which human perfectibility is related. The various faculties have, in some sense, causal or influential relationships with the other faculties, and it is important to understand his views on this in order to understand how human lapse can occur and how human perfection is obtained.

---

19. Aquinas, *ST* I.79.11; I.93.6; Aertsen, "Thomas Aquinas on the Good," 235–53; "Convertibility of Being and Good," 449–70. For a different view, see Crosby, "Are Being and Good Really Convertible," 493–94.

20. Aquinas, *ST* I-II.18.5.

Aquinas's view of the intellect in human action is intimately involved with the will. One might think that in his view the will is neutral with respect to decision-making, but this is not the case. The will is inclined. It has a hunger or appetite for goodness; that is, goodness in general.[21] But it does not by itself make determinations of goodness. The apprehension or judgment of things *qua* good is the territory of the intellect, which presents certain things under the aspect of the good to the will, whose job it is then to will it since the will is an appetite for good. In this way, the intellect can move the will as a final (but not efficient) cause since whatever is understood *qua* good moves it as an end.[22] Created by God as an appetite for the good, the will has a natural necessity to will the good, to will that which falls under the description of a good. But some things, like one's own happiness, are taken as obvious goods that are willed by the faculty of the will. Although it is determined to will the good (not by itself, of course, since apprehending something as good is the role of the intellect), it is yet free and can move itself as a self-moved mover. This in no way should be read here as claiming that Aquinas is a compatibilist, although some have read him in this way, and some place him among libertarians.[23]

In contemporary discourse, freedom ultimately relies on the sole component of the will and its ability to act autonomously. But this clouds a Thomistic understanding if one is limited to the contemporary discussion. For Aquinas, freedom of the will is a property of the human being, not a component part and the will, on his account, is not independent from intellect. There exists a dynamic interaction coupled with a natural teleology or bent and also a conditional matter of the fall. Aquinas is most plausibly construed within a libertarian viewpoint (freedom that is incompatible with determinism), but whose nuance is not typical of contemporary discussions.

As far as the intellect making the determination as to what is good and presenting that to the will, the matter is a bit complicated since the intellect can be moved by other things. First, whereas the intellect is a final cause in moving the will, the will can move the intellect as an efficient (but not final) cause. For example, it can command the intellect directly to adopt a belief (e.g., faith in God),[24] or can influence it indirectly by directing it to attend to some things and not to others,[25] supposing of course that the intellect

21. Aquinas, *ST* I-II.10.1; I.82.1.

22. Aquinas, *ST* I.82.4.

23. Pasnau, *Thomas Aquinas on Human Nature*, 221–34; Stump, *Aquinas*, 576–97. For Aquinas's view that the will cannot be coerced, but can move itself, see Aquinas, *ST* I-II.6.4.1; I.82.1; I.83.1.

24. See Aquinas, *Disputed Questions on Truth* 14.3 reply, ad2, 10.

25. Aquinas, *ST* I-II.17.1, 6.

represents doing so at that time and under some aspect as good. In short, we can choose what to set our gaze upon.

Second, the passions can influence the intellect in the case when one is in the grip of a passion (e.g., anxiety, fear, etc.) and something seems good that would otherwise not seem good if in a normal, calm state. But the intellect can resist the influence of such passion by being aware of the passion and minimizing its effects on judgment. For example, instead of making a phone call in anger today, wait until tomorrow when you are in a better frame of mind.[26]

What is also complicated is the way the will is moved by the intellect. Every willing is preceded by an apprehension of the intellect, but not vice versa. The will can be moved by the intellect to act or not to act, or to will this particular thing or that particular thing as it is presented with something under the aspect of good.[27] But it is in the will's power to refuse to think of the thing at hand and thus to not will it of necessity (other than one's own happiness, of course). If the will is presented with some object by the intellect as good under certain descriptions and not so under others, then the will is free not to will it as it is open to the will to command the intellect to consider the object in a variety of descriptions. For example, money is good in one case and evil in another. Adam's fruit might be considered in a variety of ways—healthy in one situation, but sinful in another.

Regardless of what earthly thing apart from happiness that the intellect presents to the will, the will is not constrained to will that particular thing since the will can command the intellect to consider it under a variety of descriptions. Thus, it is difficult to neatly extract the will and intellect from each other.[28] The will is influenced but not coerced.[29]

The manner in which the will moves the other active powers of the soul is as an efficient cause. Given that it is ordered to the good in general, and the other powers to the particular goods alone, the will, like a military general, moves those other powers (lesser ranking officers) under its control (except the vegetative powers not under its control), each power aiming at the good under its own jurisdiction. The power of sight's good, for instance, is color, whereas the intellect's is knowledge of truth, etc. The will has some control over the sensitive powers. For example, it can choose to close the eyes or not. The will works in tandem with the other powers, according to the design plan, to achieve the good it was designed to achieve.

26. Aquinas, *ST* I.81.3; I.82.4; I-II.9.2; I-II.10.3.
27. Aquinas, *ST* I-II.9.1.
28. Aquinas, *ST* I-II.17.1.
29. Aquinas, *ST* I-II.5.1; I-II.17.2.

While the will has no voluntary control over certain beliefs in cases where our cognitive capacities have been sufficiently moved by their objects, the will does have power over some beliefs. We can will to believe certain things and not others (e.g., empirical beliefs, memory beliefs, or perceptual beliefs; attending to certain evidences and not others, thus strengthening or changing beliefs' repression and also suppression). The will can misdirect cognitive faculties in the same way as it moves body parts if it can somehow see something as an aspect of good. So the process by which the will corrupts the intellect only requires it to have indirect control over the intellect, but the process by which the will and the intellect function together in order to produce, for example, wisdom, requires the will to have direct control over the intellect, since wisdom is a virtue and virtues are properly attached to the will. More on this later, but suffice it to say for now that the person who has faith in God forms an assent to a set of propositions under the influence of volition, which then has the effect of moving the intellect to such an assent. Yet, as we will also see, this particular volition is produced by divine grace, for which God alone is responsible. Wisdom grows out of charity, which itself depends on faith, where faith is such that the will exercises direct control over intellect on his view. So wisdom, as Aquinas treats it predominantly, depends upon faith.

As it turns out, wisdom is a dynamic and complex interaction between the intellect and will, connected ultimately to moral goodness. So the will plays a role in some, though not all, acts of the intellect. This interrelationship is crucial in understanding Aquinas's view of faith.

For our purposes, we will concern ourselves with those departments of human psychological experience that involve the intellective soul and the sensitive soul. Relative to human moral psychology, like the intellective soul, the sensitive soul also has two departments, cognitive and appetitive. Whereas the objectis of the intellective soul (being volition and thought) are the good and the true, the objects of the sensitive soul (being movement and sensation) are the particular and the universal.

Now, the appetitive faculty in the sensitive soul comprises the passions, which are the sort of things that the soul can experience through active or passive powers. Whereas active potencies enable us to do something, passive ones enable us to undergo something. The former's movements from potency to act are explained by an internal principle for their actualization, whereas the latter's movements are by an external principle. Thus, the act of such a set of potencies is either one of acting or of being acted upon. Properly speaking, within such human "acts" is the distinction between action and passion.

The passions of the soul are passive potencies whereby the soul is acted upon to bring about some state; for example, being saddened by the death of a friend. The sensitive part of the soul is essentially passive, whereas the intellective soul is essentially active. Loving (appetitive potency being realized) and smelling (cognitive/perceptual potency being realized) are essentially passive even though the grammar suggests they are active (e.g., loving God is a matter of being acted upon). Passions are individuated by their objects such that loving may be described as where the object external to the subject acts upon the subject to induce a loving state, and where the subject is intentional or attentive to the external cause, which is the object eliciting the love of the subject.

Importantly, Aquinas has analogues to the passions that pertain to the purely intellective part of the soul, which Peter King alludes to and calls "pseudo passions." But unlike the ordinary passions, these do not require bodily reactions or material basis, as their respective location is in the intellective appetite as rational acts of will. This explains how angels or other disembodied souls are capable of having "passions" (i.e., pseudo passions). Whereas animals can only have passions and angels only pseudo passions (except in embodied states), living humans are capable of both. A passion like the craving of chocolate is distinct from a pseudo passion, like the desire to eradicate chocolate consumption.[30]

Just as the formal object of the cognitive faculties is the true, the formal object of the appetitive faculties is the good. More specifically, just as the formal object of the intellective appetite (the will) is the immaterial good, so too the formal object of the sensitive appetite (the passions) is the sensitive good.[31] Now, since it is a fundamental principle of Aquinas that all creation tends toward the good, then all the passions must tend toward the good, at least toward the apparent good. His primary grouping, the concupiscible passions (love, hate, desire, aversion, joy, and sorrow), is interestingly connected to the first principle of practical reasoning (pursue good and avoid evil). We are to love good, hate evil, desire (move toward) good, be aversive (move away from) to evil, experience joy in the possession of good, and experience sorrow without the possession of good. Thus, he concludes that the passions begin with love/hate and end with joy/sorrow.[32]

Aquinas recognizes that we often explain our actions by appeal to motives, passion being one of them. For example, in the case where someone hits another person out of anger, it seems that the passion is ruling the

---

30. King, "Aquinas on the Passions," 105–6n7.
31. Aquinas, *ST* I.80.2.
32. Aquinas, *ST* I-II.25.1–2.

person. Aquinas thinks of two ways in which the passion of a man occurs: first, as just described, which he likens to the way of brute beasts where the impulse of passion is followed of necessity without movement of will or reason;[33] and second, where the man's intellective soul, reason and will, triumph. In the first case, passions literally overwhelm the individual, bringing him down to the condition of merely animal nature such that he really is not "acting" in the proper sense of human action.[34] Later, when more sober minded, the individual realizes that he was previously out of control in a fit of rage when he committed what we often call a "crime of passion." In ordinary cases, the individual, at the consent of the will, goes along with the passion rather than being consumed or overcome by it (i.e., he could have refrained, but saw in the object some apparent or real good).[35] So although the passions are of a passive nature, it does not follow that we are completely passive with respect to our passions.

Next, just because of their passive nature, it does not follow that the passions themselves are always involuntary. For one thing, the individual can choose what to set his gaze upon, such that the occasion is provided for some passions to arise. Similarly, one can to a certain extent control not only the appetitive but also the vegetative soul by choosing what if anything to consume such that the occasion is provided for digestion to take place (digestion not being ordinarily voluntary). For an action to be a proper human action, it must be voluntary, even in the cases where a passion is cited (e.g., anger) as the reason for someone's action. And Aquinas believes that passion involved in action (say, one person striking another out of anger) somehow gets mitigated in terms of the level of culpability (being less culpable than were the passion not involved in the explanation). In such a case, Aquinas says, "something seems good to an angry man that does not seem so when he is calm."[36] So the passions in such a case influence but do not determine our behavior. In any case, such actions are not purely voluntary as would be the case of, say, an act of cold blooded murder.

Aquinas divides the intellect into speculative and practical reason. Wisdom, while an intellectual virtue, consists in truly knowing the highest cause of things; in Aquinas's case, God.[37] As such, Aquinas's understanding of Aristotle's highest cause is that of mastering metaphysics, but whose

33. Aquinas, *ST* I-II.10.3.

34. Aquinas, *ST* I-II.1.1. Perhaps this is what was going on in the Fall, where there was some external principle desire to make one wise that moved the concupiscible desire, e.g., the fruit appeared desirable, etc.

35. Aquinas, *ST* I-II.10.3.1.

36. Aquinas, *ST* I-II.9.2.

37. Aquinas, *ST* II-II 45.1; I-II.57.2.

highest ontological reality, Aristotle's *theos*, is a rather thin and impoverished version of the highest cause (described as "thought thinking itself thinking"), compared to the thick and rich version considered by Aquinas, for whom wisdom is a matter of knowing God's nature, actions, and decrees—illuminating more of an Augustinian than Aristotelian theological understanding.[38] Thus, the intellectual virtue of wisdom need not be the product of both intellect and will in Aquinas. But most of what he says on wisdom has to do with wisdom as a gift rather than as an intellectual virtue acquired by human reason alone, and in this way it does involve the will connected intimately to moral goodness.

Aquinas's analogues to the passions that pertain to the purely intellective part of the soul play a large role in Aquinas's view (e.g., the intellectual love for or fear of God as exemplified not only by humans having a sensitive soul, but also angels having only an intellective soul, revealing that such passions are not necessarily grounded in some bodily state). Having faith in and loving God are both necessary conditions for the best life to be actualized, as the good life is most fully marked by the degree to which one possesses the highest good.

On Aquinas's account, a person lacking the virtues of faith and charity cannot really be said to possess some other significant virtues (e.g., the virtue of wisdom) except in a secondary, derivative, or equivocal sense. Wisdom is an outgrowth of charity, which in turn depends on faith. Faith is a case in which the will exercises direct control over intellect, in Aquinas's view.

Aquinas claims that it is the task of moral philosophy "to consider human operations insofar as they are ordered to one another and to the end."[39] "The subject of moral philosophy is human beings insofar as they are voluntarily acting for an end."[40] Human acts are attributed as such or *per se* to human agents, the sort of things whose acts are properly human, *qua* human. It is only those activities that are being knowingly and willingly engaged in that are properly termed human acts. Since free will (*liberum arbitrium*) is the faculty of reason and will, it is on account of this that whatever acts are properly done by humans are moral acts.

Aquinas's doctrines of virtue and natural law arise out of his theory of action. The dominant motif is one of *eudaimonia*. This is the ultimate end for the sake of which all other acts are done. While the medieval picture of all substances involves a teleological structure, human action in particular is

---

38. Jordan, *Ordering Wisdom*, 122. For more on Aristotle's *theos* in particular, see Kosman, "Divine Being and Divine Thinking," 165–88.
39. Aquinas, *Commentary on the "Nicomachean Ethics"* I.1.2.
40. Aquinas, *Commentary on the "Nicomachean Ethics"* I.1.3.

defined by its rational teleological action. A natural substance is what it is by virtue of having the capacity for performing a certain characteristic activity. It is the form of that particular substance which constitutes its ontological ground for that capacity, which Aquinas calls the substance's first actuality. The state in which a substance has actualized its specific potentialities is the substance's second or final actuality, its perfection or fulfillment of its potential. So he understands actuality in two different senses, and all things seek their final actuality, their perfection.

The notion "happiness" is vaguely general and is perceived as something different to particular persons (e.g., glory, wealth, pleasure, etc.). However, as is true for Aristotle, Aquinas also takes this notion to be an objective notion. There is an end or good, the ultimate end or good for man, which in itself is normatively desirable (even if not desired by each subject). Something is seen as good and attracts the will of the agent.

Aquinas relies here on two presuppositions. First, we cannot desire what is evil or bad since they are the opposite of desirable. We can only want something insofar as we see it as good (which would then, of course, be seen as good *for us*). This does not negate goods for others, even when apparently disconnected to us (e.g., successful well project providing water for Ethiopians or happy retirements for great-grandchildren). This is because the will of the agent ought to want what is good in general, which obviously includes good for each and every person, a good for that individual and not just a good to that individual. It is an objective good rather than merely subjective notion of good that is being considered. "Whatever a human being seeks, it seeks under the aspect of the good (*sub ratione boni*)."[41]

Second, there is a distinction between the thing sought and the reason for seeking it, the aspect under which it is sought. Since our good is what completes us, any object of action must be perceived as at least part of our comprehensive good. We necessarily seek the good under the assumption that obtaining the perceived good is moving toward fulfilling the kind of agents we are, human agents. Thus, the notion of the human good is implicit in any and all human acts. We act for the sake of what we *perceive* to be good, perfective of the kinds of things we are. Now, we can be mistaken about what the particular or even ultimate good is, in which case we will still act on account of what we take to be the ultimate good, and so the practical reasoning processes are the same.

---

41. Aquinas, *ST* I-II.1.6.

The Original State

Given the grandiose worldview, as might be expected, Aquinas's account of the prelapsarian state is one marked by flourishing, a normative state for human existence, variously denoted as "prelapsarian," the "state of innocence," or "integrity," in contrast to "postlapsarian," the "state of corruption," or "fallen." Things are functioning properly, the way they ought to be, when they are functioning the way they were designed to function. With respect to the hermeneutical interpretation of Genesis, the nature of the narrative about paradise (Greek, garden), Aquinas believes that it was a literal place even though having a spiritual explanation. He claims that "whatever Scripture tells us about paradise is set down as a matter of history; and wherever Scripture makes use of this method, we must hold to the historical truth of the narrative as a foundation of whatever spiritual explanation we may offer." The trees are literal even if having a spiritual signification, as the rock was in the desert.[42] Man was to learn, by experience of the consequent punishment, the difference between the good of obedience and the evil of rebellion. So it's not as though man did not know good from evil *per se* (after all, man was given a divine command), but did not know them by their consequent experiences.

In *ST* I.94, Aquinas deals with the state and condition of the first man, saying explicitly that "the first man in the primitive state of his natural life did not see God through His Essence."[43] This fact occasioned a possibility which eventuated in a pivotal point of departure from the good life, a departure fundamentally marked by man's aversion to the state of human flourishing, essentially an aversion to God, to a state of corruption, a perversion of man. The fall was possible in this state because Adam did not see God through His essence, an experience only possessed in the beatific vision in the next life. In such a state, since man cannot willingly turn away from happiness, this being the ultimate end for man, man will not be able to fall since no one who sees God's essence can willingly turn away from it (which means to sin), so firmly are they established in the love of God. Since Adam did sin, it is clear he did not see God's essence.

In the original state, indeed in all earthly states, man is distracted and occupied by sensible things potentially impeding his understanding of intelligible effects, even though "God made men upright" (Eccl 7:29, NASB). The rectitude in this state is in the sense that the body was subject to the soul, and the lower powers of the soul were subjected to the higher, where

---

42. Aquinas, *ST* I.102.1.
43. Aquinas, *ST* I.94.1.

the higher was made so as not to be impeded by the lower (i.e., as long as it remained subjected to God, a provision made possible only by God's grace). Man was happy, not with the perfect happiness, but only insofar as he was "gifted with natural integrity and perfection."[44] The first man was created in "original righteousness" or "original justice" (OJ), an accident pertaining to the nature of the species as a gift conferred externally by God on the entire human nature.

Prelapsarian man's soul was aptly designed to perfect and govern the body, the latter being entirely subject to the former without hindrance. His soul was established in a perfect state to instruct and govern others, which presupposes potentially having knowledge of all those things for which he has a natural aptitude. Aquinas says, "Now no one can instruct others unless he has knowledge, and so the first man was established by God in such a manner as to have knowledge of all those things for which man has a natural aptitude." He elaborates on this aptitude, "And such are whatever are virtually contained in the first self-evident principles; that is, whatever truths man is naturally able to know."[45]

In order to govern, man was also endowed with certain knowledge surpassing natural knowledge because the life of man is directed to a supernatural end. But among those things that were not known are those things that cannot be known by human effort or are not necessary for the direction of human life.[46] Prelapsarian man could not assent to falsehood as if it were truth since truth is the good of the intellect and falsehood its evil. This was so while the soul's rectitude in the primitive state remained subject to God. But since the intellect cannot be deceived in the state of innocence and subjected to falsehood, the lapse must be initially accounted for by some lower faculty. Aquinas initially suggests the imagination.

The key to ensuring this rectitude was in man's reason being subject to God. This was not from nature or else it would have remained after the fall, being part of human nature. But since it did not remain, it was not grounded in nature but in grace. This is a supernatural endowment. Adam, like other just souls, was gifted with God's Spirit in some degree but not as the believers who possess him now are who are admitted into eternal happiness after death.

With respect to the passions, Aquinas claims that they existed in the state of innocence, residing as they did in the sensitive appetite which has as its objects good and evil. While in the primitive state, of course, man had

---

44. Aquinas, *ST* I.94.1.1.
45. Aquinas, *ST* I.94.3
46. Aquinas, *ST* I.94.4.

no passion for evil as its object. Our sensitive appetite is not entirely subject to reason. Sometimes the sensitive appetite hinders reason's judgment. But in the state of innocence, the inferior appetite was wholly subject to reason. The passions' revolt against reason could not have occurred in the state of innocence. But then how did Adam fall from this state of innocence? Did he lack virtues thereby making such an allowance?

Aquinas thinks the rectitude of the original state required possession of all the virtues. Notably, he claims that charity, as a virtue not involving imperfection, existed absolutely in the primitive state both in habit and in act. But some virtues, like faith, are of such a nature as to imply imperfection either in their act or on the part of the matter. It is not inconsistent to conceive of the imperfection of some virtues co-existing with the original state's perfection. The perfection of that state did not extend to the beatific vision of the divine essence, the final state, so faith would have necessarily existed in the first man. Consider some virtues—for example, penance or mercy—which imply an imperfection inconsistent with the prelapsarian state such that they could exist as habit but not as act, since penance is sorrow for sin committed.[47] So Adam had the habit of penance and mercy in the sense that he was disposed in such a way that if he had sinned, then he would have repented. So Adam possessed the virtues as one created upright in the original state, key virtues of which were faith and charity.

Now, since Aquinas does not believe that Adam and Eve could have been deceived prior to the fall, yet he affirms the New Testament—including 1 Timothy 2:14, which clearly states that Eve, at least, was deceived—how does he reconcile the claim that Eve could not be deceived with the fact that she indeed was deceived? It seems open, given what was said above, that Eve's failure with respect to the forbidden fruit may have constituted a failure to consider some individual fact in the category of things not known to man. Aquinas claims, following Augustine again, that Eve was deceived before she committed a deed of sin (i.e., taking the forbidden fruit). How so? She was able to sin because the antecedent condition, her interior pride, opened the possibility. She "already acquiesced in the love of her own power, and in a presumption of self-conceit."[48] Even still, Aquinas maintains in the third reply that even if an external object were presented to the imagination or sense of the first man (and woman) not in accordance with the nature of things, then they would not have been deceived because reason would have kept it in check. So if not external and not imagination, then what caused

---

47. For a different view, see Dobbs-Weinstein, *Maimonides and St. Thomas*, esp. 89–112.
48. Aquinas, *ST* I.94.1.

it? In concluding the section, he notes that man had sinned already in his heart and thus failed to have recourse to divine aid. There was some object of desire eliciting the passions to make one wise but via illegitimate means. So how did self-love assume control over the higher faculties?

Postlapsarianism: Sin, Origin of Sin, and Original Sin

Given Aquinas's philosophy, human lapse from the original state implies an account of some sort of departure from God as the supreme good. Before considering how the first human sin was made possible (call this Primal Sin or PS), or its consequences in light of Original Sin (OS), let us look at the concept of sin.

The Concept of Sin

Sin is defined by Aquinas as "an inordinate act" whereby both voluntariness and inordinateness occur, the former being essential and the latter accidental.[49] The voluntariness refers essentially to the sinner, the inordinateness only accidentally since no one acts intending evil. And, of course, a thing derives its species from that which is essential, not accidental. Thus, sins are differentiated on the basis of their acts of voluntariness, not inordinateness. But the nature of sin consists in its inordinateness. Every sin consists in a move away from the immutable good toward the desire for some lesser mutable good for which man has an inordinate desire.[50]

Sin is inordinate, and at some level sin against God is common to all sins in that it consists in forsaking the One God for the many other created things. This is true insofar as the order to God includes every human order. If man is not rightly related to God in accordance with right reason, then other things will be disordered as well.[51] The love of God is unitive in that it draws man's affections from the many to the one such that the virtues, flowing from the love of God, are connected. But self-love disunites man's affections amongst the different things; hence, vices and sins arising as they do from self-love are disconnected. Love of God is unitive and integrative; inordinate self-love is divisive and disintegrative.[52] Given the voluntariness

---

49. Aquinas, *ST* I-II.71.2.
50. Aquinas, *ST* I-II.72.2.
51. Aquinas, *ST* I-II.72.4.
52. Aquinas, *ST* I-II.73.1.

of human action, sin is primarily in the will, but the intellect and the passions are also invoked as motives and reasons for action.[53]

Origin of Sin

At some point the first human sinned. PS lays bare an instance of morally evil action without all of the complications usually dealt with in a postlapsarian mode. In typical instances, we seek questions about antecedent conditions such as character, ignorance, and prior choices that go into influencing or determining an agent's immoral and culpable volition. In PS, however, there can be no relevant ignorance, *akrasia*, bad states or dispositions of character, or prior evil choices, because the antecedent conditions were all good.

PS brought about grave consequences which burdened all of Adam's posterity with the transmitted human condition of depravity (a certain kind of sinful disposition). Call this Original Sin (OS). Both are said to have their own problems. Taken as PS, difficulties arise about how such a fall from grace is even possible given the rich background of the good and man's condition of rectitude and disposition towards the good (i.e., sin brings about a privation). Taken as OS, difficulties arise as to how human posterity can "be all they can be" given their presently depraved condition so that they are not alienated necessarily as cosmic orphans.

Aquinas's view on the metaphysical problem of evil answers the questions about the nature and cause of evil as privation and as self-caused, while the moral problem answers the "why" question with a freewill response. The one who sins is both depraved (morally) and deprived (metaphysically). Aquinas's *De Principiis Naturae* helps us to better understand the notion of evil. He identifies three principles of change: matter, form, and privation. Now, if evil or sin is simply the privation of good, we would still be left with the problem of its causal genesis if we neglect to say something about the nature of causal explanation in Aquinas.

First, we note that all things are good in virtue of their existence, their first act of being, but also that all things seek for their final good or second actuality. Further, following Augustine, Aquinas denies that evil is a thing for it has no being in itself.[54] It is a privation, not a thing, not a substance.[55] Next, since evil is not a substance, but a real privation or lack in a good substance,

---

53. Aquinas, *ST* I-II.74.1–3. See also MacDonald, "Practical Reasoning and Reasons-Explanations," 131–59.

54. See Evans, *Augustine on Evil*; MacDonald, "Primal Sin," 110–39; Mann, "Augustine on Evil," 40–48.

55. Aquinas, *ST* I-II.75.1, 4; Aristotle, *Physics* II.3.

it follows that evil cannot wholly corrupt a good substance, for otherwise it would not be possible for it to exist in a state of privation since privation is parasitical on being, on a substance. But what is its cause? Given what has been said, evil cannot be said to have a formal cause *per se* since it has no form but is a privation of form. Nor can it have a final cause since only substances that seek their own perfection can have a final cause, and evil is not perfection. The only material cause for evil to "ride on" would be a good substance since all that is, is good. So the material cause for evil must be, at least accidentally, a good substance. Ultimately, evil can be explained by an efficient (or actually, a deficient) cause, the will of the agent.[56]

Aquinas is not naively optimistic about the noetic effects of sin. Sin can affect reason either by failure to control concupiscence or by ignorance. This is of course voluntary since, according to Aquinas, "Sin is in the reason either through being a voluntary defect of the reason, or through reason being the principle of the will's act."[57] More particularly and of interest is the fact that Aquinas claims that ignorance, as non-being, can in some sense be a cause of sin indirectly. It is a sin of omission rather than commission. He distinguishes ignorance (denotes privation of knowledge: lack of that which is known via natural aptitude) from nescience (denotes absence of knowledge). Within our natural aptitude are some items which we are obligated to know. For example, all are bound to know the articles of faith and universal principles of right. Other items, by contrast, carry no obligation (e.g., geometrical theorems and contingent particulars). Thus, through negligence ignorance is culpable. Of course, possessing such a natural aptitude is not identical to actually possessing the knowledge. Apart from sin, however, such knowledge is accessible to us were we to want it.[58] Ignorance, if involuntary or invincible (failing to know what one is unable to know or imbecility) is excusable because it is inculpable.[59] Given that voluntariness is essential to sin, ignorance diminishing voluntariness diminishes sin. For example, getting drunk creates some level of ignorance and diminishes voluntariness of sins (not of drunkenness) consequential to intoxicated states because the man's will cannot be said to fully consent to sin directly but only accidentally.[60] But it is nonetheless culpable.

---

56. Aquinas, *ST* I-II.75.1.

57. Aquinas, *ST* I-II.74.5.2. See also Snell, "Thomism and Noetic Sin," 7–28.

58. Aquinas, *ST* I-II.76.2.

59. Aquinas, *ST* I-II.76.3. More will be said about being culpable and inculpable in chapter 4.

60. Aquinas, *ST* I-II.76.4.

As already noted, passions can have influence over the will for evil. However, this can only happen indirectly since the will's proper object is the good. This can occur through a kind of distraction when the soul is so attentive to the passion as to be remiss or impeded in will for the good. It can also happen when the will's object, understood via inordinate apprehension of the imagination and judgment of the estimative power (e.g., consider those out of their mind), misleads the will away from the good to follow the passion, like taste follows the tongue's disposition, where one cannot easily turn one's imagination away from the object. The passion occasions a change in the judgment about the object of the will. So the higher mover is indirectly moved by the lower as the will never pursues evil as evil but only when falsely considering it via passionate influences as a good (ignorance or error in reason), like the fruit looking good in the garden. Hence, we mistake an evil for a good.[61] Perhaps man knows it is wrong to lie, generally, but in a particular instance it is not taken as a lie in that he is not intentionally defying what he universally knows. Or again, it is possible to have correct knowledge both generally and particularly yet not consider it or attend to it actually. Thus, it is possible for a man to act contrary to that which he would ordinarily not do were it not for the fact that he failed to consider some particular fact, or due to a lack of attending to some fact or set of facts.

Failure to attend to something because of some distraction or hindrance of something external, some bodily infirmity or passion, can bring about failure to consider some particular in light of what one universally knows. Someone in a state of passion may fail to consider in particular what he knows in general as the passions hinder him via (1) distraction, (2) opposition (to something contrary to what man knows in general), or (3) bodily transmutation (where reason is somehow fettered to not act freely or as free in cases of sleepiness, drunkenness, or ill-health; so also when man is inflamed by passions of love or excess anger, etc.) In such cases the passion draws the reason to judge in particular against what is known in general. While universal knowledge is most certain, it does not hold pride of place in action since action is about particulars. This is why it is not surprising to find passion acting counter to universal knowledge in matters of action when a privation occurs in particular knowledge. That something appears good to the reason when in fact it is not is due to a passion.

Inordinate self-love is the root cause of every sin, each of which proceeds from some inordinate desire for a mutable and temporal good. This amounts to a failure of proper self-love.[62] Concupiscence of the flesh

---

61. Aquinas, *ST* I-II.77.1.
62. Aquinas, *ST* I-II.77.4.

(sensual) or of the eyes (spiritual), as in the imagination for things inordinate, are both considered. For example, the fruit looked desirable not for its delectable taste to the tongue but to make one wise, and yet wisdom would be gained in an illicit way.

Sin occurs sometimes via defect of intellect (i.e., ignorance), sometimes defect in sensitive appetite (i.e., passion), and sometimes defect or disorder of the will (i.e., when the will chooses or loves the lesser over the greater good, it is considered disordered). The consequence of loving something lesser is that one chooses to suffer some good.[63] An inordinate will chooses some temporal over spiritual good and thus chooses to lose the spiritual, implying that a man wishes knowingly a spiritual evil or privation of some good to obtain another lesser good. This is what it means to sin through malice or on purpose. Evil cannot be intended for its own sake, but can be intended for the sake of avoiding another evil or obtaining another good.

The account, then, of PS (primal sin) for humans is that sin can be said to be irrational but not unintelligible. The answer regarding where PS originates cannot be in an efficient cause but in a deficient cause since it is a matter of defecting from what is highest to something less. But such a defect cannot be found in either an antecedent defect in the state of innocence or in God, but must be explicable in terms of human freedom as an irrational yet free choice whereby man is rendered culpable. In order to provide the resources for a defensible account of the introduction of evil and an explanation of how human moral agents can fall into evil, we must first discuss Aquinas's background assumptions, moral psychology, and ideas about human action. Morally evil choices are ordinary defective acts of will motivated by the agent's practical reasoning (or more particularly a failure to attend adequately to the reasons for which one has access). But it is actually a kind of negligence (as opposed to nescience) in practical reasoning. One turns away from the greatest immutable good and chooses lesser mutable goods.

Sin turns out to be a (metaphysical) privation in a good substance as well as a (moral) depravation. All substances are good insofar as they have being as their first act. Primal evil is a defective free choice constituting a corruption in rational nature. The sin, the moral evil, is the voluntary turning away itself. As it consists in the loving of a lesser rather than a greater good, it constitutes disorder in the soul and a novel perversion of rational nature. The characterization of turning way (*aversio*) and turning to (*conversio*) suggests that such an action initiates or gives rise to an enduring state

---

63. Aquinas illustrates this in terms of a loss of limb in order to save life. See Aquinas, *ST* I-II.78.1.

of will such as setting one's mind to or committing oneself to something in a lasting way. Sin is essentially a disordinate act of will, the turning away from the highest good, which is motivated by the fact that the sinner perceives the goodness of the object he comes to choose.

Aquinas's denial of any technical cause to PS is not a denial of utterly unmotivated acts of will. The disordered act of will is directed toward an object on account of its being perceived as a good. Thus, it is an intelligible account even if irrational. The sinner's perception of the object as a good makes his action intelligible in that he reasonably desires it, but at the same time not so intelligible in that he turns away from a greater good to the lesser. It is this irrational preferencing of the lower to the higher good that needs explaining since it is this that constitutes the disordered choice. The background assumptions in the prelapsarian state require an explanation of this cognitive and moral defect. Remember that even though he knew God, Adam did not yet have the beatific vision. It is not open, given background assumptions, for Aquinas to invoke some explanation that involves antecedent defect (e.g., *akrasia*) in PS. So Aquinas claims that the will falls when it fails to guard against sin, which it could and should have avoided. Had Adam attended to all of the reasons he possessed, he would not have fallen. Hence, his choice was thus made in some negligent sense of reasoning, some carelessness, somehow not taking into account the relevant information possessed. This was a problem of selective attention necessarily attached to finite beings.

Evidence of this may be seen in the serpent's tempting Eve by diverting attention from some things while focusing in on others, which explains how she ended up seeing the fruit as good for food, delightful to the eyes, and desirable to make one wise, all reasonable things in themselves as they accord with human nature. Unrestrained by her countervailing reasons she failed to attend to, she took and ate.

In summary, as an explanation of PS for Aquinas, we can say that the perception of certain created goods provides motivation for their being loved and turned toward but not directly motivated by love for a lesser as opposed to the greatest good. The motivation is indirect yet culpable. The culpability stems from failure to guard against sin in this way, which is why there is no essential, natural, or efficient cause of sin. So as a deficient cause, it highlights how an irrational choice can be made only as indirectly motivated since a primal sinner cannot voluntarily choose something while simultaneously seeing it as irrational. So it is grounded in a particular kind of failure in practical reasoning, failure to base one's choices adequately on one's reasons. Sin is irrational but not unintelligible. PS takes place in the context of the natural cognitive limitations of creatures, which are mutable, a necessary condition for being corruptible. Thus, we must have some nonbeing in our being rendering us capable (having potential) to fall into irrationality, but such limitation is not a defect, either moral or rational, in the original creation. It is sin that constitutes a lapse in rationality and morality. PS was a failure to act or a failure to fully attend.

Generally, inaction must be explicable in similar ways as action; but some inaction, if it requires any explanation at all, will not typically require explanation that appeals to reasons and motives one has for that inaction. Thus, it is erroneous to think that inaction essential to PS must be explicable in terms of primal sinners' reasons and motives for such inaction. That is, it is unnecessary to provide an explanation of the same sort for the defect as for the effect where the defect is an inaction (e.g., a failure to act or attend).[64] Primal sinners' ability to choose otherwise is grounded in their ability to reason otherwise. An action is either self-caused (culpable), uncaused (inexplicable), or caused by another (inculpable). PS is culpable but is not self-caused in the direct sense but only in the indirect sense.

Original Sin

If PS provides a lens by which to examine the fundamental mechanisms of culpable wrongdoing in the original, pristine state, then we should expect the results of that investigation to provide insight not only into the nature of PS but of wrongdoing generally. That is, ordinary instances of culpable wrongdoing are defective, disordered, acts of will, just as those of their primal ancestor. As such, they are (1) voluntary, which means that they are (2) motivated and also (3) avoidable, where their defect consists primarily in their being (4) less than fully informed by the sinner's reasons. Aristotle's fixity of character for vicious persons,[65] a problem generated in chapter 1, is unproblematic on Aquinas's account given the nature of culpability, but the gravity of the consequences of original sin compares to Aristotle's problem in terms of our natural and fallen inability to extricate ourselves from our poor state, thus eliminating the good life from within our grasp. If it were avoidable, then its explanation must be in the sinner's negligence in practical reasoning when she had the power to do otherwise because it was in her power to reason otherwise."[66] Each and every sin exhibits the essential features of PS.

64. MacDonald, "Primal Sin."

65. See "Habituation, the Fixity of Character and Repentance" in chapter 2 of this book; Aristotle, *NE* II.4, 1105a35; Jacobs, "Taking Ethical Disability Seriously," 141–58.

66. Aquinas does not use this language. See Aquinas, *ST* I-II.17.1.2; MacDonald, "Practical Reasoning and Reasons-Explanations," 158–59; "Aquinas's Libertarian Account," 309–328.

Even though the sensitive appetite in the fallen state, which we will look at next, makes it more difficult to pursue good and avoid evil, it is still possible in some way given Aquinas's view on the nature of free choice.

Whereas PS is an act, OS (original sin) is a habit which is relative to nature rather than to act, because it was not formed in us by bad actions leading to such habits, and so likewise cannot be annulled by good actions. It is a habit of nature like a natural disposition toward wellness or illness. It was brought about by one act but is a habit of nature inherited posterior to the one act. Aquinas does not pretend to prove the doctrine of original sin by arguments from reason alone.[67] His attempt is to reveal moral decadence with a probabilistic conclusion, but he is nonetheless bound by biblical and ecclesiastical authority to affirm it.

Aquinas says an individual can be considered either as an individual or as part of a whole, a member of a society. "Considered in the second way, an act can be his although he has not done it himself, nor has it been done by his free will but by the rest of the society or by its head, the nation being considered as doing what the prince does. For a society is considered as a single man of whom the individuals are the different members (1 Cor 12). Thus the multitude of men who receive their human nature from Adam is to be considered as a single community or rather as a single body.... If the man, whose privation of original justice is due to Adam, is considered as a private person, this privation is not his 'fault,' for a fault is essentially voluntary. If, however, we consider him as a member of the family of Adam, as if all men were only one man, then his privation partakes of the nature of sin on account of its voluntary origin, which is the actual sin of Adam."[68]

For Aquinas, OS is a paternal rather than a personal crime for Adam's posterity. It is not a habit infused or acquired (except in Adam's case), but is rather inherited via our corrupt origin.[69] OS is extensive (but not necessarily intensive) in that it extends to all parts of the soul, given that they are parts of a whole.[70]

Since the species is taken from its form, and the species of original sin is taken from its cause, it follows that the formal element of original sin is relative to original justice. As the will turned away from God in privation, all the other powers of the soul became inordinate and revealed the material

---

67. Arguably, original sin is confirmed by a broad spectrum of observers. See Chesterton, *Orthodoxy*, 15; Ching, *Chinese Religions*, 72–73, 75–77. See also atheist philosophers, e.g., Rand, *Virtue of Selfishness*; Dawkins, *Selfish Gene*; Hobbes, *Leviathan*; Ruse, "Darwinism and Christianity Redux," 19.

68. Aquinas, *Summa Contra Gentiles* (*SCG*) IV.52.

69. Aquinas, *ST* I-II.82.1.

70. Aquinas, *ST* I-II.82.2.3.

element in original sin in the other powers, turning inordinately to mutable goods whose inordinateness is denoted as concupiscence. Thus, original sin is formally privation but materially concupiscence.[71] OS attaches to the nature, not to the person. Through the origin of Adam's sin, sin entered into the world and transmitted something to his descendants as a collective, by nature (species) rather than by person (individual). OS, which is opposed to OJ, is called the sin of nature, wherefore it is transmitted from the parent to the offspring. It is transmitted to all who receive human nature from the first man, which is why it is called Original Sin, denoting its origin in nature, human nature. We need to remember that for Aquinas OS attaches to the nature rather than the person. In his summary of the Summa Aquinas writes, "The blessing of Original Justice was conferred by God on the human race in the person of its first parent in such a way that it was to be transmitted to his posterity through him. But when a cause is removed, the effect cannot follow. Therefore, when the first man stripped himself of this good by his sin, all of his descendants were likewise deprived of it."[72]

The root of original righteousness consists in the supernatural subjection of the reason to God, a grace from God. Sons of Adam may be considered as one man given our common nature. A murder committed by the sin of the hand would not be imputed to the hand, but to the whole body. OS (a state) is contrasted with actual sin (act) in one sense, but is also to be contrasted with original righteousness or justice (OJ) in another (proper state versus corrupt state). OS was a corruption in nature. Whereas the state of giftedness was to be transmitted, now disorder is transmitted.

OS is a habit, an inclination, not like a breakable bad habit but rather as a complex natural disposition that is ill-disposed. OS denotes the privation of OJ and the inordinate disposition of the parts of the soul; so it is not just a pure privation, but a corrupt habit (a bent toward evil). Though acts can form habits, it is problematic that this sort of habit cannot be broken simply by a series of acts. The principle of the spiritual life, a life in accord with virtue, is the order to the last end. If this order be corrupted, it cannot be repaired by some intrinsic principle. OS extensively infects and affects all parts of the soul in the same way as OJ did and is a universal human factor consequent to the fall.

The consequences of the fall for humanity are profound. Sin diminishes the good of human nature with regard to its teleological inclination to virtue, and it utterly destroyed the gift of original justice.[73] But it did not

71. Aquinas, *ST* I-II.82.3; I-II.84.
72. Aquinas, *Aquinas's Shorter Summa*, 223–24; *ST* I-II.81.1.
73. Aquinas, *ST* I-II.85.1.

destroy or diminish the constitutive principles and the properties flowing from them (e.g., powers of the soul). If it had, man would not even be able to sin.[74] The constitution of man is essential, whereas virtues and vices are accidental. Man as a rational being performs actions in accordance with reason, the consequence of which is to act virtuously. Sin cannot detract from man *qua* man, such that man is entirely destroyed or else there would be nothing in which sin can reside since it is always parasitical on a thing. The constitutional nature of man itself was not changed, but the moral nature or disposition was. Reason, perfected by God, had a hold over the lower parts of the soul while man was subjected to God in original justice. Bereft of this, the powers of the soul, which are naturally directed to virtue, are bereft of their proper order. Such destitution constitutes a wound of nature. The withdrawal of original justice has the character of punishment/penalty (e.g., found in bodily defects and death), whereas original sin has the character of guilt. The debt of punishment, which is really the withdrawal of grace, is a consequence of sin.

Sin incurs the character of guilt since it proceeds from the will, whereas punishment is fundamentally against the will.[75] Punishment is proportionate to sin in terms of sin's severity but not its duration. Given its turning away from the immutable good, which is infinite, its corresponding punishment is the pain of loss, being the loss of the infinite good; that is, God.[76] The effect of disturbing an order remains so long as the cause remains. Some disturbances are reparable, some are not. Some sins are not punished eternally, but sin in general incurs a debt of eternal punishment as it causes an irreparable disorder in Divine justice. Original sin incurs eternal punishment given human deprivation of grace, without which sin cannot be remitted. An eternity of punishment corresponds not to the quantity of sin but to its irremissibility.

Venial sins, unlike mortal sins, do not cause a stain on the soul because they neither destroy nor diminish the habit of charity and other virtues; rather, they hinder their acts.[77] In venial sins, man does not cleave to the temporal creature as his last end. What is for us venial, however, would have been mortal for Adam in the state of innocence. In the prelapsarian state, there was an "unerring stability of order," where man's lower parts were subject to higher and the higher to God himself, the breaking of

---

74. Aquinas, *ST* I-II.85.1.
75. Aquinas, *ST* I-II.87.1–2.
76. Aquinas, *ST* I-II.87.4.3.
77. Aquinas, *ST* I-II.89.

which constitutes mortal sin.[78] The first sin could not have been venial before it was mortal.

The Necessary Conditions for the Wayfarer State

Given the universality and gravity of total depravity extending to the whole of man, the prospects for attaining the good life appear bleak, perhaps worse than on Aristotle's account. But Aquinas is not finished yet. There is a way out, which must satisfy certain necessary conditions for the best life. In this section, we will examine the potential in the wayfarer state (the postlapsarian, post-regeneration state), ultimately realizable in the afterlife.

Faith

Would you agree with those who would say, "Faith is believing something you know ain't true"? Or as one recent author put it, "Faith is belief in the absence of supportive evidence, and even in the light of contrary evidence"?[79] The relationship of faith to living the good life for Aquinas is not unimportant. Indeed, it is a *sine qua non*. It is necessary in all states prior to the beatific vision which will render it unnecessary.[80] In contemporary literature, largely a product of post-Enlightenment thought, faith is usually contrasted with knowledge where faith is quite insubstantial in terms of increasing one's knowledge base. But not so for Aquinas who sees faith as very substantial and as part of a knowledge tradition. Here, we will consider the relation of faith to epistemology and ethics. Indeed, whereas for Maimonides faith is a moral virtue, it is for Aquinas an intellectual virtue, a virtue which perfects the intellect.[81] Now, it should be understood that reason cannot produce faith and is not the basis for faith, although it can assist faith, explain faith, and defend faith. Human reason can assist in proving natural theology (e.g., the nature and existence of one God), to illustrate or help clarify supernatural theology (e.g., incarnation and Trinity), and to refute heretical theology.[82] Faith and reason can be concurrent, but one does not cause the other. If reason forced faith, then faith would not be

---

78. Aquinas, *ST* I-II.89.3; I.95.1.
79. Stenger, "Faith in Anything is Unreasonable," 55–68.
80. Aquinas, *ST* II-II.5.
81. Aquinas, *ST* II-II.1.3.
82. Aquinas, *De Trinitate* II.3; *SCG* I.9.

a free act. But faith involves the will, and reason does not coerce the will.[83] So while interrelated, the relationship is not coercive.

When considering the adequacy of the Pauline claim, "Faith is the substance of things to be hoped for, the evidence of things not seen" (Heb 11:1, NKJV), Aquinas admits that the arrangement of the Pauline words are not in the form of a definition, but he rebuts the objection that it fails to adequately provide the points in which faith can be defined.[84] He takes faith to be a cognitive habit which, like other objects, includes two aspects, formal and material. The object of faith is known materially and formally. The formal aspect of the object of faith is the First Truth as it does not assent to anything unless it is revealed by God. Hence the mean on which faith is based is the Divine Truth. Considered materially, the things to which faith assents are not only God but all propositions of faith as they bear relation to God. And, as in the case of a habit, it is known by its act which, in turn, is known by its object. The act of faith is to believe at the will's command. For Aquinas, the proper object of genuine faith (which is the only kind of faith he is seriously considering) is something simple, the First Truth, God.[85]

In general, intellectual assent occurs either by way of the object itself or by choosing to believe (invoking the intellectual appetite), making a belief either involuntary or voluntary. The act of faith is a cognitive volition of the rational appetite related then to both the object of the will (i.e., good) and of the intellect (i.e., true). The object of faith is the substance of all things hoped for. Aquinas's own definition of faith is, "Faith is a habit of the mind, whereby eternal life is begun in us, making the intellect assent to what is non-apparent." Faith is distinguished from everything else pertaining to the intellect. Alluding again to Paul's definition, he points out that the "evidence" suggests its distinction from opinion, suspicion, and doubt, which fail to make the intellect adhere; of things unseen it is distinguished from science and understanding, according to whose objects are apparent; as "the substance of things hoped for," he claims to distinguish the virtue of faith from common so-called faith without vertical reference to the hope of beatific vision. Any other definitions given, he thinks, are simply explanations of the adequacy of Paul's points.[86]

Given the gravity of this all-important virtue, it follows that one's pursuit of the good life is handicapped if it is lacking. Even though faith is

83. Aquinas, *Disputed Questions on Truth* 14.1.2.

84. While authorship of Hebrews is disputed, Aquinas believed it was authored by Paul, as he was intent on writing commentaries on all of Paul's writings and that included his commentary on Hebrews.

85. Aquinas, *ST* II-II.1.1.

86. Aquinas, *ST* II-II.4.1.

different from and a mean between science and opinion, which are about propositions, faith lies in the middle and does not terminate in a proposition but in a thing, a person.[87] Indeed, faith that God exists is simply an assent to a propositional dictum, a *de dicto* proposition that God exists. But while that may be the desired result of Aquinas's "Five Ways," it is not his intent behind faith, which is *de re*. That is, it is also faith *in* God; it relates one *to* God and not just to a proposition *about* God.[88]

Contrary to views popularized by critics of Aquinas, like Francis Schaeffer, Cornelius Van Til, and others, Aquinas does not believe that human reason is not fallen or without natural limitations as though perfectly autonomous.[89] Van Til, for instance, states that "Thomas is unable to do justice to St. Paul's position that whatever is not of faith is sin. . . . [On Aquinas's view] faith is not required for a Christian to act virtuously in the natural relationships of life."[90] Similarly, Herman Dooyeweerd claims that the whole Greek view of nature Aquinas adopted is thoroughly pagan.[91] One problem here is that given the role of the virtue of faith where faith is an intellectual virtue, a virtue that supposedly perfects the intellect, lacking it would be problematic even absent the fall. But the whole of man was affected by the fall as Aquinas asserts in *ST* I-II: "All the powers of the soul are in a sense lacking the order proper to them."[92] What he calls the four wounds of nature claim ground in each of the major parts of the soul where a cardinal virtue should be. Contrary to many misinterpreters of Aquinas, Protestant theologian, Arvin Vos, says regarding the detailed loss in those four wounds, "there can be no doubt that a person who is ignorant, malicious, cowardly, or lustful is disordered."[93] Not only does Aquinas admit the relative loss at the fall, but he offers arguments for the insufficiency of human reason on many counts concerning things of God and for the need of revelation, before and after the fall. Following Maimonides, he gives five reasons why we first need to believe what we might later provide evidence for: (1) the depth and subtlety of the object (i.e., God), (2) the weakness of the human intellect in its initial operations, (3) the length of time needed to learn things requisite for a conclusive proof is

---

87. Aquinas, *ST* II-II.1.2; II-II.1.3.3; II-II.1.4.2; II-II.1.5.2; II-II.1.a.4; II-II.4.

88. Aquinas, *ST* I.2.1–3; Moser, *Elusive God*, 158–61.

89. Schaeffer, *Escape from Reason*, 11.

90. Van Til, *Defense of the Faith*, 56; Aquinas, *ST* I-II.65.2; Vos, *Aquinas, Calvin*, 143.

91. Dooyeweerd, *New Critique of Theoretical Thought*, 1:181–83; *In the Twilight*, 140; Kelly, *Early Christian Doctrines*.

92. Aquinas, *ST* I-II.85.3.

93. Vos, *Aquinas, Calvin*, 149, 158.

beyond reach of most, (4) some lack proper personality to engage in such philosophical pursuit, and (5) the lack of time for such pursuit beyond the necessities of life would dog most people. From the outset, we need to have some knowledge of things which are more knowable in themselves and this is possible only via faith. Faith enables us to at no time be lacking knowledge of God that we ought to possess.[94]

Given that the substance of a thing is that which is in some sense first, faith being the substance of things hoped for is preeminent among the virtues. By its very nature, Aquinas claims that it precedes the other virtues given that the end is the principle in matters of action and the end of the intellect is the First Truth. He claims that "there are no real virtues, unless faith be presupposed."[95] This is not insignificant; one wonders if some critics like Van Til even bothered to read Aquinas (in context). This vertical dimension in Aquinas has implications for Aristotelian ethics whose virtues now become *mere* virtues rather than *genuine* virtues.

In the same way in which Aristotle claims that the lack of *phronesis* (even if one possessed other virtues like justice, temperance, and courage) makes one's virtues not fully or genuinely virtuous unless done by the virtuous person who possesses such a virtue, so also now Aquinas's virtue of faith is a functional analog to Aristotle's *phronesis* in that whosoever fails to possess it cannot possess the other virtues. Thus, at best they would be mere virtues. A virtue is a mere virtue just in case it fails to be underwritten by faith, the virtue which must be presupposed for all other virtues to be real. Without faith, there is no truly good deed, and where there is no truly good deed there is the lack of the virtue of faith. While chronologically simultaneous perhaps, faith is logically prior to the fruit it produces (i.e., faithful) just as the premises to a conclusion are logically prior. But just as premises in a syllogism will produce a conclusion, so the genuine virtue of faith will produce further virtue.

Faith *per se* can either be lifeless or living.[96] Lifeless faith is not the virtue Aquinas has in mind as it is mere theistic belief or belief that God exists (as good as the devil's faith, perhaps). And while subject to reasonable belief formed by argument to show that God exists and that God is one, it is nonetheless deficient in some way. It is like matter without form. It is nominal faith. Lifeless faith is not taken to be a different species than living faith,

---

94. See Maimonides, *Guide* I.34; Aquinas, *Disputed Questions on Truth* 14.10 reply; SCG I.4.2–5; *Faith, Reason, and Theology*.

95. Aquinas, *ST* II-II.4.7.

96. Vos, *Aquinas, Calvin*, 28–30.

but is simply an imperfection. And in agreement with Aristotle, a virtue is a kind of perfection.[97]

So while lifeless faith is real, it cannot be a virtue. The genuine virtue of faith is a key virtue perfective of the intellect. But it also concerns the will to believe and so requires a virtue perfective of the will. We are now in a position to consider more acutely how genuine faith, living faith, is fully formed.

Charity

Charity is the form of faith.[98] God is the object of both faith and charity. Whereas the proper object of faith is truth and is therefore of concern to the intellect, the proper object of charity is good and is therefore of concern to the will. Aquinas's metaphysics of goodness explains the certitude of faith regarding the veracity of propositions believed, but the will's cleaving to God's goodness explains the certitude of faith regarding the tenacity of the believer. Aquinas holds that charity is the friendship of man for God. Recall that for Aquinas happiness is the ultimate end for the will and the willer wills it of necessity. But one's true happiness consists in communion with God. Therefore, the will's desire will not be satisfied until such communion or on the road to such communion.

As Norman Geisler says, "Faith draws God to man, but love draws man to God."[99] Whereas God is known mediately by us via negation, preeminence, or effects as from effect to cause, so the reverse is the case with charity as from cause to effect. We have charity with others, but only insofar as it is an overflow of a charity towards God.[100] We love God immediately and consequent to God's love for us, and it is through this love that we love others. For us to perform the act of charity there must be in us some habitual form superadded to the natural power, inclining that power to the act of charity and causing it to act with ease and pleasure. God's essence is charity, and we are said to be good, formally speaking, as we participate in Divine goodness.

While charity is not the essence of each virtue, it is no doubt the essential *motive* behind it. It is thus included in the definition of every virtue because each depends on it in the sense in which prudence, for example, is included in the definition of the moral virtues. Thus, charity is more excellent than faith and, consequently, than all of the other virtues. Charity

---

97. Aquinas, *ST* II-II.4.2; Aristotle, *Physics* VII.
98. See Aquinas, *ST* II-II.4.3.
99. Geisler, *Thomas Aquinas*, 174.
100. Aquinas, *ST* II-II.23.1.

quickens the act of faith. Faith works by love where love is its proper form.[101] No virtue is possible without charity since charity makes faith to be living faith apart from which other virtues are only virtuous in a derivative, relative, or secondary sense. Charity is impossible without God. Thus, no genuine virtue is possible without God.[102]

Good is the object of both appetites: passions (particular) and will (universal). Since that which is concupiscible is part of the sensitive appetite (the passions), the love which is in the concupiscible is the love of sensible good. Whereas Aristotle assigned love to the concupiscible (sensitive appetite, the passions), Aquinas sees charity as a kind of love, but more like a pseudo-passion in the intellectual appetite (the will). These are denoted "pseudo" because passions are typically, for Aquinas, located in the sensitive soul, not the intellective soul. In this case, it is in the intellectual appetite, the will.[103] The concupiscible cannot reach the divine good, so the concupiscible cannot be the subject of charity. Since charity is man's friendship with God and surpasses our natural faculties, it cannot be naturally acquired.[104] If he is not supremely loveable to us, given our appetite toward visible goods, then for us to love God supremely, charity must be infused into our hearts. Mortal sin does not diminish charity; it destroys it.[105]

It is quite common to view Aquinas's philosophy as Aristotle warmed over. This is especially true in his ethics. There is certainly a level of undeniable similarity. After all, they both are classical virtue theories (having a similar listing of classical virtues: wisdom, temperance, justice, and courage). Aquinas's notion of virtue acquisition and character development look similar to Aristotle's. And ethics is closely associated with reason, where the passions seem to be obstacles or, once subdued, under the control of reason. This leads Terence Irwin to claim that for Aquinas the "passions are constituents of a virtue in so far as they are subject to reason and moved by reason."[106] While holding out room for what he calls "pseudo-passions" in Aquinas, even Peter King says that contrary to Hume, Aquinas holds "that reason is and ought to be the ruler of the passions."[107] And just as Aristotle explicitly rejects any reference to the passions in defining morality, so the father of the Protestant Reformation thought Aquinas had unfaithfully

---

101. Aquinas, *ST* II-II.23.6.
102. Aquinas, *ST* II-II.23.7.
103. Aristotle, *Topics* II.3.
104. Aquinas, *ST* II-II.24.1.
105. Aquinas, *ST* II-II.24.10.
106. Irwin, *Development of Ethics*, 1:522.
107. King, "Aquinas on the Passions," 105n7.

followed Aristotle in the same way, thereby bringing erroneous views into central tenets of the Christian faith.

On the one hand, it might be thought that equating passions with emotion and eliminating it from ethical consideration is scandalously inhuman. But on the other hand, subduing or marginalizing emotions from ethics is a necessity for the objectivity of ethics. It is almost as though we must choose between the two. However, this is yet another place where Aquinas, whose ethics are objective, nonetheless breaks with his philosophical predecessor in that his ethics are not fundamentally Aristotelian in nature. Aquinas reserves a place for the passions.[108] Eleonore Stump argues, "Aquinas recognizes the Aristotelian virtues, but for him they are not real virtues. And, for him, the passions—or at least the suitably formulated analogues of the passions—are foundational to any ethical life."[109] Before discussing these pseudo-passions or analogues, we need to digress for a moment to make some distinctions with respect to virtue.

For Aquinas, each Aristotelian virtue is acquired and maintained via the agent in proper Aristotelian fashion. However, Aristotle's fashion is not Aquinas's fashion in that none of the Aristotelian virtues are genuine virtues for Aquinas. He distinguishes himself from Aristotle's common virtue theory by defining virtue this way: "Virtue is caused in us by God without any action on our part, but not without our consent." And again, but more explicit in his defense, is this: "A virtue is a good quality of the mind by which one lives righteously, of which no one can make bad use, and which God works in us without us."[110]

To be sure, Aquinas does not offer a wholesale denial of Aristotle's virtues, but simply denies that they tell the whole story (i.e., they are not fully virtues). He provides a list of the four classical virtues, but adds and understands them within the context of faith, hope, and love as theologically infused virtues. While the common Aristotelian virtues are indeed acquired in Aquinas's account much like Aristotle's, Aquinas is explicit when he considers them of an entirely different class or species of virtue altogether. "Infused and acquired virtues differ . . . in relation to the ultimate end."[111] Change the *telos* of life and you have a new motivation whatsoever you do. Not only is this true with respect to the end, but the two kinds of virtues differ "in relation to their proper objects," one being in accord with the rule

---

108. Aquinas, *ST* II-II.24.1a2; I-II.22–48.

109. Stump, "Non-Aristotelian Character," 29; Miner, *Thomas Aquinas*.

110. Aquinas, *ST* I-II.55.4. For a lengthy discussion on defining the virtues in Aquinas, see Jordan, "Theology and Philosophy," 236–41.

111. Rosati, "Moral Motivation."

of human reason, the other with divine rule.[112] One can, on Aquinas's view, possess all of the acquired virtues and still not be a moral person. That is, Aristotle could have been "virtuous" (i.e., merely virtuous), yet not moral, because mortal sins are compatible with acquired virtue while incompatible with infused virtues. In fact, Aristotle says that, an act of sin, even mortal sin, is compatible with humanly acquired virtue." On his view, a person can fail to have a relationship with God via mortal sin while possessing any number of acquired (in contrast to infused or theological) virtues.[113]

What's more, on Aquinas's account the moral life is intrinsically relational. Indeed, it is pneumatically relational.[114] The same acquired virtues bearing similarity to the infused virtues also bear similarity to gifts by God's Holy Spirit. For instance, the acquired virtue of temperance now becomes "fear of the Lord," and justice becomes "piety." Fear (filial fear) is first among the gifts, and the fear of the Lord is the beginning of wisdom, the beginning of the genuine philosophical life.[115] The gifts of the Spirit are entailed for salvation, the highest of such gifts being wisdom.[116] Regarding the gifts he says, "These perfections are called gifts, not only because they are infused by God, but also because by them man is disposed to become amenable to the Divine inspiration."[117] He speaks explicitly about the personal relationship believers have with the indwelling Holy Spirit.[118]

The gifts are not states that are wholly intrinsic to a person, say, the virtuous person, as they cannot even adequately be described in first-personal or third-personal terms. Rather, they are second-personal in character as they flow out of a second-personal connection to God. This is not, then, simply something infused into a human agent, but it is instead predicated upon the indwelling of God in the human person with the consequence of the person's heightened awareness of God and aptness to follow the inner promptings of God. This gives rise to a sort of nonpropositional knowledge of the other person via experience. Consider, for example, cases where a husband can stop short of finishing his sentence and the wife finishes it

---

112. Aquinas, *ST* I-II.63.4.1. As Frederick Copleston points out, whereas Aristotle's truly happy man is the philosopher, Aquinas's is the saint. See Copleston, *Medieval Philosophy*, 398.

113. See Aquinas, *ST* I-II.63.2.

114. This notion will be further described and characterized in chapter 4 relative to Aquinas's understanding of the Holy Spirit's role in the life of the believer.

115. Aquinas, *ST* II-II.19.121.1; *ST* I-II.62.2.

116. Aquinas, *ST* I-II.68.2.

117. Aquinas, *ST* I-II.68.1. Pinsent, "Gifts and Fruits," 475–90; Pinsent, *Second-Person Perspective*. For brevity, see Miller, "Review of *Second-Person Perspective*."

118. Aquinas, *Commentary on Galatians* 5.16.

for him by virtue of their intimate knowledge of each other. The same can be said of actions where movements are more or less predictable. The kind of knowledge in question shares features with perceptual knowledge (e.g., direct, immediate, characteristically intuitive, and reliable). Such capacities enable one to know what another is doing, her intention in doing it, and with what emotion it is carried out.

For Aquinas, such a relationship with God is possible for every person where a human person can know God's presence, mind, and will in somewhat of a direct and intuitive way analogous to the sort of second-personal knowledge we can have with other human persons, but in this case it is with a divine Person in light of an eternal perspective. Aquinas speaks of a general way in which God is in all things (e.g., as a cause is in the effects via participation), but a special way appropriate for a rational being,

> wherein God is said to be present as the object known is in the knower, and the beloved in the lover. And since the rational creature by its operation of knowledge and love attains to God Himself, according to this special mode God is said not only to exist in the rational creature but also to dwell therein as in His own temple.[119]

The Holy Spirit fills a person with a sense of the love of God and his nearness and friendship, for Aquinas. Through this second-personal connection, the individual united in love with God and for God because of God's love for her will tend to grow more like God, coming to know intimately God's judgments and intuitions, taking on "the mind of Christ," as it were. The person will not always strive to simply reason things out with respect to ethics, but will instead be pneumatically-relationally disposed to think, do, and feel, in morally appropriate ways. Aquinas does not locate real wisdom, the gift of wisdom, in the reason but in the will. He says, "Now this sympathy or connaturality for Divine things is the result of charity, which unites us to God, according to 1 Corinthians 6:17: 'He who is joined to the Lord, is one spirit.' Consequently, wisdom which is a gift, has its cause in the will, which cause is charity, but it has its essence in the intellect, whose act is to judge aright."[120]

Let us now return to our discussion of the passions. Aquinas's bedrock passion is love. But love appears on three separate lists of passions (i.e., it is tri-level). In its most basic sense, a passion is a response of the sensory appetite to direct and intuitive perceptual stimuli. As we said much earlier, such a passion can have a detrimental moral result by influencing the intellect via

119. Aquinas, *ST* I.43.3.
120. Aquinas, *ST* II-II.45.2.

making something seem good that would not have seemed good otherwise. But such a passion can also enhance the moral life by influencing the intellect towards what is really good with greater fervor. In this way, a basic passion in an Aristotelian sense is morally praiseworthy or blameworthy only as it is related to the intellect. Otherwise, it is neutral. However, a passion may not merely be in the sensitive appetite but in the intellectual appetite, the will. In this second sense, a passion is a responsive desire that is produced based upon information coming from the intellect rather than the senses alone. Love in the first sense is sensitive love, but in the second sense is rational love.[121] This is love untethered to the material part in that some of the passions in this sense can even be had by God. This may seem odd if God is taken to be impassible, but the impassibility is clearly problematic with passions in the first sense given the necessary tie to the sense perception of physical beings, of which God is not. But this impassibility seems to be irrelevant to the second sense where God loves. This has obvious connection then with the statement in certain context about God as "the God who suffers."[122] Love, in this second sense is an infused virtue and as such cannot be morally neutral as the basic sense of passion is. Indeed, not only is it always good, but it is the essential motivation behind all of the genuine virtues. Finally, as the virtues have analogues in the gifts of the Spirit, so the passions have them in the fruits of the Spirit. The fruits are second-personal in nature as the outflow of someone intimately connected with God. Citing an oft quoted verse by Augustine, Aquinas says that "[God] is love. Hence it is written (Rom 5:5): 'The charity of God is poured forth in our hearts by the Holy Ghost, Who is given to us.' The necessary result of the love of charity is joy, because every lover rejoices at being united to the beloved. Now charity has always actual presence in God Whom it loves."[123]

To summarize, the basic passion is grounded in the sensitive appetite as a direct perceptual response to stimuli, and is *per se* morally neutral without connection to reason. The second sense is also a response, but a non-physical response to graciously infused virtue in the non-resistant will and whose passions are always good rather than morally neutral. And, finally, a passion like love as a fruit of the Spirit is a strong motivational response in light of an intimate relationship with God and as a natural consequence of a flourishing life, the good life. The gifts and fruit of the Spirit are relational rather than intrinsic. And it is this pneumatically-relational ground that provides the basis for all real virtue and the good life.

121. Aquinas, *ST* I-II.26.1.
122. Aquinas, *ST* I.20.1.
123. Aquinas, *ST* I-II.70.3.

So in the end it is clear that for Aquinas the fruits of the Holy Spirit relative to the moral life are not an Aristotelian set of passions governed by reason, but instead these emotions, spiritual analogues to the passions ("pseudopassions"), are transformed in the second-personal relation to God. The relational connection radically heightens motivation for the *vita activa* and *vita contemplativa* far more than "thought thinking itself thinking" à la Aristotle. This is in harmony with the way in which Augustine, not Aristotle, would summarize ethics: "Love God and do as you please."[124] Not only is love necessary to perfect faith, but grace is necessary to produce it.

Grace

Aquinas believes that man is created in God's image irrespective of what state man is in. Like Aristotle, Aquinas believes that we have a fundamental desire to understand, to understand being universally.[125] This includes the world and all that is in it. Aristotle's epistemology is such that one knows things by grasping their causes, which raises the question of what caused the world, the question of God. According to Aquinas, then, all human beings have a natural desire to know God. This aspect of man's nature does not change just because of the fall. Man retains the capacity for the eternal. Given human limitation and Aquinas's epistemology, we can know God's effects but not God in himself in his essence. But knowing that God exists and whatever must belong to such existence cannot satisfy the longing we have naturally as humans. The goal of intellectual being is to know. In light of Aquinas's restrictions, knowledge of God in himself (i.e., his essence) would seem to be an unattainable goal, naturally speaking. It is not that God is actually unknowable, but that he is not naturally knowable to us, to our natural human understanding. Faith can extend this, but even faith is insufficient. Yet a total *via negativa* is untenable for Aquinas because "God promises us complete happiness."[126] He says:

> The ultimate happiness of a man consists in his highest activity, which is the exercise of his mind. If therefore the created mind were never able to see the essence of God, either it would never attain happiness or its happiness would consist in something other than God. This is contrary to faith, for the

---

124. Augustine, *Treatise on the Epistle of John to the Parthians* 7.8.
125. Aquinas, *ST* I.78.1.
126. Aquinas, *ST* I-II.3.2.

ultimate perfection of the rational creature lies in that which is the source of its being.[127]

Thus, he concludes that it must be possible, in some way, for humans to apprehend God's essence. But this cannot be via natural knowledge alone, nor can it simply be via the extension of faith, not even prelapsarian faith. For if it were possible, the fall would not have been possible. For no one can see God in his essence and turn from it; hence the fall proved man did not see God's essence. He says, "Man is not able by his own operation to reach his ultimate end, which transcends the capacity of his natural powers, unless his operation acquires from divine power the efficacy to reach the aforesaid end."[128] The good life is within man's grasp. Yet, while man has a teleological demand suitable for his nature, the transition from nature to *telos* is not sufficiently grounded in his nature itself. The demand expresses not that which is actually impossible but only that which is humanly impossible. Man's nature is, however, designed for its end, and the means by which this is accommodated depends upon grace making possible the wayfarer's life of faith. Although grace was necessary in both pre- and postlapsarian states, it was needed for more reasons in the postlapsarian state. The experience of seeing God in his essence, that for which we were made, the good life, is ultimately obtainable only by the blessed in the beatific vision, reminiscent of the statement by Augustine: "Thou madest us for Thyself, and our heart is restless, until it repose in Thee."[129]

Although contrary to popular opinion, Aquinas does not hold that human reason is without limitations, due both to issues of finitude and rectitude. He argues that revelation is necessary given the human finite and fallen conditions. Revelation is a kind of gift or grace, of course, just as faith is, but the grace that is most substantial insofar as humans are concerned from Aquinas's perspective pertains to its infusion. Eternal life is an end that exceeds that which is proportionate to human nature such that man cannot attain it by his natural endowments but is designed nonetheless to attain it. Thus, divine aid is required. So while he can do a human good (e.g., toil in the fields, have friends, acquire virtues, etc.), these are deeds conducive to a man in a natural way alone.[130] There are two ways man could fulfill the ethical commands of God's law. First, the substance of the works, say, of justice, fortitude, and other acquired virtues, can be fulfilled whilst in a state of perfect nature. But in corruption, man cannot do so without

---

127. Aquinas, *ST* I.12.1.
128. Aquinas, *SCG* III.147.5.
129. Aquinas, *ST* I.12.1; Augustine, *Confessions*, 1.
130. Aquinas, *ST* I-II.109.2, 5.

healing grace. Second, they can be fulfilled not merely in the substance of the act, but also the mode of acting (i.e., the acts done out of charity). In this way, man cannot fulfill the commands either in innocence or in corruption without grace. He cites Augustine: "Without grace men can do no good whatever," and then he adds, "Not only do they know by its light what to do, but by its help they do lovingly what they know."[131]

Although he must prepare himself, man cannot *by himself* prepare himself for grace without external aid. The preparation for the human will to good is two-fold. First, it requires the habitual gift of grace which is the principle of meritorious works. Second, it requires the preparation for this gift.[132] Recall that man incurs a triple loss by sinning: (1) stain, (2) corruption of natural good and a disordered will that is not subject to God, and (3) debt of punishment deserving of damnation. God's grace is required for all three and at both points: the habitual gift, and God moving us freely to himself.[133]

Aquinas does not hold that the good of nature is unimpaired after the fall. He distinguishes (1) good inherent in the principles constitutive of this nature, (2) the inclination of virtue following from such principles, and (3) original justice. The principles were neither destroyed nor lessened, the inclination was severely diminished, and the OJ destroyed. Sins are not actions done in accordance with reason and are thus irrational for an otherwise rational being to do. Nonetheless, even though "a person can add sin to sin, he can raise countless obstacles; yet the inclination itself cannot be totally destroyed since its root always remains.[134] The inclination is not destroyed, and so the ability to extricate oneself (with divine aid) is available.

With respect to his view about nature, Aquinas held that man has a natural desire to know God, yet the *summum bonum* is an end that nature cannot by itself achieve. "Beatific vision or knowledge is, in one way, above the nature of the rational soul, for the soul cannot reach it by its own power." Couple that with, "But in another way it is in accordance with its own nature, in so far as the soul by its very nature has a capacity for it, being made in the image of God."[135] Just because a thing has a capacity, it does not follow of necessity that it can self-actualize that capacity. There is a human nature, a human *telos*, and a means by which the capacities of human nature sometimes include the transcending of self-actualizing capacity, the *summum bonum* being a prime example. Aquinas defines for us his understanding

---

131. See Augustine, *On Corruption and Grace* II.
132. Aquinas, *ST* I-II.109.6; I-II.113.7.
133. Aquinas, *ST* I-II.109.7.
134. Aquinas, *ST* I-II.85.2.
135. Aquinas, *ST* III.9.3.

of nature in one of two ways: (1) the sufficient principle in a thing (e.g., an Aristotelian physical object with natural downward movement), and (2) that to which a thing has an inclination even if it cannot gain it by itself. For example, it is natural for a woman to have a baby even though she cannot do so without a man.[136] Similarly, the soul has a natural inclination for the vision of God, but it cannot obtain it without divine aid. Contrary to the Aristotelian assumption that a desire will not extend beyond one's natural capacity to fulfill it, as later Thomists assumed, for Aquinas, humans are "ordained to an end higher than that which is proportionate to their natural powers."[137] So grace presupposes nature, not in the sense that grace is merely additive to nature, but in the sense that human nature is inclined to an end without a self-sufficient principle to attain it, requiring grace.

In the state of innocence, without habitual grace, man's position was *posse non peccare* (i.e., it was possible not to sin) in both mortal and venial senses. Nonetheless, man could not do it without God's "conservational" help since, if this had been withdrawn, even his nature would have dissolved. But in this postlapsarian life, including even that of the wayfarer, the healing is in the mind; the carnal appetite is not yet restored (cf. Rom. 7:25, on the law of the mind versus the law of flesh). So the case is *non posse non peccare*—venial sins seem inevitable—except for mortal sin that man can abstain from which takes its stand in his reason. Venial sin is inevitable given corruption of man's lower sensual appetite. He can repress each of its movements but not all of them. But mortal sins are inevitable in the postlapse, preconversion state. So man can avoid each but not every act of sin via grace. Nonetheless, because he culpably does not prepare himself to have grace, the inevitability of sin without it fails to excuse him.[138]

Man still needs grace after justifying grace to persevere against the attacks of the passion (passions here are taken in more of a negative sense). While in innocence, he stood at a crossroads as it were where it was both *posse non peccare* and *posse peccare*. But in heaven, not only will he be able to persevere, but he will be unable to sin (*non posse peccare*).[139] Sanctifying grace is first manifested by living faith. Grace is not a virtue, but is a certain disposition presupposed in the infused virtues.[140] Grace is the principle of meritorious works through the medium of the virtues

---

136. See Aquinas, *Disputed Questions on Truth* 24.10.1.
137. Aquinas, *ST* I-II.91.4.3.
138. Aquinas, *ST* I-II.109.8.
139. Aquinas, *ST* I-II.109.10.
140. Aquinas, *ST* I-II.110.3.

and, in a respect, it is unmerited favor.[141] But how are we to understand the nexus of grace and living faith?

Aquinas provides an account for the accommodation of living faith. When a person transitions into the wayfarer state toward the good life, God operates on him in order to bring him to the assent of faith by infusing into him operating grace wherein he participates in the divine. Aquinas is often misread in theological circles for being Pelagian (or Semi-Pelagian) given his connection to Aristotle.[142] But regarding the Pelagian heresy—"they believe that without grace man can fulfill all the Divine commandments"— Aquinas demurs.[143] Nonetheless, it is sometimes imagined that the central motif for Martin Luther's version of the Protestant Reformation hinged on ridding Aristotle from Christianity via ridding Aquinas, who baptized him so deeply based on the understanding that, in Aquinas's opinion, the fall had relatively little impact on human reason; and so he generously assimilated Aristotle wherever revelation fell short. Luther scholar, Ron Frost, stakes virtually the entire Protestant Reformation on the contention that Luther's *real* reason for it was none other than overturning the pervasive influence of Aristotle via Aquinas which shaped the medieval moral tradition.[144] Admittedly, Aquinas is big fan of Aristotle and so it is easy to misread Aquinas and throw the baby out with the bath water, as it were. Luther, following the later Augustine, affirms the affective model (i.e., compatibilism on the free will debate) as the motivating feature of salvation, whereas the alleged Aristotle-Aquinas model was grounded on an autonomous will apart from any influence of the affections or passions, leading to a cooperative model of salvation that Luther rejected. The context of Luther's polemics pertaining to God's grace in salvation was the Augustinian-Pelagian controversy. Aquinas's view of grace, it might be thought, combines human responsibility and divine enablement in the cooperative model of faith wherein love as part of the will is crowned with merit, rather than the affective model which as a faith response is non-meritorious. It is this conception of love that supported Aquinas's crucial living faith (*fides caritate formata*) in progressive justification, and consequently Aquinas's model is semi-Pelagian. Or so goes the possible theological objection that serves as a foil to understanding Aquinas's views.

But this invites closer consideration. First, Aquinas's actual view would be more in keeping with the Synod of Orange (AD 529), which rejected

---

141. Aquinas, *ST* I-II.110.1–4.
142. Evans, *Pelagius*; Shelley, "Pelagius, Pelagianism," 897.
143. Aquinas, *ST* I-II.109.4.
144. Frost, "Aristotle's 'Ethics,'" 225–26.

Pelagianism, siding with Augustine but without fully accepting Augustinianism. The Synod was essentially semi-Augustinian, which should be a better description of Aquinas's views.[145] For Aquinas, no meritorious acts, in part or whole (*meritum de congruo* and *meritum de condigno*), were possible before grace, and any following were so only on the grounds of grace, not the ability of the human will *per se*.[146] According to Aquinas, without living faith none of the other virtues or good deeds are genuinely good or virtuous, and without grace such faith is not available. So he is not even semi-Pelagian. It is possible to misconstrue Aquinas's interpretation of the fall and its role in human reason, will, and the passions if his view is seen as too closely approximating Aristotle's or perhaps Pelagius's view. But this seems to be a misunderstanding. And while it might be thought on Aquinas's account that the detrimental effects of original sin would preclude the free will required for morality, this is not a problem on his account because such freedom cannot be taken away by original sin since it is part of human nature grounded in the *imago Dei*.[147] Suffice it to say that although Aquinas's views are similar (non-identical) in ways to Aristotle's on human agency,[148] he sided neither with Aristotle's view of human nature nor with Luther's views of fallen human nature. Fallen humans have been created in and still maintain the image of God, "as the apogee of God's creation." It is significant to note that the *imago Dei* is not at the periphery of what it means to be human. Luther may have held that at the fall man lost the *imago Dei*, but that is just Luther.[149] Being human entails being made in the *imago Dei*; to lose that entails that we cease to be human. Given our humanity, then, we have a natural *telos* for God. Aquinas depicts human nature in two ways: (1) "in its integrity, as it was in our first parent before sin," and (2) "as it is corrupted in us after the sin of our first parent."[150] Aquinas endorsed and adopted Aristotle at many points but not uncritically and wholesale.

---

145. Not all Reformed Protestants see Aquinas's views on grace and justification as objectionable. See Kyle, "Semi-Pelagianism," 1089–90; Oberman, *Archbishop Thomas Bradwardine*, 145, 148–51; Muller, "Scholasticism, Reformation, Orthodoxy," 81–96.

146. Aquinas, ST I-II.114; I-II.109.5; Oberman, *Forerunners of the Reformation*, 123–40.

147. For more on the free will debate see Stump, *Aquinas*, 277–306; van Inwagen, *Essay on Free Will*; Kenny, *Will, Freedom, and Power*; Helm, *Providence of God*; Flint, *Divine Providence*.

148. MacDonald, "Practical Reasoning and Reasons-Explanations," 133–49.

149. Copan, "Original Sin," 519–41; Pelikan, *Reformation of Church and Dogma*, 145; Plantinga, "Essence and Essentialism," 138.

150. Aquinas, ST I-II.109.2.

So what is his actual view, then, of the relation of free will and grace? We have already talked some about his anthropology, so we will make specific his account of how the two relate. Basically, sin is a privation of being where being ought to be, like a hole in your stocking where more stocking ought to be. A privation is not an absence in a thing, but lack in a good thing. Aquinas says, "For it was shown that good is the subject of evil. But evil has no formal cause, rather is it a privation of form; likewise, neither has it a final cause, but rather is it a privation of order to the proper end; since not only the end has the nature of good, but also the useful, which is ordered to the end. Evil, however, has a cause—by way of an agent, not directly, but accidentally." Aquinas is not suggesting that sin is not real. God created everything. Evil or sin is not a thing. That is, it is not a substance. It does not exist in itself, but only as inhering in a good substance. He says, "As the term good signifies "perfect being," so the term evil signifies nothing else than 'privation of perfect being.' In its proper acceptance, privation is predicated on that which is fitted by its nature to be possessed."[151]

God can fix the defect in the will without breaking the will, provided only that the will does not resist God. When the will stops clamping its teeth shut against God's grace, when it just ceases to resist without yet willing anything positive, then God can slip in the grace needed for the longing for God. That longing is the beginning of a process of someone in the wayfarer state in that a human is justified when God graciously operates on him in a way to bring him to faith with its two-part act of will (a longing for goodness and a detesting of sin, the latter derivative on the former).[152]

Aquinas affirms libertarian agency in his belief that nothing, not even God, operates on the will with efficient causation, claiming that "every motion of the will must proceed from an interior principle."[153] He affirms what he takes as Augustine's view: "The necessity of compulsion cannot in any way apply to the will."[154] This is the case even with respect to the infusion of grace: "There is no motion from God to justice without a motion of free choice."[155] Following this quote is the section where he affirms that this act of free will is produced by God. And still,

> Now it might seem to someone that a human being is compelled to some good action by the divine aid . . . but it is characteristic

---

151. Aquinas, *ST* I.49.1; *Aquinas's Shorter Summa*, 125. For more, see section in this book on the Origin of Sin.

152. Aquinas, *ST* I-II.113.5–7.

153. Aquinas, *SCG* III.88.

154. Aquinas, *Disputed Questions on Truth* 22.5 reply.

155. Aquinas, *ST* I-II.113.3.

of a human being (and every rational nature) that he acts voluntarily and is master of his own acts . . . and compulsion is contrary to this. Therefore God does not compel a human being to good action by his aid.[156]

Yet he also says, "God can change the will with necessity, but he cannot compel it."[157] So just what does he mean by necessity yet without compulsion?

Aquinas answers with respect to those in the wayfarer state by providing an illustration about a stone. A stone has a natural disposition or inclination to fall and if thrown upward while having that inclination, then violence or coercion is used in that it is moved contrary to its inclination. However, it is possible to change that natural configuration or inclination by removing the prior inclination downward. Then it can be given an inclination to move upward instead of downward, wherein at that time compulsion cannot be invoked with respect to the upward motion since it is not now contrary to the inclination.[158]

In God's infusion of grace, it is the infusion of a created form following the removal or expulsion of a prior form, the form of corruption. He says, "Grace which is and inheres expels guilt—not that guilt which is but that guilt which previously was and is not. For grace does not expel guilt in the manner of an efficient cause. . . . Rather, grace expels guilt in the manner of a formal cause."[159] He speaks about the transition happening in an instant, saying:

> This happens when the two endpoints of a motion or change are . . . privation and form. . . . And so I say that the endpoints of justification are grace and the privation of grace. Between these there is no mean . . . and therefore the transition from one to the other is in an instant. . . . And so the whole justification of an impious person occurs in an instant.[160]

So the will of someone just prior to entering the wayfarer state is in a situation characterized by guilt and culpability. God cannot simply will that that person wills to hate sin and love God without violence against the will. The endpoints of the change at God's infusion of grace are not two opposite forms but a privation of a form *and* a form. So the guilt is first removed, leaving a privation with respect to sin and goodness. Then God adds the

---

156. Aquinas, *SCG* III.148.
157. Aquinas, *Disputed Questions on Truth* 22.8.
158. See Aquinas, *Disputed Questions on Truth* 22.8 reply.
159. Aquinas, *Disputed Questions on Truth* 22.8–9.
160. Aquinas, *Disputed Questions on Truth* 28.9.

form of grace to the will, not by restructuring the same inclination but by adding a new one where there is a lack. Thus, grace operates on the will formally but not efficiently. This may seem like semantics, but it is not. Consider what accounts for this privation.

For Aquinas, it is not merely that one can assent or dissent, for one can do nothing at all. The will in a particular situation can remain inactive or quiescent. So with respect to God's overtures of grace, the will can accept (hate sin and love God), reject (love sin and hate God), or simply be turned off. All of those decisions are in its power. For Aquinas, prior to the wayfarer state yet in a postlapsarian situation, the will is in a state of rejection of grace until at some moment it gives way to privation or quiescence, and it is at that time that God can infuse grace into the will, bringing about justifying faith.

Now, the human willer has the power to move from rejection to quiescence or vice versa, but one ought not to invoke the charge of Pelagianism or even semi-Pelagianism at this juncture.[161] For on that note, Aquinas would have to hold that a human being is capable of some good act without grace, which is not his view. To will rejection or even quiescence (i.e., not to will), the two capable motions prior to grace, is not to will something good. The will's ceasing to act is not a good act because it is not an act at all. Any good act by the willer is brought about by grace. He affirms that "God is prepared to give grace to everyone. . . . But the only people deprived of grace are the ones who provide in themselves an obstacle to grace."[162]

So man's movement in justification toward the final consummation of the good life begins at the nexus of operating grace and the cognitive volitional act of living faith whereby the process of restoring man to rectitude culminates in the next life and sins are remitted. Justification, therefore, is a process. It should be noted that while grace is the same, Aquinas distinguishes between operating and cooperating aspects on the basis of the effects brought about in the believer's mind. In particular, it makes distinct the will's role acted on by grace or in accord with grace to produce some good act. Either way, it is God's grace.[163]

Conclusion

Like Aristotle, Aquinas claims that the function which characterizes the human agent is rational activity by virtue of which the agent is made good, enabling her to live the good life. For Aquinas, human activity is a relationship

161. Aquinas, *ST* II-II.2.5–7; II-II.6.1.
162. Aquinas, *SCG* III.159.
163. Aquinas, *ST* I-II.111.2.

between the cognitive and appetitive powers. But what happens when this activity is somehow curtailed by a dysfunctional lapse in the human condition owing to sin, an inordinate activity of self-love, is that all hell breaks loose in corruption and there exists universally extensive total depravity in man. On final analysis, it becomes clear that the good life is not really a good life without certain necessary conditions that transcend Aristotle's notion of good, namely, theological goodness attendant with the virtue of living faith at the nexus of God's grace. These conditions are necessary in all states outside the beatific vision itself.

Regarding Aristotle's view, we realized that there was a problem of tragic proportion. The gap between human nature and its natural *telos* rendered the good life elusive for most if not all. On the surface it seemed available, but in reality it was quite esoteric at best. But none of the problems that plagued Aristotle are problems on Aquinas's account. First, Aquinas's man has no ultimate issue with fate and sufficiently required external goods before one can even commence towards the morally good life en route to the contemplative good life. One did not have to be part of Aristotle's gentlemen's club to qualify. For Aquinas, man's justification by faith on the basis of God's grace available for those made in God's image makes the possibility universally realizable (the intramural Christian debate on election notwithstanding).

Even given the parallel fixity of character problem for Aristotle and the doctrine of OS for Aquinas, the accessibility for change affected only the Aristotelian vicious man, not the Thomistic man, given what we have said about God's grace making potential change, in principle at least, available for all. Aquinas's account of the good life is not simply an ideal but a reality. The problem with OS relative to human nature and the demand of the human *telos* seems prima facie to widen the gap, hence exacerbating the problem for Aquinas, but is remedied because of the availability (in principle) of the necessary conditions, living faith and God's grace. This does not reduce the demand, but in a modified Kantian view where "ought implies can" is corrected to be "God's ought implies can by God's grace," a pneumatically relational design plan where grace is not merely added to some Aristotelian "autonomous" human nature, but where human nature was designed for the presence of God's grace for ultimate flourishing and proper function. Moreover, the motivational force in the Thomistic viewpoint is enhanced over Aristotle's "thought thinking itself thinking," due to its fundamentally relational nature.

Aristotle's *theos* is not identical to the Judeo-Christian *theos*, given that it is essentially deistic. While the theistic viewpoint has experienced resurgence among philosophers given relatively novel discoveries entering into contemporary design and cosmological arguments (e.g., the cosmic fine tuning of the universe and big bang discoveries), deism has likewise gained in adherents. Indeed, the arguments are immune from the infamous "problem of evil," given that they reveal nothing about the moral character of the designer/creator. However, the motivational force behind relating to the "God" of deism versus the God of theism is vastly different. The former, but not the latter, treats God as though transcendentally absent and this has wide ranging effects on our seeking to "be like God," especially in matters of moral goodness. If there is a moral law akin to physical laws, then it seems a bit awkward to claim that God would instill such moral laws in his creation without further care or concern for the creation on such matters.[164]

---

164. Flew and Varghese, *There Is a God*; Helm, *Providence of God*, 69–90.

4

Maimonides and Aquinas in Dialogue

While it was impossible for Maimonides and Aquinas to have had an actual dialogue in light of their timeline (Maimonides died in 1204 and Aquinas was born in 1225), it is possible to consider them in dialogue as contemporaries converging within similar yet divergent traditions. Aquinas read and commented on Maimonides. Maimonides lived in Christian Europe for a period of time, and so he may have read sources in the Christian tradition that influenced Aquinas as much as he read sources in the Islamic tradition, thus sharing similarities with Aquinas in their intellectual histories. For our purposes, it is possible to construct a kind of dialogue based on certain views held and implications that their respective views have for one another. We will want to take stock, then, and explore some important comparisons and differences that make a difference in these two medieval Aristotelian philosophers' conceptions of the good life.

In this chapter, we will compare conceptions by taking stock on some points of convergence and divergence. We'lll consider implications based on a particular parable in Maimonides's *Guide*, which begins to surface a potentially problematic area. We'll consider an initial evasion of this problem in the context of a controversial area in Maimonides, and we will explore a potential obstacle for both in terms of the ultimate goal, the knowledge of God. But our focus will then be on exploring and developing Aquinas's pneumatically relational approach in light of God's immanence and with some consideration to modern developments in social and neuroscience.

Comparing Conceptions

In previous chapters, we examined a broadly plausible interpretation of Aristotle to set up the philosophical background, and then we traced the basic Aristotelian structure of the human good by considering raw human nature, its ultimate end, and how to get from man as he is in the raw to man as he could become—the good life for man. The Aristotelian vision is one way to mark out the good life. Others have followed although not necessarily meeting with success.[1] The concept of the good life for man is prior to the concept of a virtue. The understanding of virtue and the human *telos* is also intrinsically connected to one's understanding of *theos*. The account of this Aristotelian teleological structure was shown to exhibit certain systemic problems according to which attaining the human end, the knowledge of God, is rendered elusive for most people in light of certain preconditions for the attainment of the good life. In considering a narrow path by which a few might obtain it, we saw that it becomes elusive even for the best of men as a mere human idealistic façade, or else so rare and episodically unsustainable as to render man a being who seems somehow severed from his natural end.

Like Aristotle whose views on human perfection reveal a striking two-tier notion of moral virtue in light of *phronesis* (a necessary precondition to the ultimate perfect life of intellectual virtue), both Maimonides and Aquinas are committed to making a similar Aristotelian move given a certain nexus without which the virtues are less than fully virtuous (or even non-virtuous) and virtue itself is less accessible than even Aristotle's understanding supposed. The considered features found lacking were grace and the virtue of faith, something of a functional analogue to the Aristotelian *phronesis*. These notions were made more salient against the background of the fall as explicated respectively by the two medievalists.

Like Aristotle, both of their systems can be duly characterized as personally transformative. This is no surprise, however, since classical and medieval virtue theories in general focus on the character of the person whereas many modern ethical theories ignore personal character altogether. This is true not only of virtue ethics as commonly thought of, but also of virtue epistemology.[2] The process by which one approaches the good life leads to genuine transformation of character, but character transformation takes on a vastly different nuance for each thinker. The comparative approach helps highlight aspects of each thinker's position that might otherwise be ignored or simply missed by focusing on one thinker in isolation.

Through a comparative approach we can mark out a salient distinction by describing their respective viewpoints. Comparatively speaking, Aristotle's approach may be characterized as informational, Maimonides's as instructional (presupposing information, of course, but adding divine gift in the form of external instruction or Torah), and Aquinas's as pneumatic-relational (presupposing information and instruction, but adding a more intimate

---

1. MacIntyre, *After Virtue*.

2. Wood, *Epistemology*; Annas, *Morality of Happiness*; Anscombe, "Modern Moral Philosophy," 1–19.

internal way of knowing and transforming so as to be relating with God the Holy Spirit as internal guide rather than merely external guide). This has implications for how each approach describes the way to imitate God.

Having the proper philosophical reflection serves the purposes of reinforcing, internally motivating, and sustaining the good life. These systems are in a sense based firmly in the study of human motivation given that, in these systems, virtue ethics and epistemology are grounded in the common normative teleological structure. It is designed to move people beyond being merely virtuous to being fully virtuous and God-like, enjoying the good life via *imitatio Dei*. But imitating the divine requires some kind of conception of the divine, some kind of knowledge of God or *theoria*, which is constitutive of the good life. Aristotle's vision seems less than motivational in that imitating God reduces to (ideally) sustainable contemplation because God is, under Aristotle's description, little more than thought thinking itself thinking.[3] The contrasting visions of the knowledge of God will be something we will need to address to see how faith connects with the knowledge of God.

Both Maimonides and Aquinas take faith to be a virtue. Aquinas approvingly cites Maimonides on the necessity both of faith and of divine revelation. Aquinas provides reasons for the necessity of faith, including the difficultly of the subject matter, weakness of mind in the early years, lack of training in preliminary knowledge by many, without which many would be destitute of knowledge of God, physical incapacity of many, and a busy life.[4]

Far from being a deficiency, as some in secular society might suppose, both consider faith essential in their approach to the good life as part of a knowledge tradition. It is a difference from Aristotle that makes a difference in fundamental ways. For both, faith involves a moral component. Indeed, for Maimonides, faith, while having an intellectual aspect, is essentially a moral virtue approximating the notion "faithful" or "faithfulness." It is required for moral perfection, and without moral perfection one cannot reach intellectual perfection. For Aquinas, faith is an intellectual virtue. But without the essential moral component (the virtue of love) involving the will, faith is relatively inert (i.e., dead faith). An ordinary belief can simply be intellectual (e.g., belief in the proposition 2+2=4), but not so for faith. For faith to have any muscle it must be a certain kind of faith, which includes both the intellect and the will in what Aquinas calls "living faith." It requires believing in God (material aspect, *credere deum*), believing God (formal aspect involving God's self-revelation, *credere deo*), and believing unto God

---

3. Kosman, "What Does the Maker Mind Make?," 343–58; Nagel, *View from Nowhere*.

4. Maimonides, *Guide* I.33–34; Aquinas, *ST* I-II.1.1.1; 2-2.2.4.

(indicating the relation of faith to the will, *credere in deum*).⁵ At this point, Maimonides and Aquinas together make their most fundamental break with Aristotle such that we begin to see the unraveling of their convergence into some pretty stark divergence with implications for each other in a more radical sense than either had in diverging with Aristotle. To see this, let us look at the end of Maimonides's *Guide of the Perplexed*.

Maimonides and the Cosmic Orphan

The highest human aspiration according to Maimonides is that which considers intellectual perfection to be merely a necessary condition to ultimate human perfection (just as moral perfection is necessary to our intellectual perfection). This ultimate objective, however, is not always captured adequately by commentators. The content of the moral/political dimensions of the intellectually perfected Jew seems to derive from the commandments, and thus it is reasonable that we adopt an interpretation that maintains Maimonides's strongly observant Jewishness while also respecting Maimonides *qua* philosopher.

It is also not a secret that Maimonides sometimes intentionally contradicts himself in the *Guide*. One reason he does this is pedagogical; in other words, until the student is better equipped he is kept under a tutor. He also uses contradiction in the *Guide* where the vulgar should not be made aware of it and the author takes all measures to conceal it.⁶

Astonishingly, in the same place where his use of contradiction is explicit also resides his treatment of the issue of human perfection *qua* apprehension of the intelligibles. Additionally, we find he also provides in the same chapter his exposition of Jeremiah 9:22–23 where he claims that Jeremiah does not limit the noblest ends only to the apprehension of Him, but also in the knowledge of His attributes (i.e., His actions).⁷ The person in question is not only one who knows God but who knows God's ways and imitates them. Hence, the goal of *theoria* ends up being *imitatio Dei*. It appears that the *vita activa* and not the *vita contemplativa* is the ideal, in a sense. Various schools of thought have developed regarding this Jeremiah passage. One common view contends that the ultimate perfection is imitating God's moral qualities.⁸ Another view maintains that it is imita-

---

5. Aquinas, *ST* II-II.2.2. Aquinas posits three distinct aspects of faith as it relates to God.

6. Maimonides, *Guide* I (18).

7. Maimonides, *Guide* III.54 (637).

8. Guttmann, "Editor's Introduction," 34; Guttmann, "Commentary," 225;

tion of God's governance of the world through the creation of just states, a decidedly political interpretation.[9] So it is either moral or political by these two schools. A third interpretation, however, retains a strong sense of Maimonides's Jewishness. Isadore Twersky says, "Maimonides believed that knowledge stimulates and sustains proper prescribed conduct [i.e., halakhic (legal) obedience] which in turn is a conduit for knowledge, and this intellectual achievement in return raises the level and motive of conduct."[10] The point is that while intellectual perfection is the prized perfection, it is not *per se* the final end of human existence, but is a means of deepening, enriching, and elevating observance of the *mitzvot*.

While the correct interpretation in light of Maimonides's esotericism is perhaps impossible to determine for certain, I think the best interpretation, at least as plausible as the others and the one I will represent for our purposes, is that of Manechem Kellner who, in the spirit of Twersky, defends this other "halakhic" (i.e., legal) interpretation as superior.[11] Let us unpack the salient part on human perfection at the end of Maimonides's *Guide* III.51–54. While in chapter 2 we discussed Maimonides's notion(s) of perfection, there is a particular section that draws our attention to it now at greater length.

Guide III.51 is Maimonides's (in)famous Parable of the Palace, which is introduced by the following words: "I shall begin the discourse in this chapter with a parable that I shall compose for you."[12] He then presents the parable that created more divisiveness and outrage in the Jewish community than anything else he wrote in the *Guide*. Traditionalists were outraged that he seems to hold that "men of science" could attain a higher degree of perfection and closeness to the divine than the halakhists, who were immersed in the Torah. Some questioned whether he wrote it, or said that if he did it should be burned. For example, Kellner cites Shem Tov as saying: "How could he say that those who know natural matters [physics] are on a higher level than those who engage in religion, and even more that they are with the ruler in the inner chamber, for on this basis the philosophers who are engaged with physics and metaphysics have achieved a higher level than those who are immersed in Torah!"[13]

Schwarzschild, "Moral Radicalism and 'Middlingness,'" 65–94. For variants of this position, see Frank, "End of the Guide," 485–95.

9. Berman, "Maimonides, the Disciple of Al-Farabi," 154–78; Berman, "Political Interpretation," 53–61; Berman, "Maimonides on the Fall of Man," 1–15.

10. Twersky, *Introduction*, 511.

11. Kellner, *Maimonides on Human Perfection*.

12. Maimonides, *Guide* III.51 (618).

13. Shem Tov quoted in Kellner, *Maimonides on Human Perfection*, 15.

Maimonides divides all human beings into several different categories. Kellner summarizes Maimonides's explanation of these categories as follows: (a) Those outside the city are individuals without doctrinal belief (brutes); (b) Those in the city facing away from the palace, who have adopted incorrect beliefs; and the farther they walk, the farther they are from the palace (They are worse than the first group and "necessity at certain times calls for killing them"); (c) Those who seek to enter the place but have not yet seen it. These are the Jewish masses, "the ignoramuses who observe the commandments"; (d) Those who have reached the habitation and circle it, seeking a way in. These are halakhists who hold to the true beliefs or views but "who do not engage in speculation concerning fundamental principles of religion." They "are engaged in studying the mathematical sciences and the art of logic"; (e) Those who have entered the gate and walk around the antechambers. They "have entered into speculation concerning the fundamental principles of religion" and "understood the natural sciences [i.e., physics]"; (f) Those who have entered the inner court of the palace and are there with the ruler. This is he [Maimonides uses the singular here] "who has achieved demonstration, to the extent that that is possible, of everything that may be demonstrated; and who has ascertained in divine matters, to the extent that that is possible." These are the "men of science" who "are of different grades of perfection."

One of those grades consists of those who, after attaining perfection into the study of metaphysics, "turn wholly toward God . . . and direct all the acts of their intellect toward an examination of the being with a view to drawing from them proof with regard to Him." These are the prophets. Another of these grades consists, apparently, of Moses, who "attained such a degree that it is said of him, 'And he was there with the Lord'" (Exod 34:28, KJV).

It has been suggested that Maimonides posits two routes to perfection here, one by the philosopher and the other by the Talmudists. The first is via speculation, the second via divine assistance (i.e., God guides him who seeks him). Kellner claims that this is based on a false reading since Maimonides never claims that philosophers attain a higher degree of perfection than *halakhists*. So he proffers an interpretation of the parable, rejecting the interpretations of Maimonides as being either a naturalist/secularist or an Al-Farabian philosopher who did not really affirm Judaism.[14]

Kellner's view is that the parable is exclusively taken to be referring to Jews, at least from the third and possibly the second class onward (the first being "sub-human," non-Jews). The comparison is simply between *halakhists* simpliciter and ones who have perfected themselves in the sciences

---

14. Kellner, *Maimonides on Human Perfection*.

and philosophy. There is no discussion, at least not here, of Aristotle or non-Jews and immortality. And the *Guide* as a whole is addressed to Rabbi Joseph ben Judah.

The second group at times requires a death sentence because of incorrect beliefs.[15] It cannot be concluded that these people are Jews, because in "Laws of Kings," it is claimed by Maimonides that any heathen under Jewish command is to be put to death if he refuses to accept the seven Noahide commands.[16] Most of these, except idolatry, deal with behavior. The third group consists of Jewish "ignoramuses," observers of the law, nothing more. The fourth are "jurists" of the law held on the basis of traditional authority, but who do not speculate and rationally justify belief. The fifth class consists in Talmudists who are competent in physics but not quite yet competent in metaphysics, and are of variant ranks. They also engage in the "fundamental principles of religion." So from groups three onward we see a narrowing focus of Jews: (3) ignoramuses (Jewish masses), (4) *halakhist* jurists with no speculation, (5) Jewish speculators of religious fundamentals and physicists, (6) metaphysicians, and (7) graded prophets (again, Jewish), and Moses (clearly Jewish).

Given the symmetrical relationship of all these groups as graded subsets of the previous (i.e., filling out a set of relative concentric circles, the larger being more inclusive than the smaller), it would follow that the speculators and metaphysicians are Jews as well. Since both the *Guide* as a whole and the parable in particular have as their intended audience Talmudists, it makes sense to interpret the fifth class to be scientifically trained Talmudists. The sixth class of people achieved philosophic perfection, not just achievement in the natural sciences as was true of the fifth class but also of divine science (i.e., metaphysics), making this a subset of the fifth class. Achieving philosophic perfection requires moral perfection without which metaphysical perfection is impeded.[17]

Now, can anyone achieve this moral perfection? Yes, in principle. But perhaps it is unachievable outside of Judaism, at least in the pre-messianic world. Maimonides cites the *Talmud*: "When the serpent came to Eve, it cast pollution into her. The pollution of [the sons of] Israel, who had been present at Mt. Sinai, has come to an end. [As for] the nations who were not present at Mt. Sinai, their pollution has not come to an end" (Shabbat 146a).[18]

15. See Deut 13; 20:16–18; Maimonides, *Guide* I.36 (84), 54 (127); *Mishneh Torah*, s.v. "Laws of Kings and Their Wars" I; IV; "Laws of Idolatry" IV; V.1–5; "Laws of the Murderer" IV.10; "Laws of Testimony" XI.10.

16. Maimonides, *Mishneh Torah*, s.v. "Laws of Kings" VIII.9.

17. Maimonides, *Guide* I.34 (76–77); III.27, 54.

18. Maimonides, *Guide* II.30 (357).

Commentators are unanimous on this passage. Man is subverted by imagination in the fall, but thanks to the Torah, the Jews are able to overcome and achieve the requisite moral perfection to lead to intellectual perfection. The Law functions to restrain the undisciplined exercise of our appetites to which we originally succumbed. As indicated, most of the *mitzvot* serve no other end than moral perfection. One might think, however, that it is not necessary where the functional equivalent of the Torah is something akin to the lessons of instruction found in the lectures of Aristotle's *Nicomachean Ethics*. But then again, per the nations not benefitting from Sinai still have their pollution to contend with. Not insignificant is the fact that in *Guide* III.53, Maimonides calls faith a moral virtue. It is exceedingly difficult to imagine how Maimonides could expect Aristotle to have that virtue. But without it, moral imperfection endures, and thus no intellectual perfection is possible in that no ultimate *imitatio Dei* is possible.

While the Parable of the Palace indicates one way of categorizing, Maimonides's elitism (bifurcating the elite from the masses) is well-known and perhaps establishes a further ethical bifurcation than just elite and vulgar, but between Jew and Gentile, making some hierarchy: Jew-elite, Jew-vulgar, Gentile-elite, Gentile-vulgar.[19] This provides further reflection in thinking through how he divides them, on Kellner's thoroughly Jewish interpretation of the Parable, into eight classes: (1) Gentiles who are subhumans without doctrine, (2) idolaters (unclear of their gentile/Jewish commitments), (3) Jewish masses, (4) Jewish jurists, (5) Jewish speculators on the fundamentals of religion/study of physics, (6) Jewish metaphysicians, (7) Jewish prophets of various grades, and (8) the Jew, Moses, human author of the Torah.

Even those who have reached the sixth class do not necessarily "see the ruler or speak to him." This requires that "they should make another effort," thus joining the seventh class, a subset of the sixth. Now, the seventh class is also divided into four: (a) those who see the ruler from afar, (b) those who see the ruler from nearby, (c) those who hear the ruler's speech, and (d) those who speak with the ruler. This extra effort is explained by Maimonides:

> There are those who set their thought to work after having attained perfection in the divine science, turn wholly toward God ... renounce what is other than He, and direct all the acts of their intellect ... so as to know His governance ... insofar as possible. These are those present in the ruler's council. This is the rank of the prophets.[20]

---

19. See Harvey, "Islamic Philosophy and Jewish Philosophy," 354.

20. Kellner, *Maimonides on Human Perfection*, 29. Maimonides can be blamed for giving some legitimacy to this interpretation. See Maimonides, *Guide* II.36.

Kellner argues here that those in this class, having achieved the rank of prophet, are not simply "super philosophers" with highly developed imaginations, as they are often depicted. Rather, they are individuals whose love of God dominates their entire lives.

So the seventh class is prophets, a subset of philosophers (like the ideal reader of the *Guide*), which is a subset of physicists. While Maimonides affirms the theoretical possibility that non-Jews could prophesy, he thought that practically speaking it was impossible for them to achieve this since moral perfection is a prerequisite and, as we have seen, a Gentile cannot be morally perfect in this life, lacking, at least, the virtue of faith. Thus, Maimonides maintained that not even Aristotle achieved prophecy or divine overflow.[21] Aristotle reached the highest human level of intellectual perfection available without prophecy. If not Aristotle, as highly as Maimonides regarded him, then the likelihood that other Gentiles could achieve moral perfection is bleak. Thus, the Parable of the Palace sets up various levels of human perfection (interpreted by Kellner as open only to Jews): those obedient to Law, those with juridical competence, experts in principles of religion and physics, and experts in metaphysics, prophecy, and Mosaic prophecy.[22]

Guide III.52 reflects the idea that along the path to human perfection, the individual must acknowledge that God is ever watchful, whose knowledge is supposed to evince fear and awe in the individual. The actions required by the *mitzvot* have the function to bring this about, hence their importance for achieving human perfection. But the doctrines of the Torah also teach us the love of God. But superiority seems to rest with the doctrines rather than the actions of the commands, since service out of love is greater than service that is done out of fear, and the first of the 613 commandments is to love God.[23] Perhaps this supports the position that ultimate perfection is intellectualist. Yet he also claims that the love of God finds expression in the fulfillment of commands.[24]

Guide III.53 discusses certain terms like loving-kindness (*hesed*, shown in the creation of the world), judgment (on relative good and evil in the world), and righteousness (providence over living beings via their own natural powers), terms Maimonides claims apply to God's actions whose actional attributes are paramount for imitating.

21. Maimonides, *Guide* II.57; Ivry, "Islamic and Greek Influences on Maimonides's Philosophy," 139–56.
22. Maimonides, *Guide* III (623–24).
23. For doctrine over practice see Maimonides, *Guide* III.27 (510). For love over fear, see Maimonides, *Mishneh Torah*, s.v. "Laws of Repentance" X.
24. See Maimonides, *Guide* III.24 (500–501) about Abraham; *Guide* III.44 (574); "Laws of Repentance" X.2; Twersky, *Introduction*, 363.

Guide III.54 discusses wisdom. The wisdom of him "who knows the whole of the Law in its true reality" is constituted by "the rational virtues comprised in the Law and in respect of the moral virtues included in it."[25] The Torah teaches only the results of (consistent) philosophical speculation (e.g., God's existence, unity, and incorporeality), while philosophy provides the actual proofs of the rational content. Kellner suggests that it ennobles our lives because such obedience is not performed, as it is for the vulgar Jews, in order to earn a reward as though there is a tit-for-tat reward; rather the elite act purely out of love of God and to imitate Him. Maimonides ends with talk of the four perfections, the last of which is intellectual. But remember, one need not conclude an intellectualist interpretation here, since Maimonides is clear in his interpretation of Jeremiah 9:22–23 and Exodus 33:13 that one not only glory in the apprehension of God but in his attributes, by which he means his attributes of action.[26] And as Jeremiah 9:23's interpretation makes clear, those actions that ought to be imitated are lovingkindness, judgment, and righteousness, actions Moses desired to imitate in governing the Jewish people. To know God was to know His ways, by which Moses thought, in Exodus, that He might find grace to govern rightly. Thus, upon achieving the fourth perfection, intellectual/philosophical perfection, one will naturally seek orthopraxy.

To summarize then, all four chapters of Guide III.51–54 end up serving a practical end, which is to bring certain individuals to full devotion toward God after having achieved knowledge of Him, which seems to be the whole point of the Guide. The Parable of the Palace shows us that prophecy requires intellectual perfection, which itself requires *halakhic* perfection. Prophets are sophisticated Talmudists, while the Patriarchs (including Moses) were exalted prophets who contemplated while living the life and guiding others to God's ways. Thus, their imitation of God is in *halakhic* terms, which, while having a political aspect of course, was not primarily in political terms (especially not construed naturalistically). Kellner claims "the political life is not the best life; rather, the best life has a political dimension."[27] So we have two distinct kinds of *imitatio Dei* (before, out of fear; and after, out of love).[28]

---

25. Maimonides, *Guide* III (633).
26. Maimonides, *Guide* III (637).
27. Kellner, *Maimonides on Human Perfection*, 39.
28. Maimonides inherited two distinct schools of thought on *imitatio Dei*: (1) Greco-Islamic and (2) Biblical-Rabbinic. For more on the first, see Berman, "Political Interpretation," 53–61; "Maimonides, the Disciple of Al-Farabi," 154–78. For more on the second, see Lev 19:2; Deut 10:12; 28:9.

One imitates God by acting godly, which is acting on our knowledge of God's actional attributes (e.g., God acts mercifully, so we should act mercifully). Acting godly also includes obeying God's commands. In the end, how one is to imitate God by becoming like Him depends on how one understands God. There is a strong link between one's *theos* and one's understanding of one's *telos*. If Aristotle's god is in view, for example, then one is pursuing a never ending intellectual quest toward the ideal of intellectual perfection. But Maimonides's understanding of human perfection, while intellectualist, is not austerely intellectualist.[29]

Perfecting our intellects does make us fully human, but the imitation of God should make us more than fully human, something Godlike. Kellner says, "By perfecting our intellects, that is, by perfecting ourselves as human beings, we also earn (or, perhaps, create) our own immortality."[30] But the imitation of God is done out of love, not for reward.[31] Whenever Maimonides connects intellectual perfection as he does with immortality, we should note that this is not the highest state since this extrinsic reward (or consequence of activity) would taint the purity of love of the highest state. Kellner claims that the *Guide, qua* guide, should make us expect a different reality from the beginning to the end such that the beginning reflects a lower state than the end.[32] So at the beginning, intellectual perfection is set as the goal, whereas imitating God via *hesed*, righteousness, and judgment is possible at the end after such perfection is attained. *Imitatio Dei* expresses love of God post intellectual perfection.

Various texts seem to show that Maimonides's *summum bonum* is intellectual perfection as he makes clear that immortality is a function of the perfected intellect. The most perfect individuals apprehend God to the greatest extent possible to them but recognize that they need to imitate God via God's loving-kindness, righteousness, and judgment as asserted in *Guide* III.54. *Guide* III.51–54 shows intellectual perfection is the penultimate state available to humans, more specifically to Jews. This interpretation is *halakhic* in nature. The end, therefore, is a contemplative yet social activity of "bringing into being a religious community that would know and worship God."[33] This has a political aspect but is ultimately realized via obedience to the *mitzvot*. Intellectual perfection is therefore not the final end of human existence. *Imitatio Dei* is not construed in terms of becoming like God but

---

29. Schwarzschild, "Moral Radicalism," 68–69.
30. Kellner, *Maimonides on Human Perfection*, 56.
31. Maimonides, *Mishneh Torah*, s.v. "Laws of Repentance" X.1–2, 4–5.
32. Kellner, *Maimonides on Human Perfection*, 56.
33. Kellner, *Maimonides on Human Perfection*, 62.

like His actions; God being ineffable in nature, but discoverable via creation and providence. We can know that God exists, not what God is, but also how God has acted as guidance to how we should act. *Halakhah* is the way in which God has commanded the Jews to imitate Him.

Maimonides's theology is a developed theology, not of God, nor of his own views of God, but pedagogically developed for the perplexed ones, and this extends from God as intellect and our obligation to contemplation to God as active, emulated by lovingly keeping his commands. Maimonides's goal of the *Guide* mirrors the Torah in that it is practically transformative rather than merely theoretically informative. This bit of instruction via divine aid in the form of Torah provides the Jew an advantage en route to human perfection, rendering the non-Jew, including someone like Aristotle, to be at a significant disadvantage or perhaps beyond the scope of achieving genuine human perfection.

Aristotle's view made the good life elusive for most, something Maimonides's view initially seemed to evade given divine aid (Torah) and repentance. But now his view seems to be quite exclusivistic and parochial in the sense of being very narrow or limited in scope or outlook, no less elusive than Aristotle's account. Aware of this, Oliver Leaman asks whether this is not "inexcusably elitist?" He goes on to answer: "In its fully fledged sense it is . . . because God has created everyone differently and if, as a result, we have different chances of attaining perfection, then we might justifiably complain about this situation." Pawning this off simply as a piece of typical medieval philosophy, he concludes, "The important thing is that for everyone there should be a route available to salvation, while it is not necessary that everyone should be able to achieve the highest level of perfection."[34]

But in accordance with the Parable of the Palace, the whole thing seems quite parochial and exclusivistic. How does this not saddle Maimonides with a worse problem than Aristotle faced since on the former's account there is not merely a natural *telos* but a divine image in each man that God created? This seems to render most as severed from their natural end. Indeed, since they are all created in God's image, then they are severed from their supernatural end as some sort of cosmic orphans. What hope for the non-Jew created in God's image? Much of Maimonides's thrust is to root out idolatry. He claims that the worst form of idolatry is a cognitive error, "believing God to be different from what He really is."[35] He even says that Jews who affirm the unity of God but think such unity to be compatible with multiple attributes are no better than Christians who say that God is one and

---

34. Leaman, "Ideals, Simplicity, and Ethics," 119.
35. Maimonides, *Guide* I.36 (84).

three.[36] The faith aspect of Maimonides has some dire implications for many, including someone like Aquinas who affirms the Trinity. By Maimonidean lights, Aristotle was somewhat ignorant without Torah, but Aquinas is an idolater. Of course, Aquinas's views with respect to articles of faith have implications for Maimonides as well. Aquinas distinguishes between articles of faith and preambles of faith. A preamble includes certain truths about God that "we can know by our natural powers of reasoning like "God exists." An article, by contrast, comprises matters that are "set before the whole human community for belief."[37] This faith aspect now creates a divergence between Maimonides and Aquinas, whereas initially it brought about their greatest convergence in departing from Aristotle.

The applicable concern here with Maimonides's position is with the parochial or limited scope of availability. It seems somewhat responsible for the elusiveness for most to participate in the good life, whose participation seems promissory according to nature but not so promising according to actualizing that nature. This has a strong religious intonation with egalitarian and existentialist overtones, given that man is said to be created in God's image. One possible way of overcoming the problem is to show that it is not so parochial after all. If the Torah at minimum places the Jew in a position of clear advantage to attaining the good life, perhaps having a means outside of the Torah can be found for the same end. This brings up the issue of natural law, a law available and therefore potentially accessible for the non-Jew in order to elude the problem.

Maimonides on Natural Law and an Initial Evasion

Although many (perhaps most) Jewish thinkers object to the claim that Maimonides's ethical theory is a species of natural law ethics or that it is even compatible with such, evidence seems supportive for the claim, implying that perhaps these objectors are simply wrong. Maimonides's views fit with the paradigm case of a natural law theorist. That paradigm is Aquinas, who is mentioned in virtually all such discussions. For Aquinas, natural law is *law* insofar as it is morally ordered by God as a matter of its being rationally binding, and it is *natural* insofar as it is in accordance with human nature, whose nature is a rational nature and thus finds universal applicability. Aquinas says, "Whatever is contrary to the order of reason is contrary to the nature of human beings as such; and what is reasonable is

36. Maimonides, *Guide* I.50 (111).
37. Aquinas, *ST* I.2.2; II-II.1.5.

in accordance with human nature as such." Others have defended the claim that Maimonides affirms natural law but we will not do so here.[38] What is more important for us relative to our concern is what the implications are behind the opponent's objection to Maimonides being a natural law theorist. For this reason we will focus on the objections. 'Natural law theory' is often used to designate theories of ethics, politics, civil law, and religious morality.[39] I will use it to denote a particular ethical theory.

To be sure, Maimonides never uses the term *natural law* to describe his system.[40] But simply lacking the label does not suffice to show that Maimonides's view necessarily excludes natural law or that he himself did not affirm it conceptually. Nonetheless, let's consider the objections by those who think Maimonides would have rejected, or did in fact reject, natural law, not to determine whether or not he did, but to see whether or not it would really help him with our present concern even if he did.

First, it might be argued that a natural law ethic is objectionable to Judaism, generally, on theological grounds for the same reason that some have objected to it in other similarly revealed religious traditions, Islam and Christianity. Marvin Fox, perhaps the greatest contemporary opponent of the view that Maimonides affirms natural law, says that "in Judaism there is no natural law doctrine, and in principle there cannot be. . . . [A] correct understanding of Maimonides will show why he could not affirm a theory of natural law."[41] For him, it seems to undermine the value of special revelation. The source of the apparent conflict is found not in the first feature of the paradigm case of natural law (*law* as morally ordered by God) but in the second feature about it being *natural* (human nature renders it universally discernible). It might be thought that if one could rationally discover God's moral law via natural means, then revealed law is superfluous.

But this theological objection seems misguided. It seeks to show that if natural law applied to Judaism, then it would undermine the revealed law, the Torah, by subordinating the infallible word of God to the human (and therefore fallible) reason of man. But why think this? If taken seriously, the argument would also undermine human reason's ability to receive revealed law, either as a prophet or layman, not just natural law. For in any case, it is the same created reason in humanity that is to be the receptacle of God's revealed law specially found in the Torah as it is the receptacle of natural

---

38. Levine, "Maimonides," 11–15.

39. Buckle, "Natural Law," 161–74; George, "Natural Law," 460–65; Aquinas, *ST* I-II.71.2.

40. Novak, *Image of the Non-Jew*.

41. Fox, "Maimonides and Aquinas," 10, 26; Bleich, "Judaism and Natural Law," 5–42.

law generally. It is the same author, God, and same recipient(s), rational man. The only differences are the occasion and scope of the revelation, be it special or general.

Now, if natural law is construed for Maimonides as an aspect of divine providence, as is true of the paradigm case above, and there is no good theological reason to deny it, then there is no relevant distinction that afflicts natural law receptivity without also afflicting revealed law receptivity. In fact, Maimonides says,

> I do believe that providence goes with reason and is a necessary consequence of its possession. This is because providence is exercised by a rational being, namely the One who is reason so perfect that no greater perfection is thinkable. Therefore, providence extends to everyone who is affected by this emanation to the extent that that being is gifted with reason.[42]

And, of course, what is common among humans is their rational nature (even if it comes in varying degrees among individuals). Not only does he specifically state this aspect of providence in accordance with human reason, welcoming the second feature of natural law, but his whole project behind giving reasons for Torah commandments implies that human reason can discover reasons for the laws of Torah and even some of the laws themselves (e.g., Noahide laws, which will be discussed below) since the law is of itself rational. Explanations as to the ultimate source and justification of moral norms in terms of God need not rule out a doctrine of natural law. Nor would the fact that some receive moral and legal knowledge via special revelation necessarily imply that *basic* moral principles are not universally binding and knowable, in principle, to all via human reason.

Second, perhaps there is a legal reason why Maimonides would have rejected natural law. It might be claimed that natural law introduces an element of selectivity, allowing its proponents to retain precepts from the Torah necessary for a just and well-ordered society while disregarding all ritual or cultic laws for which no rational basis could be posited. While this may have been acceptable for Aquinas, who distinguished between moral and ceremonial aspects of the Torah and saw natural law as only applicable to the moral (e.g., laws prohibiting murder versus laws prohibiting the wearing of two kinds of clothing), is it acceptable for Maimonides?[43]

This is only problematic if the natural law theorist here claims that reason grasps *all law* without special divine aid, which is not the claim. Are there not in Judaism distinct covenants according to occasion and scope

42. Maimonides, *Guide* III.18 (169, Rabin).
43. Fox, *Interpreting Maimonides*, 145.

for God's own purposes, which include some laws and not others (e.g., Adamic, Noahic, Abrahamic, Mosaic, Davidic, etc.)? Some of these covenants seem to have specific audiences in mind, while others have a more general audience, implying both occasional historical laws for particulars and universal natural laws in general which are those that would constitute that body of moral norms in accord with practical reason found in nature.[44] In fact, one area of biblical support for such distinction is Noahide law, law that points to natural law.

While the revealed law addressed to Jews is binding on Jews, what about non-Jews? Maimonides believes that "moral virtues are a prerequisite of intellectual virtues."[45] Clearly, he took Aristotle to be one of immense intellectual virtue. But how so unless Aristotle, a non-Jew, had some conception apart from biblical revelation of what was moral and what was not? In addressing the question of the relevancy of the image of God for the non-Jew, our concern is how, in the absence of revealed law, non-Jews, or those who have never heard of Torah, come to know the moral law, which Maimonides clearly thought someone like Aristotle could grasp via unaided reason. In light of this, Maimonides approvingly cites the Rabbis who say, "If they [i.e., moral laws] had not already been written in the Law, it would have been proper to add them."[46] This might imply that the moral law is rationally discernible through natural lights. Perhaps revealed law to the Jews constitutes a larger set of moral norms than that portion of overlap it has with natural law as discernible by human reason, which is just where Noahide law comes in. David Novak nicely captures this, saying, "The Torah of the world is learned through human nature; the Torah of the covenant is learned directly from God."

In *Natural Law and Judaism*, Novak gives several scriptural examples demonstrating that the normative content of the Sinai covenant need not be regarded as originally instituted at the event of the Sinai revelation, indicating also that the natural law concept was not one grafted onto Judaism from Hellenism, but that Judaism had the concept well in place for the appropriate terminology. While Novak affirms natural law himself and thinks that Maimonides affirms it, he rejects what he sees as Maimonides's

---

44. This is precisely what Joseph Albo, the Spanish Jewish theologian, argued. Specifically, he said that the Noahide and Sinaitic (or Mosaic) codes, although both religious laws (read "divine law or revealed law" for Aquinas), they differ in their particulars because they address different audiences.

45. Maimonides, *Guide* I.34 (61, Rabin).

46. Maimonides, *Maimonides Reader*, 378.

Greek teleological basis in favor of a view that gives greater account for the notion of Covenant.[47]

The debate over natural law in the Jewish tradition centers on the status of the Noahide laws, which are the "seven commandments of the children of Noah," which some tradition considers universally binding. Genesis 9:4–6 is the famous biblical passage that Rabbis have interpreted to comprise seven fundamental laws applicable to all man with extensive application: (1) establishment of courts of justice, (2) prohibition of blasphemy, (3) prohibition of idolatry, (4) prohibition of incest, (5) prohibition of murder, (6) prohibition of robbery, and (7) prohibition of eating flesh cut from a living animal. These bear remarkable resemblance to that culminating in the Mosaic code in the Decalogue.

Those who reject these laws laws as the primary locus of that body of natural law that is universally binding and knowable interpret Noahide laws to be law made by Jews for non-Jews over whom they had political power who were living in their midst as resident aliens. However, as Novak points out, the Rabbis who formulated the doctrine of Noahide law did not have any such power over any group of non-Jews, indicating that what was really going on was the abstracting of principles from generalizations.[48] Further, that the Rabbis used these verses in their speculative enterprise does not mean that they were regarded as the actual sources of these laws, but rather they are used as allusions since the Rabbis were engaged more in speculating about the overall teaching of Scripture and its analogues in the outside world when they were developing the doctrine of Noahide law. Noahide law functions more as a system of abstracted principles than as an actual body of rules. It is likely that Maimonides saw the "completion" of Torah in Moses in the Aristotelian sense of final cause where the Noahide would be seen in *potentia* to the Mosaic.[49]

One should not think that natural law first originated in Judaism within Noahide law. For natural law to be truly natural it must be recognizable throughout the world (universal via nature) and even before the special revealing of Torah itself. Novak argues using numerous biblical examples that natural law is presupposed via nature before Torah was specially revealed at SinaiTake the story of Cain and Abel, for example, which shows that Cain

---

47. Novak, *Natural Law in Judaism*, 27–61, 92–148; Miller, "Review of *Natural Law*," 488–92.

48. Novak, *Natural Law in Judaism*, 149–51.

49. Novak, *Image of the Non-Jew*, 280.

was held accountable for murder of his brother Abel, something for which he has no explicit command, implying that this was known via nature.[50]

As history presupposes nature, so also revealed law presupposes natural law. So, for Maimonides, not only does natural law serve those already converted by giving reasons for the law, but it actually temporally precedes the acceptance of the Torah given the rational plausibility structure already in place in accord with human reason. Even the prescription for capital punishment for murder in the Noahide law presupposes a prohibition of murder already in place such that one cannot simply interpret this prohibition of murder as just another case of revealed, covenantal law. The reason for capital punishment in Genesis is stated in the verse, which is because man's nature is that which is in the image of God. Hence, it was not because it was elsewhere revealed in another historical covenant, even the Noahic covenant, but that it was revealed in nature (i.e., natural law). "The Noahide commandments," says Jonathan Jacobs, "are such that they could have been known without revelation, but that does not imply that they are knowable utterly without reference to God, since our capacity for understanding is owed to God, and we can come to see that even without revelation."[51] Our epistemic route to the ontological basis for ethical requirements may differ via natural and divine law, but the basis for them is arguably the same.

Natural law is therefore a precondition to the rational acceptability of revealed law, both of which are dimensions of Torah.[52] The error of some is to confuse the pre-condition of revelation (human reason) with its ground (God). In an important passage, Maimonides comments about the Noahide laws:

> Any man [i.e., any non-Jew] who accepts the seven commandments and is meticulous in observing them is thereby one of the righteous . . . and he has a portion in the world to come. This is only the case if he accepts them and observes them because God commanded them in the Torah, and taught us . . . that the children of Noah were commanded to observe them even before the Torah was given. But if he observes them because of his own conclusions based on reason, then he is not a resident-alien and is not one of the righteous . . . nor is he one of their wise men.[53]

---

50. Novak, *Natural Law in Judaism*, 31–61.

51. Jacobs, *Law, Reason, and Morality*, 202; Plantinga, "Evolutionary Argument against Naturalism," 30.

52. Novak, *Natural Law in Judaism*, 185–87.

53. Maimonides, *Maimonides Reader*, 221–22.

Problematic here is why Maimonides thinks that a non-Jew should accept the Noahide on the basis of their revelation in Torah. What about those who never heard of Torah? Aside from these problems, he does not say that the Noahide are unknowable outside of revelation. Aside from the fact that they were known to Noah and sons prior to Sinai, he thinks that they can be known through natural reason. He is only saying that to observe them because of one's own conclusions *based on reason* will not satisfy conditions for being counted among the righteous or wise men, while accepting them because God commanded them will. That is, he is making the theological versus legal-moral distinction. If this stipulation is salvifically problematic, it does not follow that it is in necessary conflict with natural law theory per se. For perhaps natural law is not intended to procure "salvation," or the best life, but to minimally provide a rational basis for civility in society and a plausibility structure for further revealed law which is intended towards that end.

According to the paradigm account, natural law ethical theory has two broad features—the roles of God and of man. With regard to the first feature, God (the giver), natural law constitutes one aspect of divine providence, another of which is revealed law, and both of which are grounded in God's eternal law. With regard to the second feature, man (the receiver), natural law is that body of moral norms which constitutes for us the principles of practical reason as grounded in a specifiable human nature, whose principles are by nature, therefore, universally binding and knowable. Maimonides's teleological framework bares remarkable similarity to that of Aquinas's in accounting for practical reason based in human nature. He clearly shares the first feature. The second feature is also shared and is most fundamentally seen under the heading of Noahide laws. Hence, in affirming both of these features, Maimonides can thereby be counted a proponent of natural law ethics. Perhaps his understanding of the good life is not so parochial or so limited, but is more readily available to a broader audience than one might otherwise think given the universality of natural law.

This at least attests to God's "Torah of the world," as suggested by David Novak who comments, "God has not deprived the world of Torah. According to Scripture and rabbinic tradition, God gave the complete Torah to Israel and a partial Torah to the world. . . . Both relationships are governed by the same Torah: the former one, by the Torah's more specific precepts; the latter, by its more general precepts."[54]

---

54. Novak, "Election," 126–27. Here, Novak is dealing with the problem of Jewish election and seems to deflect that overly exclusivistic criticism that Judaism is so by claiming a global Torah.

However, one problem that still persists here, as Novak noted and Fox is keen to point out: natural law still seems to lack (at least for Fox) the motivational force of moral authoritativeness such that possession of which without the faith ethic is problematic. What makes these laws robustly binding is their divine status. Thus, for Fox, many would be left out including the likes of Aquinas since Aquinas, as we will see, does not consider the Old Law binding. To buttress this, Maimonides even holds that Noachites need to believe in revelation. Fox intimates that Maimonides makes the final validity of Noahide laws dependent upon their belief being of divine origin.[55] So while Maimonides's view may be consistent with natural law theory (whether or not he's an advocate), this does not avoid the problem we are concerned with, namely, making the good life available only for a select few even though all are marked by being created in God's image. Marvin Fox comments, comparing Maimonides and Aquinas on natural law:

> If both Maimonides and Aquinas may be thought of as seeking the conditions of salvation, then their differences might be understood in the following way. For Aquinas, the Christian, salvation is neither by works alone nor by rational knowledge, but by grace. Natural law tells men how to behave, but it cannot lead them to their final and true fulfillment. For Maimonides, the Jew, salvation depends on good works, leading to rational apprehension of the highest truth. There is . . . only the law of God, which teaches us to live our lives in such a way that we are worthy of our claim to have been created in His image.[56]

The Maimonidean passage problematic for many is found in "Laws of Kings," where Maimonides claims that those who accept the seven Noachite laws and fulfill them has a share in the world to come, but only "if he accepts and practices them on the ground that God commanded them in the Torah. . . . But if he practices them on the basis of his own rational considerations," then he has no such part in the world to come.[57] Steven Schwarzschild underscores why this Maimonidean position of exclusivism is profound:

> [Maimonides] adds a prerequisite [to "salvation" or "the world to come"] which is normally not encountered in the relevant Jewish discussions of this subject. . . . Maimonides is not only the greatest philosopher in all of Jewish history . . . the thinker who most explicitly acknowledged his intellectual indebtedness to non-Jewish, pagan, and Mohammedan predecessors, and

---

55. Fox, "Maimonides and Aquinas," 13.
56. Fox, "Maimonides and Aquinas," 36.
57. Maimonides, "Laws of Kings" VIII.2.

who is, therefore, rightly expected to be more appreciative of the merits of non-Jews than most others. Aristotle in particular is venerated by him almost on a par with biblical authority, and thus ... one cannot help but have some sympathy with Spinoza's expression that ... 'Aristotle (whom he considered to have written the best ethics) ... yet this was not able to suffice for his salvation, inasmuch as he embraced his doctrines in accordance with the dictates of reason and not as Divine documents prophetically revealed.'[58]

Indeed, Schwarzschild says, "Maimonides insists repeatedly on the prerequisite of faith in God for the attainment of salvation. He does not say so in so many words, but he clearly leaves room for his doctrine that 'the virtues' can be acquired only through revelation."[59] For Schwarzschild and others it is unmistakable even in light of post rabbinic Judaism that Maimonides teaches "that ethics must necessarily be religious ethics and involve a definite religious commitment, (for all this is clearly involved in the prerequisite of belief in the divine revelation of the Torah)."[60] It is no wonder, Novak claims, that both Jews and Christians are convinced that people are doomed if left on their own, and that "grace is a necessity for the human condition. The difference between them," he continues, "is whether one is connected to the grace of God by the Torah or by Christ."[61]

To see things from the other side, Aquinas thinks that there are certain articles of faith that all must believe and that the Old Testament lacks binding authority following the inauguration of the New Testament, which Maimonides would consider anathema. The instance of law which, according to Aquinas, is not natural or rational (and, thus, not binding any longer) is the Old Law. Some of the commandments are in accord with the natural law, and people are thus bound when they are. But this is not simply because it is part of the Old Law given that it is now obsolete in many respects after Christ. Rather, he eliminates the ceremonial and civil aspects of law and retains only that part of the law, the moral law, which is properly known as natural law.[62] To continue after Christ to observe these simply because they are derived from the OT would be a mortal sin as it would be tantamount to a denial of Christ.[63] If Aquinas is right, this is not good

---

58. Schwarzschild, "Do Noachites Have to Believe?," 80.
59. Schwarzschild, "Do Noachites Have to Believe?," 40.
60. Schwarzschild, "Do Noachites Have to Believe?," 45.
61. Novak, *Natural Law in Judaism*, 30.
62. Aquinas, *ST* I-II.98.5.
63. Aquinas, *ST* I-II.104.3; cf. I-II.103.4.

news for Maimonides.[64] So it may not be sufficient to be part of natural law theory if it does not have the desired effect of authoritativeness of divinely revealed law or other requirements that have salvific and or motivational implications relative to the good life.

Hence the problem still seems to be on the table of rendering the masses as cosmic orphans. If human perfection requires moral perfection, and Torah provides a serious advantage to aiding in repentance and the moral life as well as pointing to God, natural law in Judaism does not seem to do much as it does not necessarily provide the moral motivation according to which such law is grounded. If God designed man for this good life, entailing the knowledge of God, then one wonders why he sets up a program that seems to be either so exclusivistic or, at least, elusive for most.

The Ways of Negativity and Knowledge of (the Simple) God

Maimonides and Aquinas can be compared at various points, but perhaps some are more salient than others. Central is the question about our knowledge of God. In this and the following sections we will look at the nature and extent of the knowledge of God one might have in Maimonidean and Thomistic viewpoints and how one can best be expected to worship and imitate God in light of this. We will compare and contrast their perspectives on negative knowledge and what it amounts to. Then we will home in on Aquinas's indispensable foundation for the good life and how this becomes the basis for a more immanent knowledge of God. Our discussion is based primarily on his mature works in the biblical commentaries. Following this will be our exploration of this more immanent knowledge connects the virtue of faith and testimonial knowledge. Finally, we will offer a contemporary elucidation on Aquinas's view of knowing God and spiritual formation in light of contemporary neuroscience and social science.

Negative Knowledge and the Tension between Transcendence and Immanence

It is well known that Maimonides (and to a certain extent Aquinas) affirms negative theology. But this is sometimes misunderstood by confusing various theses pertinent to negative theology. For example, one commentator and defender of negative theology, Isaac Franck, seems to conflate

---

64. Coolman, "Romans 9–11," 101–112.

epistemic and semantic theses.[65] Joseph Buijs points out others who similarly conflate Aquinas and Maimonides on this point, claiming they have superficial differences but share substantially the same position. They do this either by playing down Maimonides's "linguistic excess" on the issue or by claiming that alleged differences are a matter of "residual contrast of emphasis" due in large part to their respective religious pressures and available philosophical resources.[66] But Buijs contends that there are significant philosophical differences between Maimonides and Aquinas in both knowledge and language of God.

In Franck's case, for instance, he takes the unknowability of God's essence to be the central commitment of negative theology, but interchanges it with the semantic element (his more radical view of unknowability might be contrasted with a moderate view of our inability to know). Conceptually, however, our inability (or ability) to know God is non-identical with our inability (or ability) to talk about God. Ability to know does not always correspond with ability to talk of or about some subject or object. For instance, we often lack the ability to talk about our knowledge of our own mental or emotional states. Being aware of and being able to describe such states may differ. As well, we might consider children (or even young college freshmen) who use words (e.g., *God, rights, justice*, etc.), but do not know the meanings of the terms or concepts which remain intelligible nonetheless. There is a semantic and epistemic relationship present, but it is not always clear. Let E refer to the epistemic thesis and S to the semantic thesis. Buijs elucidates Franck's depiction as the following:

E: With respect to God's existence, we can know that God is; with respect to his essence, we cannot know what he is and thus we can only know what he is not.

S: Only terms predicated negatively of God are meaningful; terms predicated positively of God are meaningless.[67]

The conjunction E and S perhaps characterizes Franck's more radical notion, but it does not accurately represent either Maimonides or Aquinas on the matter. It is not problematic for them to deny E and accept S. S can be disambiguated by S(1) and S(2) whereby

S(1) 'God' cannot be the subject term in anything but negative propositions, and

---

65. Franck, "Maimonides and Aquinas," 591–615.
66. Buijs, "Negative Theology," 723–38.
67. Buijs, "Negative Theology," 727.

S(2) Meaningful language about God's nature can be expressed only in negative description.

As we will see, both Maimonides and Aquinas, in developing their cosmological arguments for God's existence (where Aquinas mentions and somewhat follows Maimonides), affirm E, but they divide when S is clarified.[68] And, likewise, we will see that both deny S(1), but Maimonides affirms and Aquinas denies S(2). Maimonides takes his cosmological argument to demonstrate that God exists as a necessary existent, having no cause for either existence or essence. He also concludes from this that God is absolutely simple (not complex) and incomparable (not compared).[69] Maimonides says, "We are only able to apprehend the fact that He is and cannot apprehend His nature."[70] Aquinas also concludes that we know that God is and, as some might contend, only what God is not in terms of attributes. That is, we know that God exists, but via negativa seems to provide us with *only* negative knowledge (e.g., 'God is not a body'). Of course, we will see that Aquinas's interpretation is nuanced so as to accommodate more than "as some might contend, only what God is not."[71]

Linguistically, Aquinas begins following Maimonides in his belief that corporeality and potentiality are denied in reference to God.[72] Some attributes may properly be said of God, namely, "God is infinite" (i.e., not finite) and "God is eternal" (i.e., unending), but when it comes to attributes of goodness and wisdom it is another matter. For they imply neither corporeality nor negative connotation, yet for Aquinas they denote pure perfections, and as such they are predicable of God substantially.[73] He draws a distinction, enabling him to both affirm and deny such predicates of God by distinguishing between the thing signified (affirmed as *res significata*) and the way in which it is signified (denied as *modus significandi*). They are predicated analogically of Creator and creatures, enabling him to carve between univocal and equivocal language with reference to God in terms of our having imperfect and limited knowledge of what God is.[74] So he affirms E just so long as it is understood to exclude only comprehensive knowledge of God, but he denies both S(1) and S(2).

---

68. Craig, *Cosmological Argument*, 131–204.
69. Maimonides, *Guide* I.57 (132–33); II.1 (243–52).
70. Maimonides, *Guide* I.58 (135).
71. Aquinas, *ST* I.3.
72. Aquinas, *ST* I.13.2; *SCG* I.14.
73. Aquinas, *ST* I.13.2.
74. Aquinas, *ST* I.13.2.ad1, 3, 5.

Maimonides rejects S(1) along with Aquinas because 'God' can be the subject of an affirmative proposition when it is an attribute of action or where some predicates signifying perfections amount to saying "God is God."[75] But he contrasts with Aquinas in that he affirms S(2) in that we can only say what God is not, not what God is. He says, "Know that the description of God . . . by means of negations is the correct description . . . we have no way of describing Him unless it be through negations."[76] We may be convinced about God's existence but must be agnostic about His essence. Thus, he affirms E without qualification.

In sum, Maimonides's negative theology amounts to conjoining E and S(2); Aquinas affirms a qualified E and denies S(1) and S(2). Concerning God's nature, then, Maimonides is completely negative and Aquinas is not. Their approach on the logical relationship between the two theses differs. Maimonides argues from E to S(2). If God's essence remains unknowable, then we cannot meaningfully describe it. Actional attributes do not violate either thesis because, while flowing from it, they do not describe an essence. Where S(2) derives from E, E derives from Maimonides's metaphysics which derives from his cosmological argumentation. E is true following on cosmological proofs of God's existence and their entailment about God's nature. Language depends on thought which depends on reality. By contrast, Aquinas seems to deal with the epistemological and semantic theses separately, yet both are derived from his metaphysics. From the denial of S(2) he moves to a modification of E (i.e., given that some attributes truly, even if imperfectly, describe God's nature, then we can know something positive about the essence). Given his metaphysics, then, he denies S(2). But since E seems to entail S(2) which he denies, this leads him to deny E (without qualification). So for Aquinas, both language and thought are contingent upon reality.

The main difference between Maimonides and Aquinas turns on Aquinas's analogy and Maimonides's notion of divine action. Both face the philosophical problem of how to use veridical and meaningful language about God, as well as the religious problem of speaking of God positively. Both recognize human limitations. Maimonides's solution is in turning to God's actional attributes to talk positively about God (avoiding God's essence directly), and Aquinas's analogical language allows adequate positive talk about God's essence (although more fully in the hereafter).[77]

---

75. Maimonides, *Guide* I.51.

76. Aquinas, *ST* I.58.

77. Burrell, *Knowing the Unknowable God*, 51–70; Buijs, "Maimonidean Critique," 449–70.

Like Maimonides, Aquinas derives his doctrine of divine simplicity from his cosmological argument. Maimonides is extremely intent on rooting out idolatry. Aquinas affirms in his discussion of simplicity what Maimonides affirms, namely, the need to purify our understanding of God by removing notions of complexity. It is understandable why some would see a sort of agnosticism about God's nature in Aquinas due to simplicity as one finds in Maimonides. Simplicity is important for Aquinas. In fact, Eleonore Stump maintains that "[divine simplicity] is also fundamental to the Thomistic worldview. It is foundational for everything in Aquinas's thought from his metaphysics to his ethics."[78] Simplicity can seem to render God radically transcendent, impersonal, and stoic.[79] But this appearance may be an indication that the understanding of God communicated from the typical Thomistic account of divine simplicity is wrong; other ways of understanding Aquinas's doctrine of simplicity are possible. Andrew Pinsent asserts that "God is 'simple,' but not frozen and unresponsive." Aquinas's interpretation of simplicity is intended to keep it from rendering us Maimonidean skeptics. His view of God is quite immanent and relational compared to Maimonides. Beginning his discussion of divine simplicity in his prologue in *ST* I, he says,

> When we know with regard to something *that* it is, we still need to ask what it is like . . . in order to know with regard to it what it is. . . . But because we are not able to know with regard to God what he is, but what he is not, we cannot consider with regard to God what he is like but rather what he is not like. . . . It can be shown with regard to God what he is not like by removing from him those things not appropriate to him, such as composition and motion and other things of this sort.[80]

It is easy to see how one might infer a view of agnosticism from this, but only if it is read without its context. Aquinas does explain simplicity in terms of what God is not, but in so doing he relies on positive claims about God. God is not a body (i.e., incorporeal), for example. He argues that "God is incorporeal" on the basis of other claims like "God is the first mover," "God is pure actuality," "God is the first being," "God is the most noble of beings," etc. In arguing against God being composed, he says this: "A form which is not able to be received in matter but is subsistent by itself (*per se subsistens*) is individuated in virtue of the fact that it cannot be received in

---

78. Stump, *Aquinas*, 92.

79. Ruse, "Not Reasonable but Not Unreasonable"; Davis, "Three Conceptions of God," 491–508; Hughes, *Complex Theory of a Simple God*.

80. Aquinas, *ST* I.3.

something else. And God is a form of this sort."[81] If there were nothing we could know about God's nature, then it would seem difficult to suppose that one has proved the existence of something that one only knows what it is not. Indeed, as Stump points out in her defense of Aquinas, in the very act of knowing that something exists, one already knows something more about what it is than what it is not.[82] Furthermore, in dealing with the names of God, Aquinas explicitly rejects the sort of agnosticism sometimes attributed to him and associates it specifically with Maimonides:

> And so these people say that when we say that God is living, we signify that God does not exist in the manner of an inanimate thing, and so on for other such names. And this is the position of Rabbi Moses. Others say that these names are imposed to signify a relationship of God to created things, so that, for example, when we say "God is good," the sense is "God is the cause of goodness in things." And the same point applies in other such cases. But both of these opinions appear unsuitable, for three reasons.[83]

He goes on to point out the inconsistency of such reasoning. God is the cause of bodies the same as the cause of goodness, so if when we say "God is good," nothing more is meant than that God is the cause of good things, in the same way we should be able to maintain that "God is a body" because God is the cause of bodies. But this corporeality is precisely what Maimonides insists on avoiding and yet seems committed to by confining such positive statements about God as mere actional attributes. Aquinas goes on, then, to point out that names of the sort "God is good"

> signify the divine substance and are predicated of God substantially, but they fall short in their representation of him.... Therefore, when one says "God is good," the sense is not "God is the cause of goodness" or "God is not evil." But this is the sense: "What we call goodness in creatures pre-exists in God and in a higher mode.... Because he is good, he diffuses goodness in things."[84]

Aquinas then responds to an objection concerning a view sometimes inappropriately applied to himself by saying, "Damascene says that these names do not signify what God is because no one of these names expresses

81. Aquinas, *ST* I.3.3.
82. See Stump, *Aquinas*, 92–130.
83. Aquinas, *ST* I.13.2.
84. Aquinas, *ST* I.13.2.

perfectly what God is, but each of them signifies God imperfectly."[85] This, of course suggests that implying agnosticism about God's nature is not what Aquinas meant in his prologue to *ST* I.3.[86]

Both medievalists have no problems admitting human limitations in our knowledge of God and compensatory adjustments in accordance with the nexus of faith and grace (Aquinas adds to this issue of human epistemic finitude a robust notion of lacking proper rectitude, and then compensates by a more robust notion of grace than Maimonides).[87] As we have seen, in Maimonides's reasoning even with compensatory grace, our knowledge of God is quite limited in comparison to Aquinas's. Their respective conclusions about knowledge of God make a difference concerning the good life, its availability, as well as increasing our motivation in pursuing it.

For Maimonides, knowing that one God exists is the basis and near exhaustion of our knowledge of God. He says with regard to the one God's oneness, "There is no oneness at all except in believing that there is one simple essence in which there is no complexity or multiplicity of notions, but one notion only."[88] From this austere unity, Maimonides concludes that there cannot be moral dispositions, plurality of faculties, essential or non-essential attributes or relations in God. In response, Paul Helm notes, "Perhaps we know positively that God is one; but we do not know one what, and perhaps if we do not know what one God is we cannot know that he is one. To be one has to be one something."[89] God is literally incomparable. Kenneth Seeskin comments, "If there is a comparison to be made, it is not between God and us but between the results of our actions and the results of God's."[90] Maimonides says, "Every attribute that is found in the books of the deity . . . is therefore an attribute of His action and not an attribute of his essence."[91] One may speculate over whether God's actional attributes (assuming that they are not themselves equivocal) allow us to predicate things about God's essence (e.g., from "God acts justly" we can perhaps infer "God is capable of acting justly.") Seeskin claims that for Maimonides, "our chief way of knowing God is to deny that the consequences of effects resemble their source."[92] This may plausibly strike one as not being very informative.

85. Aquinas, *ST* I.13.2.
86. Aquinas, *ST* I.3. See Stump, *Aquinas*, 95–96.
87. Dobbs-Weinstein, *Maimonides and St. Thomas*, 141–70, esp. 164.
88. Maimonides, *Guide* I.51 (113).
89. Helm, "Maimonides and Calvin on Divine Accommodation," 152–53.
90. Seeskin, "Metaphysics," 87; Leaman, *Moses Maimonides*, 27.
91. Maimonides, *Guide* I.53 (121).
92. Seeskin, "Metaphysics and Its Transcendence," 88.

He adds that this is consistent with the biblical record where Moses is able to see "God's goodness" via God's ways, but not able to see God. If the only thing we can know about God is what God is not, then double negatives in this way usually reveal a positive. "God does not not exist" means "God exists." "God does not lack power" means "God possesses power." In fairness to Maimonides, he is doing more than this trivial word game. Maimonides's intent is to get us out of the simple comparative-superlative mode of thinking about God as is common in everyday usage about created things and also common to "Perfect Being Theology" which he rejects. He makes the point by referring to a wall that does not see because the wall neither sees nor lacks sight, but is not in our categories at all.[93]

Even negative predicates, however, are problematic for Maimonides in that God is still the subject about which the negation pertains and so has some degree of specification. Maimonides's response to this problem is that the purpose of negative predicates is not to provide literal truth but to "conduct the mind towards that which must be believed with regard to Him."[94] That is, even they are not truly representative. All God talk is a distortion. Yet even this will not do. For a distortion presupposes something being distorted. He argues that the best response to God is silence.[95] Perhaps Maimonides has a pedagogical purpose in mind with all of this; in other words, a heuristic intended to graduate people toward the truth. Seeskin claims that the best way to think of what Maimonides is up to is to think in graduated steps. First, avoid anthropomorphisms. Second, see God's effects rather than God (e.g., "God is merciful" is really meant to say "God acted mercifully"). Third, metaphysically positive attributes like power, intelligence, unity, and existence cannot be univocal or analogical affirmations when applied to God and man. Finally, fourth, even the negations are not problematic according to Seeskin because we are placed in awe of God's transcendence. Silence, then, should be taken in the sense of what Seeskin calls "learned ignorance rather than inarticulateness."[96] Maimonides concludes in the *Guide* that "None but He himself can apprehend what He is."[97] One is tempted to ask whether the statement, "God knows himself" is itself a positive statement about God. Clearly, questions remain.

Seeskin argues for negative theology's positive contribution, claiming that there is much to be gained by denying that God's power, existence, or

---

93. Maimonides, *Guide* I.58 (136).
94. Maimonides, *Guide* I.57 (133).
95. Maimonides, *Guide* I.59 (139).
96. Seeskin, "Metaphysics and Its Transcendence," 90.
97. Maimonides, *Guide* I.59 (139).

intelligence are incomparable to ours. But these denials cannot replace the silent contemplation of the next step. These steps are helpful steps, but not the ultimate goal which is silent contemplation. In comparison to Maimonides, Aristotle's view is hierarchical, and up at the top God's essence is knowable: thought thinking itself thinking. Seeskin says that Maimonides's position is more complicated than Aristotle and amounts to the recognition that "human effort to know God is destined to fail."[98] If true, then Maimonides's God seems more transcendent and perhaps beyond reach than even Aristotle's. So most if not all are precluded from attaining the good life.

In the end, for Maimonides, metaphysics is helpful in removing our conceit of an egocentric universe and humbling us; it is more heuristic than demonstrative; and it points more than it proves. Maimonides says, "When a man reflects on these things . . . his love for God will increase . . . as he becomes conscious of his lowly condition."[99] Seeskin compares God to the sun where the sun is hidden from us, not because it emits no light but because it emits so much light. "This makes God inaccessible not because God is cold and aloof but because the difference between God and us is too great for us to fathom."[100] One wonders how merely contemplating the unfathomable per se can compel love. I cannot fathom what our universe is expanding into, but I am not sure I love it more because of this. If "one cannot love God in ignorance," then one might ask what virtue there is in being epistemically agnostic about God's nature.

Seeskin again defends the intelligibility of Maimonides's position in that negative theology serves a practical and pedagogical end, namely, preparing the mind for genuine religious experience.[101] He argues that religious language is not referentially denoting a metaphysical reality. Its function is preparative for a kind of reflection, in that for Maimonides, "true piety is not a matter of knowing God but of knowing that we do not know."

In the *Guide*, Maimonides says this: "All men . . . affirm clearly that God . . . cannot be apprehended by the intellects, and that none but he himself can apprehend what he is, and that apprehension of Him consists in the inability to attain the ultimate term in apprehending him."[102]

Diana Lobel claims that by negating, Maimonides helps conduct the mind toward what must be believed and denied about God; in other words, this exercise helps remove idolatrous accretions from our concept of God and

---

98. Seeskin, "Metaphysics and Its Transcendence," 91.
99. Maimonides, *Mishneh Torah* IV.12.
100. Seeskin, "Metaphysics and Its Transcendence," 102.
101. Seeskin, "Sanctity and Silence."
102. Maimonides, *Guide* I.59 (139).

come closer to the true reality, asymptotically closer to the positive knowledge of the divine via the process of elimination.[103] When the moment of awe occurs, the mind humbly stops. Then, positively, the mind moves in love and worship. Lobel says, "Informed negation brings us to contemplate and love the Necessary One, whose essence our minds can never fully grasp."[104] Maimonides says in a famous passage in the *Mishneh Torah*, "This sublime, awesome God, it is a commandment to love and revere; as it is said, 'You shall love the Lord your God,' and it is said, 'You shall revere the Lord your God.' And what is the way to the love and awe of Him? When a person contemplates his great and wondrous works and creatures and from them obtains a glimpse of his wisdom which is incomparable and infinite."[105] Hence, it is that the negative way in *Guide* I is complemented by a positive way in *Guide* III.51–54. In light of this fact that we can never know the weaver, but yet we can sense his presence and be awed by the tapestry woven, Lobel asks, "And then do we not, in some sense, know the weaver?" And she continues, "Negative theology brings correct knowledge of God—knowledge through negation—which inspires love and awe."[106]

Commenting on the Maimonidean language about God in the Torah, Paul Helm claims that the problem is that it is "intellectually inert."[107] It does not serve but to preserve the radical transcendence and unknowability of God. I will take this a step further and say that because it is intellectually inert, it extends this inertia to the motivational and practical spheres of moral psychology and moral epistemology. Whereas Seeskin claims virtue from such epistemic agnosticism regarding what God is like, it may in fact be a vice. As pointed out earlier there may be severe motivational problems pursuing the Aristotelian notion of the divine that is characterized by thought thinking itself thinking. Something similar can be said of Maimonides's conception. Indeed, at least something of what God is like is known to Aristotle.

Now if the knowledge of God constitutes human perfection, then human imperfection is somehow constituted by a lack of the knowledge of God. As Kenneth Seeskin puts it, "One cannot love God in ignorance."[108] Thus, if mastery of divine science is needed for human perfection, it is impossible to fulfill the commandments without it because one must know something

---

103. Lobel, "Silence Is Praise to You," 43; Maimonides, *Guide* I.59 (139–40).
104. Lobel, "Silence Is Praise to You," 45.
105. Maimonides, *Mishneh Torah*, s.v. "Foundations of the Torah" II.1–2.
106. Lobel, "Silence Is Praise to You," 48.
107. Helm, "Maimonides and Calvin," 157.
108. Seeskin, "Metaphysics and Its Transcendence," 82.

to love something. So Seeskin's claim, along with Maimonides's, is on the border of being incoherent. In this case, Maimonides's thoroughgoing negative theology, while perhaps not unintelligible (since it posits knowledge of what God is not), does not really help human perfection much. Nor does it provide much by way of moral motivation.

For Maimonides, asking what is the purpose in God's mind for willing or failing to will something is futile. He says, "As we shall not inquire into the purpose of the existence of God, so we shall not inquire into the purpose of his will, according to which everything past and future is happening in the way it happens."[109] This is consistent with his skepticism in other areas about God (e.g., *via negativa*). In contemporary philosophical jargon, his response would amount to a position known as "skeptical theism," namely, such things lie outside of our epistemic ken.[110]

An objector wanting a response merely about God's existence cannot have an answer to his question. The distinction between epistemic questions about God's existence cannot be separated and treated aside from the question of God's nature, which Maimonides insists we remain agnostic about. We must say what *God* means before we can say something could answer that description. The history of Judaism in general and Maimonides in particular are focused on avoiding idolatry. The ancient polytheistic gods were anthropomorphic. God is hidden to most but the prophets who heard his voice in history. The children of Israel were constantly sliding back into idolatry and the prophets were trying to bring them back. When properly worshipping, it was the one invisible God whose works alone were visible in history and whose Torah became the unique guide. This, Jacob Ross explains, is Maimonides's tradition.[111]

Ross admits that this is in character an elitist ideal and unattainable by the Jewish masses who continue to retain a more emotional or distorted understanding of God's nearness, an imaginative distortion which enables the masses to live moral and holy lives imitating God's actional attributes. God's nature requires agnosticism as God cannot accurately be described in humanlike terms accommodating to the masses. The Jewish thinker Judah Halevi captures nicely the tension for the western Judeo-Christian perspective between transcendence and immanence: "Lord, where shall I find You? Your place is lofty and secret. And where shall I not

---

109. Maimonides, *Guide* III (157).

110. Draper, "Skeptical Theist," 176–77; Ross, "Hiddenness of God," 181–96.

111. Ross, "Hiddenness of God," 190; Maimonides, *Guide* I.18 (43–44). See Maimonides, *Maimonides Reader*, 45–46.

find You? The whole earth is full of your glory."[112] While comparable with Maimonides at some level regarding the transcendence of God, Aquinas's view of God is vastly different in terms of divine immanence which has implications for our knowledge of God and our motivation in pursuing the good life via relationship with God.

The Immanent Foundation of Aquinas's Model of Spiritual Formation

Exposure to and perspectives on Aquinas's thought varies. Many see him as a philosopher, highly influenced by Aristotle. Others see him as a systematic theologian, standardizing and extending the thought of Augustine in catholic tradition. Less appreciated, however, is how Aquinas's views were steeped in and shaped by the Bible itself as reflected in his many commentaries. Indeed, he produced commentaries on five Old Testament books, two Gospels, and on over half of the New Testament, including virtually all of the Pauline corpus (numbering fourteen if one takes Paul to be the author of Hebrews as Aquinas does), which is probably good reason for why Paul ("the apostle") is cited more by Aquinas than Aristotle ("the philosopher"), and even more than Augustine.[113] Aquinas thinks God puts a revelation of himself into history and so reveals His mind and will to human beings in a way that goes beyond what is merely in the written text. This serves to buttress the point about Aquinas's doctrine of simplicity being less problematic in comparison to Maimonides's when it comes to one's religious experience of God. Aquinas, by contrast, depicts a God that can be experienced in some way as immanent. For this reason, we ought not ignore the data mined from his commentaries that aids us in our understanding of his views on important matters related to our project in philosophical theology and especially to elements of his views on spiritual formation. It is generally agreed that his commentary on John is part of his second period at Paris and thus a mature work composed near the end of his life (1269–1272). Another of his mature works is his *Commentary on Romans*, a commentary on Paul's *magnum opus* of the New Testament. While many of Aquinas's smaller epistles stay closer to the text, his commentary on Romans is perhaps the richest and most

---

112. Halevi, "Lord, Where Shall I Find You?"

113. Stump, "Biblical Commentary and Philosophy," 252–69. Aquinas of course is not alone in thinking highly of the mind of the Apostle Paul. Indeed, the once famous atheist said in his testimonial transition from atheism to theism that Paul was "a first class intellectual" and that he had "a brilliant philosophical mind." See Flew and Varghese, *There Is a God*, 186.

sophisticated of all of his Pauline commentaries, including discussions of the nature of a divided will and how the will is affected by grace and the role of the Holy Spirit. Aquinas apparently used more than one version of the Latin Vulgate Bible, there being several versions of it available by the thirteenth century.[114] In these biblical commentaries, one finds plenty of citations from Aristotle, Plato, and Democritus, to Cicero and Seneca. In terms of the content of his important mature works like commentaries on *John* and on *Romans*, as expected he cites those of his religious tradition, but perhaps unexpectedly for many is that he also discusses views from Aristotle quite regularly.[115] Indeed, as Norman Kretzmann observes about Aquinas's commentary on *Romans*, "he refers to Aristotle far more often than in any other of his commentaries on Paul's epistles."[116] These commentaries were written in the same time period as his work on the *Summa* and so provide important insight into his mature views.[117] At the heart of the good life for Aquinas is knowledge of God's immanence by means of the Holy Spirit. This suggests a distinction between two propositions, both of which Aquinas would affirm: (1) "Aquinas knows *that* God is present in the Eucharist," and (2) "Aquinas knows God's presence in the Eucharist." The knowledge of persons is not reducible to knowledge *that*. Pneumatology is the study of the doctrine of the Holy Spirit. Aquinas affirms a pneumatically relational kind of moral epistemology relative to spiritual formation.

In noting what he calls a "pneumatological deficit" among the posterity of the Latin Western churches (Roman Catholic and Protestant), Bruce Marshall observes that among actions of the triune God in theological literature, specified actions by the Holy Spirit are noticeably empty, especially when compared to the actions of the Father and of the Son. Indeed, substitutes are often used where one would expect traditional theology to speak of the Spirit (e.g., grace, the Church, the Virgin Mary). Among many critics, Marshall writes, "Augustine is usually assigned the chief blame for this unhappy state of affairs, with Thomas Aquinas a close second."[118] By contrast with these critics, and while not attempting to exonerate Augustine, Marshall contends that Aquinas actually assigns quite a few particular temporal actions and outcomes to the Holy Spirit in his *Commentary on John*, many of which are unique to the Spirit. These generally range, on the

---

114. Weisheipl, *Friar Thomas D'Aquino*, 246–47, 369; Tugwell, *Albert and Thomas*, 246.

115. For example, see Aquinas, *Commentary on John* 1.1, where he discusses the nature of signs, citing Aristotle's *De interpretatione*.

116. Kretzmann, "Warring," 181.

117. Boyle, "On the Relation," 75–82.

118. Marshall, "What Does the Spirit Have to Do?," 62.

one hand, from the Spirit being sent upon Christ and marvelously given to the apostles in such ways indicative of how the apostles themselves would spread the grace and teaching upon being "filled with the Holy spirit,"[119] similar to a later imperative that all believers are to be filled with the Spirit (Eph 5:18), to, on the other hand, being involved in both the crucial saving action that leads men generally to love God (forgiveness of sins) and the effect of that action (our love for God).[120]

A wide range of unique activities and effects are attributed to the Spirit and rooted in the Spirit's *propria* (especially *amor* as a personal characteristic). We, in turn, possess some characteristics via a participated likeness such that they are in us "just as the properties of fire are in a piece of burning wood."[121] In fact, "everyone who is born of the Spirit is just like (*sicut*) the Holy Spirit."[122] The Spirit "raises up our hearts from love of the present age to a spiritual resurrection, in order that they might find their way totally into God."[123] He cleanses the hearts of the apostles so that they might convict the world of sin.[124] He moves our hearts to obey God and consecrates us to God.[125] As the *amor Dei* in person, the Spirit "gives us contempt for earthly things and makes us cling to God."[126] Indeed, the Spirit—"*amor* taken notionally"—is "the source (*principium*) of all the gifts which are given to us by God."[127] For Aquinas, the Holy Spirit actually has quite a bit to do.

In Aquinas's *Commentary on the Gospel of St. John*, he actually focuses on two particular actions: making us the Father's adopted children (ontological) and teaching us the truth (epistemological), both having moral implications in the spiritual formation of our lives. "In both cases," Marshall contends, "the action of the Spirit is to bring about a specific relationship of human beings to the Son."[128] The Spirit's mission in this respect is unique to Him as it is only He that is sent by both Father and Son. "The Spirit's mission, Aquinas argues, "implies a certain power of movement (*impulsionem*), and every motion has an effect appropriate to its source . . . consequently the Holy

---

119. Aquinas, *Commentary on John* 2.4.
120. Aquinas, *Commentary on John* 2.4.
121. Aquinas, *Commentary on John* 3.2.
122. Aquinas, *Commentary on John* 3.2.
123. Aquinas, *Commentary on John* 7.5.
124. Aquinas, *Commentary on John* 16.3.
125. Aquinas, *Commentary on John* 14.6.
126. Aquinas, *Commentary on John* 15.5.
127. Aquinas, *Commentary on John* 5.3.
128. Marshall, "What Does the Spirit Have to Do?," 66.

Spirit makes those into whom he is sent similar to him whose Spirit he is."[129] He gives us a share in Jesus's own eternal sonship. In Aquinas's words, he "has conformed (*configuravit*) us to the Son, in that (*inquantum*) he adopts us as children of God."[130] All of this reveals something far different than utter transcendence in terms of man's conception of and relationship with God. Aquinas's writings reveal a God who is also immanent and intends for us to be, in some respect, participants of the divine nature.

Given Aquinas's abundant references to Paul, it is instructive to see something of Aquinas's comments related to the heart of Paul's greatest theological work, *Romans*, and his comments elsewhere on Pauline thought relative to the spiritual lives of believers. In commenting on the first verse of the epistle, Aquinas explains that the word "gospel" means the same thing as "good news" ("good annunciation"). And here is why: "For in it is announced the union of man to God, which is the good of man."[131] Aquinas thus interprets the content of the gospel in reference to "the union of man to God" that happens in three ways. The first has to do with the Incarnation (i.e., "the Word became flesh"), the third with the beatific vision (i.e., "the glory of fruition" as Aquinas calls it). Only the second of which will concern us here. He says, "The second is through the grace of adoption, as is introduced in Ps 82:6: 'I said: You are gods and all sons of the Most High.'"[132] This mode of union of man with God is filial adoption, designated here by Aquinas's expression "grace of adoption." He specifies that it is "sanctifying grace" that is the "grace of adoption."[133] This sanctifying grace is distinct from charisms where, for example, prophecy unites a person to God "as regards an act of God (God inspires the prophet, God gives to the prophet knowledge of events to come)"; the gift of sanctifying grace unites "to God himself."[134] The rest of his commentary will show that this filial adoption comes from Christ who gives it by the Holy Spirit, and is applied only to human beings to whom Christ communicates a participation of his filial divinity. In the prologue, Aquinas makes explicit by citing the Psalm above that this filiation by grace constitutes a sort of divinization. Elsewhere, Aquinas contrasts the bodily sign of God's people in the OT, circumcision, with the spiritual sign of those in the NT, the Holy Spirit. Whereas one

---

129. Aquinas, *Commentary on John* 15.5.

130. Aquinas, *Commentary on John* 14.6; *ST* III.2; Marshall, "Action and Person," 379–408, esp. 390–92, 397–99.

131. Aquinas, *Commentary on Romans* 1.1.

132. Aquinas, *Commentary on Romans* 1.1.

133. See Rom 1:4 in Aquinas, *Commentary on Romans*.

134. Aquinas, *Commentary on Romans* 1.3.

might expect that the sign of the NT believers would be baptism, Aquinas claims here that it is the Holy Spirit.

Gilles Emery says that, as a whole, "the commentary of St. Thomas does not dwell at length on the Holy Spirit in the immanent life of God the Trinity ("theology"), but rather explores the work of the Holy Spirit in the gift of salvation ("economy")."[135] The commentary demonstrates that by his actions "the Holy spirit is revealed as a person, because he accomplishes the actions that are properly the actions of a person—even as the Holy Spirit reveals himself as God by accomplishing actions that belong exclusively to God."[136] Aquinas says that the Holy Spirit "proceeds as Love,"[137] proceeding as he does from "the Love of the Father and the Son."[138] Aquinas is concerned above all to emphasize the "economic" repercussions of this teaching; being Love in person, the Holy Spirit diffuses charity, as Emery notes, "because he proceeds from the Father and the Son, he unites the faithful to God the Father and he conforms them to Christ from whom he comes (this is the 'economic' stake of the doctrine of the procession *a Patre et a filio*)."[139]

Aquinas's *Commentary on Romans* 8:14–17 contains profound teaching on filial adoption relative to the Holy Spirit. After procuring salvific justification by living faith, the Holy Spirit makes his beneficiaries children of God because he is "the Spirit of adoption of sons" (Rom 8:15), that is the Spirit "by whom we are adopted as sons of God."[140] Emery says, "This adoptive filiation is manifested by the gifts of the Holy Spirit . . . and by the testimony of the Holy Spirit himself."[141] While others may perceive effects consonant with the work of the Holy Spirit in the lives of believers, the believer has a unique second-personal experience with the Holy Spirit communicating via His own witness or testimony and on His own authority. There is a constant underscoring by Aquinas of the tension from the inauguration to the consummation of this adoptive filiation: "For this adoption begins through the Holy Spirit justifying the soul . . . but it shall be consummated through the glorification of one's body."[142] To participate in the inheritance of God via divinization is to be "co-heirs with Christ"

---

135. Emery, "Holy Spirit," 133.

136. Emery, "Holy Spirit," 134.

137. Aquinas, *Commentary on Romans* 11.5.

138. "*Qui est amor Patris et Filii*" (Aquinas, *Commentary on Romans* 5.1). See Keaty, "Holy Spirit Proceeding," 533–57.

139. Emery, "Holy Spirit," 135.

140. Aquinas, *Commentary on Romans* 8.3.

141. Emery, "Holy Spirit," 144.

142. Aquinas, *Commentary on Romans* 8.5.

(Rom 8:17). Aquinas comments, "For the adoption of children is nothing other than that conformity [*conformitas*]: he who is adopted as a son of God, is conformed to his true Son."[143] Divinization in this sense is a participation in the glory of Christ; when Christ enlightens believers via wisdom and grace, he makes them to be conformed to himself. This has an ontological dimension concerning the renewal of the human being adopted as a matter of eternal filiation of Christ who is said to communicate a certain conformity of his filiation to others.[144] Adoptive filiation is a certain participation in the natural filiation of the Son enabling believers to bear the image of the Son. There is thus a moral dimension in terms of the imitation of Christ's human condition. Spiritual formation begins with justifying grace provided by the Holy Spirit. Spiritual formation in Christ is the process through which disciples or apprentices of Jesus take on the qualities or characteristics of Christ himself, every essential dimension of human personality.[145] Aquinas explains that just as Christ attained to the inheritance of glory via his sufferings, "for that reason it is necessary even for us to arrive at that inheritance through suffering. . . . For we do not immediately receive an immortal and impassible body, in order that we might suffer with Christ."[146] Part of this spiritual formation takes place as believers undergo trials or struggles in their faith, during which their proper responses further develop their character and increase in living faith.

With Paul, Aquinas emphasizes that it is by the Spirit of adoption that those who are children of God address God as "Father" whereby "this greatness of intention proceeds from the affection of filial love, which the Holy Spirit effects in us. And therefore the Apostle says in whom, namely, in the Holy Spirit, we cry out Abba, Father (Rom 8:15)."[147] Aquinas notes that this interior testimony is that of "filial love, which the Spirit produces in us" and is comparable to the voice of the Father in his declaration of Christ, "This is my beloved Son, in whom I am well pleased."[148] When Aquinas discusses the "instinct of the Holy Spirit," he ties it directly to filiation in a passage by Paul that Aquinas loves to cite:

> "For they who are led by the Spirit of God, these are sons of God" (Rom 8:14). What, in particular does it mean to be "led"

---

143. Aquinas, *Commentary on Romans* 8.6.

144. Aquinas, *Commentary on Romans* 8.6.

145. "Put on the Lord Jesus Christ" (Rom 13:14). See Willard, "Spiritual Formation," 1–6.

146. Aquinas, *Commentary on Romans* 8.3.

147. Aquinas, *Commentary on Romans* 8.3.

148. Aquinas, *Commentary on Romans* 8.3.

in this way? It involves the action of the Holy Spirit directing as a guide, "insofar as the Holy Spirit illumines us interiorly about what we ought to do."[149]

This relates to the epistemic dimension. But Aquinas does not stop at this dimension of illuminating our minds as to what we ought to do. He goes on to talk about how the Holy Spirit moves our heart. In this case, the "spiritual man" acts under the impetus of the Holy Spirit. Aquinas comments:

> For those things are said to be led [*agi*], which are moved by a certain superior instinct [*superiori instincti*]. Whence concerning brute animals we say that they do not lead but are led [*non agunt sed aguntur*], because they are moved by nature and not from their own motion for the purpose of doing their actions. However, similarly, the spiritual man [*homo spiritualis*] is inclined to do a certain thing, not as though from his own will principally but from the instinct of the Holy spirit [*ex instinctu Spiritus Sancti*]. . . . And so it is said in Luke 4:1, that "Christ was led by the Spirit into the desert" [*Christus agebatur a Spiritu in desertum*]. Nevertheless, it is not excluded through this that spiritual men operate through the will and free choice, because the Holy Spirit causes the very movement of the will and of the free choice in them, accordingly, Phil 2:13: "For it is God who works in you both to will and to do for His good pleasure."[150]

While the gifts and virtues are obviously going to be important in their own right in the process of spiritual formation, according to Michael Sherwin, "Grace transforms the source and character of moral excellence."[151] Similarly, Servais Pinckaers observes that "the first source of moral excellence is no longer located in the human person, but in God through Christ."[152] Further on, Aquinas explains that God acts "as the one moving chiefly" while man "as by one acting freely."[153] Lest one think that this pneumatic relational model of spiritual formation in the life of the believer is relegated to an elite class, this "instinct of the Holy Spirit" as treated in Romans 8 is directly linked to filiation as a constitutive aspect of all Christian life.[154] This is in stark contrast to the elitism of Maimonides. Moreover, were there elite Christians, Paul would certainly have been named among them. Yet even he,

149. Aquinas, *Commentary on Romans* 8.3.
150. Aquinas, *Commentary on Romans* 8.3.
151. Sherwin, "Infused Virtue," 29; Aquinas, *ST* II-II.19.9.
152. Pinckaers, *Morality*, 71.
153. Aquinas, *Commentary on Romans* 9.
154. Aquinas, *Commentary on Romans* 9.3.

representing Christians everywhere, is still susceptible to spiritual struggles in the spiritual life. Romans 7:14–25 is a classic NT example of Paul struggling between following the Spirit and the deeds of the flesh. While contemporary scholarship may not share this view, Aquinas (following Augustine) holds that this text reveals the spiritual struggle all believers can identify with and which was demonstrated in the life of the Apostle. On Romans 7, "it has become common place, perhaps even a majority opinion in some NT circles, that the 'I' of Romans 7 is not autobiographical." Ben Witherington claims it is a rhetorical technique known as "impersonation" and that this is how some of the earliest Greek commentators on *Romans*, such as Origin and John Chrysostom, took this passage. Indeed, they take it to denote those Gentiles and Jews outside of Christ.[155]

In his *Commentary on Ephesians*, Aquinas reflects on Paul's famous declaration: "For by grace you are saved through faith: and that not of yourselves, for it is the gift of God," saying that, from the side of man, faith "is the foundation of the whole spiritual edifice." Grace is the source, but faith—a gift to be sure—is the condition and foundation of salvific justification.[156] Explaining the work of grace in salvation, Aquinas says, "By grace the will of a human being is changed, for grace is what prepares the human will to will the good."[157] For him, it is a habit or disposition bestowed in virtue of Christ's passion by the Holy Spirit on a person, inclining that person to freely comply with God's ways.[158] God "infuses the gift of justifying grace that at the same time he moves free choice to accept the gift of grace."[159] And this movement of the free will is the first act of faith, thus beginning the most significant process of moving toward God in the forgiveness of sins whose goal is not mere forgiveness but also union via infusion. Stump comments, "The process of the infusion of grace and the consequent effects of grace on the mind of the person receiving it is the process of sanctification, in which a person's sinful nature is slowly converted into a righteous character."[160] But there is more to sanctification or the whole process of spiritual formation.

Aquinas is a sacramentalist. God offers special aid via the sacraments. Grace is procured by Christ's passion and death, and the special method (in contrast to the more general method of daily walking with the Spirit) of

---

155. Aquinas, *New Testament Rhetoric*, 133; Raith, "Portraits of Paul," 238–61.

156. Aquinas, *Commentary on Galatians and Ephesians* 2.3.

157. Aquinas, *Disputed Questions on Truth* 27.1.

158. Aquinas, *Disputed Questions on Truth* 27.3.

159. Aquinas, *ST* I-II.113.3.

160. Stump, *Aquinas*, 445.

bestowing grace is via the sacraments.[161] According to Aquinas, "One must hold that the sacraments of the new law are, in a certain way, the cause of grace." Neither the sacraments nor any created thing can give grace in the manner of a cause acting *per se* . . . but the sacraments function as an instrument of grace. . . . The humanity of Christ is an instrumental cause of [our] justification, and this cause is applied to us spiritually by faith and corporeally by the sacraments. . . . The passion of Christ is said to work in the sacraments of the new law, and in this way the sacraments of the new law are the cause of grace, working as it were as an instrument of grace.[162]

Grace is involved in all the sacraments, but the one most important for Aquinas's understanding of the atonement is the Eucharist: "The most perfect sacrament is that in which the body of Christ really contained, namely the Eucharist, and it is the consummation of all the others." Furthermore, the nature of the Eucharist is such that when a believer partakes of it, he does not turn the sacrament into his substance, as happens when he eats other food. Rather, he becomes part of the body of Christ and is incorporated more deeply into the body of Christ.[163] The result of merits of Christ's passion flowing into that person by appropriating the sacrament is that his mind and will are strengthened against future sin because his love of God and goodness are stimulated and strengthened. Aquinas goes so far as to say that the soul is inebriated by the sweetness of divine goodness indicative of an increase in moral motivation.[164] This is so because, when the person freely acts out of living faith (faith formed by love) in the sacrament, the free will is directed both towards past sins and future acts, withdrawing from things contrary to God and moving toward God. Simultaneous with this free act, God infuses grace into the believer's soul, adding to the believer's intellect and will an increased disposition toward God and away from sin.

The repetition of this cooperative action of free willing and infusion of grace is the process of gradually conforming the believer's mind and character to Christ's, a process which culminates in the beatific vision.[165] So on Aquinas's account of the atonement, not only is there forgiveness (past sins), but also resources for strengthening the bond of union via communion (preventative maintenance against future sins). Whatever else the mystical body of Christ may be, it is (or at least essentially includes) a union of minds and wills when the believer values and wants what Christ

161. Aquinas, *ST* I-II.109.10; II-II.137.4.
162. Aquinas, *Disputed Questions on Truth* 27.4, 7.
163. Aquinas, *ST* III.73.3.ad2.
164. Aquinas, *ST* III.79.1.2
165. Aquinas, *Disputed Questions on Truth* 28.1.

wants. In this respect, we can make some sense of what Aquinas has in mind with his claim that Christ's grace is transferred to a believer through the Eucharist. It is not like magically plucking some moral disposition from Christ and transferring it to the believer. Rather, in loving Christ because the believer thinks Christ loves him and desires his love in return as depicted in the passion, the believer takes on a frame of mind of sacrificial love, and thus forms, in the words of Stump, "a second-order willing to have first-order willings" to will what God wills.[166] In this way, Christ's grace is transferred similar to the way in which understanding from one mind to another is transferred.

Trust and the Transmission of Testimonial Knowledge

Faith, for Aquinas, is a virtue. And it is an expression of trust or confidence. Recall that in his third lecture of *Romans* chapter 8, Aquinas affirms that there is a testimony of the Holy Spirit along with Paul's statement about those *led* by God's Spirit who can somehow sense Him testifying to their spirit that they are children of God (Rom 8:16). He does this "through the effect of filial love he produces in us."[167] Let us consider what this transmission of knowledge from the Holy Spirit in relation to man might look like as an ongoing experience, something more than simply the single confirmation that the Holy Spirit gives to believers that they are children of God.

It is commonly agreed that testimony can transmit knowledge. We rely on testimony in our grasp of science, history, geography, and a host of other areas. Which bus to catch, what to eat for a proper diet, etc., are all decided based on some one's testimony. Memory beliefs parallel testimonial beliefs. Beliefs about the past are not infallible, and yet we have confidence in memory beliefs. Memory is a psychological mechanism that conveys beliefs across stages of a life, whereas testimony is social and conveys beliefs across lives at a time. Some testimony we can and do check or confirm in a normal day, but most testimony is not checkable (often due to a lack of time and resources). Thomas Reid spoke of God implanting in our natures two principles that tally with each other (1) propensity to speak truth (principle of credulity), (2) a disposition to confide in the veracity of others (principle of veracity). He says, "It is evident that in the matter of testimony, the balance of human judgment is by nature inclined to the side of belief; and turns to that side of itself, when there is nothing put into

---

166. Stump, *Aquinas*, 451.
167. Aquinas, *Commentary on Romans* 8.3.

opposite scale. If it was not so, no proposition that is uttered in discourse would be believed, until it was examined and tried by reason; and most men would be unable to find reason for believing the thousandth part of what is told them."[168] Trust is an important element for the character of knowledge transmitting testimony. The one bearing testimony can invite trust, and the other one accepting the invitation voluntarily gives the trust. In this way, knowledge can be transmitted from the testimonial sender to the testimonial receiver. Indeed, in some cases knowledge can be transmitted because of the testimony and not just through it, where the receiver and not the sender possesses knowledge because of it (e.g., when the sender contributes a portion to the receiver's whole that adds up to other portions previously possessed to result in knowledge by the receiver).

Some privilege interpersonal relations in their account of testimony. For example, in describing her position, one author says,

> Certain features of this interpersonal relationship—such as the speaker offering her assurance to the hearer that her testimony is true, or the speaker inviting the hearer to trust her—are (at least sometimes) actually responsible for conferring epistemic value on the testimonial beliefs acquired.[169]

For those who take knowledge gained to be the product of an epistemic virtue, it is not immediately obvious how this might be so in this situation.[170] Why would simply accepting the testimony of someone else be counted virtuous? What is it about the notion of trust that contributes to knowledge via testimony? And what, precisely, is it for one to give trust to another?

It is easy enough to understand how one person gives trust to another to gain, say, scientific knowledge via testimony when shared by an expert scientist in the relevant field, or perhaps someone receiving classroom directions on the first day of class by an older student in the hallway. In some such cases, perhaps the willingness of one to give trust to another relies upon some evidence related to the credentials of the one providing testimony (e.g., expert scientist) or upon the presumed likelihood of the other to give correct information (e.g., older student in the hallway), rather than something grounded in an ongoing and developing interpersonal relationship since the receiver of the testimony may never have met or seen the person prior to the deliverance of the testimony.

---

168. Thomas Reid quoted in Sosa, "Testimony," 503–5.

169. Lackey, "Testimony," 78.

170. For a wide range of epistemic virtues considered, see Greco, *Achieving Knowledge*; Wood, *Epistemology*.

Or consider a case of a love story where one person, Patty, gives trust to another, Seth, where the giving of trust is the primary or only basis for the acceptance of the putative testimony and resultant knowledge of Seth's love for her. What is the connection between her willingness to trust him (a state of her will) and her knowledge that he loves her (a state of her intellect)? And, further, why think her belief counts as the product of an intellectual virtue when acquired in this way versus her simply being gullible or guilty of wish fulfillment? Her giving trust is equivalent to her willing to believe that he loves her. Now, one presupposition here is that it is possible to will to believe something and that doing so is justifiable. Obviously, it would be problematic if she were told by him that 2+2=5 and she willed to believe this. Can she have any confidence in some beliefs she wills and not in others? How so? If she cannot will to believe, then she also cannot will to trust. If some belief, and trust in particular, is such that there can be no voluntary component, then it follows that trust is not the sort of thing one can give or be invited to give as the expression "trust me" suggests. This would differ little, if at all, from belief generated by evidence. But it seems that there is such an element such that someone can withdraw trust as much as give it. For example, a child gives trust to the parent who teaches her about Santa Claus only to later withdraw trust in particular areas after having found out that her mother was not being truthful in this one area.

We have already seen Aquinas's account of faith and his general psychology of how will and intellect relate.[171] He holds that some beliefs have a voluntary component.[172] Certainly, as we have seen, this is the case with his view of faith. Aquinas goes on to relate faith to wisdom, a process that begins with the will and issues in an intellectual virtue. And living faith is a case where the transmission of knowledge occurs through testimony. Indeed, one's spiritual formation develops—at least in part—via a pneumatically relational sort of epistemology whereby the Holy Spirit plays a central role in communicating God's love and will to us. On his account of the relation of faith to wisdom, interpersonal trust functions to generate intellectual virtue and also to sustain it.[173]

For Aquinas, it is not the intrapersonal interactions between one's will and one's intellect that are the most notable for our present purposes. Rather, the most notable case in which the will can command the intellect involves interpersonal interaction whereby an individual comes to faith in God and

---

171. See chapter 3. Aquinas, *ST* I-II.17.1, 6.

172. Adams, "Involuntary Sins"; DeWeese-Boyd, "Self-Deception and Moral Responsibility"; Cook, "Deciding to Believe"; James, "Will to Believe."

173. Stump, "Wisdom," 28–62.

gains wisdom, which will have implications for further decisions and opportunities for growth in spiritual formation. We recall from previous discussion that Aquinas thinks the object is sufficient to move the will in the case of God as mover because God is the ultimate good for a person. What every person wants as the greatest good is his own happiness, and on Aquinas's view that greatest happiness is none other than union with God. Thus it is that propositions of faith present this greatest good both as happiness and as union with God. For him, the will is working with the design plan of the intellect in light of the fact that propositions of faith are true. Because they are true and such truths have radical epistemic impact on the intellect, then for Aquinas faith contributes to the perfection of the intellect and is thus considered to be an intellectual virtue. And because in faith the will desires what is in fact its ultimate good, faith contributes to the perfection of the will as well and is thus a moral virtue, coming together in living faith.

For Aquinas, then, in the act of faith an intellectual virtue is generated by the state and actions of the will rather than by acts of the intellect itself. Most significant for our purposes, however, is that faith results from an interpersonal interaction between a person and God in that the person coming to faith is attracted to God and God's goodness. For Aquinas, as Stump notes, "the generation of faith is followed by the next step in the process of faith's leading to wisdom."[174] In this act of faith and love of God and his goodness a mutual second-personal relation emerges whose personal interaction is characterized by trust in God, and further openness to God grows in the individual. Consequently, the person develops what Aquinas denotes as "connaturality" or "sympathy with God." When the person is in this second-personal relation with God, then his or her mind is attuned to God's, forming a resonance or sympathy. Such sympathy enables the development of particular dispositions of intellect in the person. Given her openness to God she understands things and has insight into things in ways she otherwise would not have apart from her new openness to the mind of God. According to Aquinas, these dispositions are the most significant or real of the intellectual virtues (e.g., wisdom). Wisdom enables a person to form excellent judgments about what is good both theoretically and practically. Aquinas connects this intellectual virtue with the will in distinction from the exercise of the intellect. He says,

> wisdom denotes a certain rectitude of judgment according to the eternal law. Now rectitude of judgment is twofold: first, on account of perfect use of reason, secondly, on account of certain connaturality with the matter about which one has to judge....

174. Stump, "Faith, Wisdom," 210.

> Now sympathy or connaturality for divine things is the result of love, which unites us to God. . . . Consequently wisdom [in its highest form] . . . has its cause in the will, and this cause is love.[175]

So in the connaturality grounded in the second-personal divine-human relationship, we see the development of the intellectual virtue of wisdom whereby the person will be disposed to understand intuitively what is good in a way she would not have known otherwise or not as well or as readily known. This does not entail, on Aquinas's account, that a person will instantly arrive at being an excellent moral philosopher, but it does entail that one is significantly aided to be on one's way, both as a child or as an adult, who takes this relationship seriously. The young or least educated in faith will have some basis for intuitive theoretical and practical knowledge of the good insofar as connection with the mind of God maintained and developed by God's grace.

For Aquinas, coming to wisdom in this way indicates that there are two sequences of states whereby the will exercises influence over the intellect. First is the establishment of a trusting second-personal relationship. Second, with that relationship comes sympathy and then wisdom. In connaturality, the will's desire for God is sufficient for the will to move the intellect to accept propositions of faith. Following this comes the acquisition of an intellectual virtue. So the establishment of connaturality whereby a person is willing to give trust to God results in the intellectual disposition of wisdom. On one account of testimony, God's intentionally sharing some part of his mind with a human person counts as testimony.[176] In this way, knowledge can be transmitted to a person from God's mind via testimony. In short, the second-personal relationship generated by faith in God has the result that God can transmit knowledge through a witness of trust, and then the intellectual virtue of wisdom develops in a process that began with the will.

Not only is there a virtue of wisdom, but even greater is the gift of wisdom. All of this is grounded in second-personal experience.[177] Individuals suffering from cognitive abilities on some level seem to lack this experience, whereas those who are capable of experiencing it are able to experience triadic "joint attention," wherein both individuals in the relationship can have their attention fixed on some third object such that their attitudes and responses can be shared in a manner that is intuitive and direct. This social insight can shed light on the sharing of minds between God and another person. A person fails in terms of the ability to be "moved" affectively by

---

175. Aquinas, *ST* II-II.45.2
176. Lackey, "Testimony," 71–73.
177. Stump, *Wandering in Darkness*, 75–76.

God when they suffer from an analogical form of autism, spiritual autism. The infused non-Aristotelian virtues and gifts heal and remove such spiritual autism. The virtues and gifts can be seen as two interrelated and complementary sets of dispositions. Pinsent argues that first personal dispositions (e.g., the virtue of wisdom) are had by someone without entailing a shared stance or interpersonal relationship since they are habitual dispositions where a person exercises self-determination via his or her own reason,[178] an individually based evaluative judgment. By contrast, second personal dispositions involve the shared experience of embodied relationship, a mutual presence and shared stance. The person so identifies with the other that they take on something of the other's psychological disposition such that in the gift of wisdom they come to a "shared evaluation." Andrew Pinsent says, "By means of the gifts, one's cognition and appetites are moved [by God] in a second-personal way, a gift could be characterized as a second-personal disposition, classifying a virtue, by contrast, as a first-personal disposition."[179] With the virtue, one moves oneself in the context of grace; but with the gift, one is moved by God.[180] The transformation of a person's character circles around a motivational shift. In the first-personal virtue, one loves God for one's own good. By contrast, second-person motivation is concerned with loving with God what God loves and in the manner in which God loves.

Contemporary Elucidation on Aquinas's Pneumatically Relational Model

Aquinas's account of faith and wisdom is helpful background in considering the role of trust in the testimonial transmission of knowledge. At its core is connaturality (or sympathy) and its establishment by trust. It is unclear, however, what mental capacities are involved in forming and developing connaturality between the person and God. We cannot invoke mere intellect, nor the combination of intellect and will as sufficient. Aquinas's account is not developed at this point, but it does resemble features in the current phenomenon of mind-reading, the knowledge of persons and their attending mental states. We will be in a better position to understand his view of faith and wisdom in spiritual formation after looking at how current studies in neuroscience and social science might elucidate his view.

Recent work in developmental psychology and neurology, especially work on the impairments among children suffering on some level of autistic

178. See Aquinas, *ST* I.2.
179. Pinsent, *Second-Person Perspective*, 62; "Gifts and Fruits," 475–90.
180. See chapter 3 of this book. See also Pinsent, *Second-Person Perspective*, 87, 95.

spectrum disorder, has brought about new discussions even in philosophy and theology about the possibilities of mind-reading and sympathy. The most salient characteristic of the disorder severely impairs the cognitive capacities required for mind-reading.

It isn't entirely clear among philosophers what the precise nature of mind reading is. It seems to be taken analogously to the ambiguity in perception. The notion of perception can be taken as (1) perception, (2) perception as, and (3) perceptual belief." Here, we might say that (1) the cup is an object of perception for Michelle, (2) Michelle perceives the cup as a cup, and (3) Michelle perceives that that is a cup. In reference to both perception and its analogue, mind reading, Eleonore Stump prefers (2). Others such as Alvin Goldman understand the phenomenon of mind reading in terms of (3). He says, "By 'mindreading' I mean the attribution of a mental state to self or other. In other words, to mind read is to form a judgment, belief, or representation that a designate person occupies or undergoes (in the past, present, or future) a specified mental state or experience." For him, it wouldn't be true to say that autistic children are mind reading impaired because it is still possible for them to form judgments about others' mental states. Patty can use the cognitive capacity to read the mental states of Seth in a similar way in which perception can be understood as "perception as" (i.e., Michelle perceives the cup as a cup).[181]

The alleged knowledge which is impaired in autism is not knowledge *that* such and such is the case because pre-linguistic infants are not capable of knowing that a particular person is his mother even if he can know his mother and some of her mental states. An autistic child can know that a particular object is his mother and even some of his mother's mental states, but he can know this without mind-reading. For instance, he might be able to know of his mother's happiness simply because he has learned to associate a smile with a happy state in general. But this is non-identical to the child's knowing his mother's mental state.[182] According to researchers, that which is impaired is the mind-reading capacity for non-propositional knowledge of persons and their attending mental states.[183]

New research reveals that this kind of knowledge of persons is partly subserved by what is now denoted the "mirror neuron system" which makes possible such knowledge when it shares something of the phenomenology of perception. Like color perception, mind-reading of persons is

---

181. Stump, "Faith, Wisdom"; Goldman, "Mirroring, Mindreading, and Simulation," 312; Gallagher, "Neural Simulation."

182. Moore et al., "Components of Person Perception."

183. Gallagher, "Practice of Mind," 83–108.

direct and intuitive. When neurons in this system fire at the time when one does some action and also when one sees the same action done by someone else, this makes such mind-reading possible. Shaun Gallagher says that they "constitute an intermodal link between the ... perception of action or dynamic expression, and the first-person, intra-subjective ... sense of one's own capabilities."[184]

We can think more clearly about this by considering the notion of empathy, which has considerable literature, as something resulting from the cognitive capacity subserved by the mirror neuron system.[185] Some person—Patty—sees an emotion in someone else—Seth—and as a result the mirror neuron system produces in Patty a similar emotional state to Seth's. In empathizing with Seth's pain, Patty will feel something of his pain but as his and not hers, being alert that she is not herself in any sort of physical pain. Yet she is able to take something of his mental state into herself. Consequently, she knows on this basis that Seth is in pain which shows that emphathic feeling of his pain is a reliable ground for knowledge that Seth is, in fact, in pain.[186] As Stump says, "The ability to mind-read is part of what enables human beings to function as the social animals they are. Mind-reading connects people into smaller or larger social groups which can function as one because mind-reading unites people psychically to one extent or another."[187] Gallese explains mind-reading on the part of infants by noting that research shows there is an innate mechanism allowing them to map observed behavior on the part of others to their own behavior which has been denoted "active intermodal mapping" since it enables the brain to translate visual to motor information.[188] By means of visual observation, the child's neuro-system is able to take actions and facial expressions and translate them into motor programs that it would use if it were doing the same action. In this way, it feels from the inside what the outsider is doing and is able to run the motor programs necessary for that action with more or less successful mimicry. This is why newborns can mimic facial expressions of their care-takers. In adults, Gallese contends, "a mirror matching neural mechanism can represent content *independently of the self-other distinction*."[189] Thus, the mirror neuron system takes data from vision and other perceptual and/or non-perceptual sources whereby the content is

---

184. Gallagher, *How the Body Shapes the Mind*, 220.
185. Goldman, "Two Routes to Empathy," 31–44.
186. Gallese, "Being Like Me," 101–118; Nagel, "What Is It Like to Be a Bat?," 436.
187. Stump, "Faith, Wisdom," 211.
188. Gallese, "Being Like Me," 105.
189. Gallese, "Being Like Me," 110.

available from the inside.[190] These mirror neurons, he continues, map this multimodal representation across different spaces inhabited by different actors. These spaces are blended within a unified common intersubjective space, which paradoxically does not segregate any subject. Profoundly, this space is "we-centric."[191] Gallese goes on to explain empathy:

> Self-other identity goes beyond the domain of action. It incorporates sensations, affect, and emotions. . . . The shared intersubjective space in which we live from birth continues long afterward to constitute a substantial part of our semantic space. When we observe other individuals acting, facing their full range of expressive power (the way they act, the emotions and feelings they display), a meaningful embodied link among individuals is automatically established. . . . We have a subpersonally instantiated common space.[192]

He therefore concludes that "it is just because of this shared manifold that intersubjective communication, social imitation, and mind-reading become possible."[193] Thus far we have caught a glimpse of the burgeoning development of the science of the second-personal as a mode of knowledge of other persons.

Given the neurology on mind-reading and empathy, there is only one thing lacking to elaborately connect empathetic mind-reading with Aquinas's connaturality. Empathy is the ability to feel another's emotion, like pain or excitement. But empathic mind-reading capacities make room for more far-reaching interpersonal connections that can be responsive to moral characteristics of another person; that is, to somehow sense and perhaps even be able to love what another loves or hates.

When Seth is doing some action that seems morally repugnant to Patty, Patty's mind-reading of his actions can connect her to his moral characteristics. Consider graphic films and the impact that the activities by say, child abuse actors, have on viewers, and, further, consider the author of those films or narratives and the intended impact they have on viewers.[194] The mirror neuron system gives the viewer some limited awareness of the moral character of the abuser and some sense of what it feels like to do such reprehensible actions. Watching such actions and the response it evokes is

---

190. Stump, *Wandering in Darkness*, 64–82.
191. Gallese, "Being Like Me," 111.
192. Gallese, "Being Like Me," 111, 114.
193. Gallese, "Being Like Me," 115.

194. A number of films come to mind that are intended to elicit strong responses of one kind or another: *Braveheart*, *Schindler's List*, *The Passion*, etc.

not a purely scientific matter given that it evokes evaluative notions. It is possible to read goodness in another when, for instance, we detect directly and intuitively some acts of compassion, and such awareness might even serve to motivate action of like mind. We detect actions to be morally praiseworthy or blameworthy and not merely as providing us with scientific facts (e.g., discerning the difference between a bribe and a gift lies in the motivation for the act and confers on it vice or virtue).

Stump claims that Aquinas's account of "the way in which faith leads to wisdom relies in two places on such an empathic intuitive recognition of goodness, one gained through stories and descriptions of God and the other exercised in second-personal experience with God."[195] First, when someone comes to living faith, he or she begins by having some feel for the goodness of God portrayed in narratives and descriptions of God and, in accordance with Aquinas's philosophical anthropology, they have a desire for that goodness.[196] In this empathic state, mediated as it were by the mirror neuron system where God is, for the person, perhaps still in narrative form, he or she may be willing to assent to the propositions of faith. If so, then they will be open to second-personal experience of God (rather than mere second-personal account via narrative) where, in virtue of the trust of such a connection, mind-reading is established. Second, resultant to this second-personal experience of God and openness for more of it, the person will be even further inclined to be moved by God the Holy Spirit. In this divine-human relationship, something of the mind of God will be communicated via testimony. So on Aquinas's view of faith and wisdom there can be knowledge of God transmitted via testimony in consequence to trust, a phenomenon akin to mind-reading. It is the person's trust in God and his goodness that first establishes a connection, followed by a connaturality with God, the basis for the transmission of knowledge through trust from God to him.

What the scientific story of mind-reading adds to Aquinas's account is the introduction of a new cognitive capacity, which is not part of Aquinas's philosophical psychology; namely, the capacity for mind-reading. This capacity is consistent with Aquinas's philosophical psychology and theology. If this cognitive capacity is reliable, then its operation can result in knowledge. Stump comments:

> On Aquinas's account of faith and wisdom, the process of acquiring knowledge bypasses the usual operations of the intellect in acquiring evidence and assessing reasons; the result of the

195. Stump, "Faith, Wisdom," 216.
196. Smith, "Come and See," 195.

operation of will on intellect nonetheless results in knowledge, because it depends on the mind-reading capacity, which is itself reliable and which connects a person with a highly reliable source of information; namely, God.[197]

There is also a design plan for the system that involves the mutual interactions of the intellect, the will, and the mind-reading capacity such that when the system is employed in the appropriate circumstances in accord with its design plan, it is also a reliable cognitive system. The implications of this goes beyond mere knowledge *that* God exists, but brings us into an active relationship with God where one is able to discern not merely another mind but in some cases even intentions, character, emotions, and will. In Aquinas's commentaries in both *Romans* and *Galatians* we see evidence on knowing the mind, will, and intentions of God.[198]

Aquinas's account of faith and wisdom provides a promising avenue in considering ordinary cases of the transmission of testimonial knowledge, which helps us understand a possible way of elucidating Aquinas's pneumatic relational model of spiritual formation.

Let us bring things together by thinking of Patty, beginning with a certain resistance to trust Seth's overtures and perhaps even skepticism about his testimony to her that he loves her. As she experiences his presence, she experiences some second-personal understanding. She comes to some awareness of his goodness and goodness toward her, and she desires it. This is analogous to Aquinas's process just prior to a person's acquisition of living faith.

Next, in accordance with her desire, her will moves her intellect to believe or give trust to Seth's love for her. This trust may at this moment be tacit and even fall below her conscious radar. This is analogous to when a person has just now come to faith. She releases more of her previous resistance to trust him, thus providing a basis for a deepening of her second-personal experience of him. She becomes more trusting and more open. In this voluntarily increased receptivity, her empathic mind-reading capacities also become more attuned to him, resulting in increased empathic awareness. This is analogous to Aquinas's connaturality. At this stage she may lack propositional evidence sufficient to support Seth's claim to love her, but when she hears him express this love she believes in light of the intersubjective space provided by the mind-reading capacity. She feels his love for her. And so she then believes that he loves her. Such a belief is the

---

197. Stump, "Faith and Wisdom," 217; Bergmann, "Epistemic Circularity," 709–727.

198. Aquinas, *Commentary on Romans* 8.1; 12.1; *Commentary on Galatians and Ephesians* 5.4.

result of a cognitively reliable capacity operating under the appropriate circumstances and in accordance with the design plan working together with her intellect and will.

Further, it takes place in a context that lacks defeaters, or at least overwhelming defeaters. In this case, when she accepts the belief that Seth loves her, she acquires knowledge of his love for her. In Aquinas's case, at this point a person possesses both the intellectual virtue and the gift of wisdom because of connaturality with the mind of God, whose gracious overtures have intentionally produced in the person of faith a disposition that functions as a means of channeling understanding of God's goodness in theoretical and practical ways.

With time and experience, trials of life test the resolve of Patty's relationship with Seth and, depending in part on how Patty responds in these various circumstances, can result in her increased knowledge and love of Seth. Consequently, her life progressively displays the fruitful effect born out of the increasingly loving and trusting relationship. This is, for Aquinas, analogous to the evident fruit of the Spirit on display when someone is walking in the Spirit and being led by the Spirit through faith.

So what is it for Patty to give Seth her trust, and what about this contributes to her acquisition of knowledge through testimony? Further, why would such knowledge of Seth's love for her be considered to be the product of an intellectual virtue in Patty? On Aquinas's account, with help from the insight of contemporary developmental psychology and neurobiology, Patty's giving her trust to Seth consists in the dynamic interaction between her will and intellect, mediated through mind-reading, and results in her belief that Seth is good. Subsequently, and similarly, mediated by a deeper empathic form of mind-reading, she comes to a belief that he loves her. This is just what it means for her to give trust. Further, through intrapersonal interaction between will and intellect in her intellective soul, we see the role of will in her belief-forming processes. The mind-reading capacities help to elucidate why the process can yield knowledge. The capacity considered is as reliable as other cognitive capacities. And beliefs grounded in it are likely to be true as are beliefs in perceptual faculties which are likewise generally reliable and yet fallible. An essential element in the testimonial transmission of knowledge is trust because trust is necessary to exercise the mind-reading capacity which provides the basis for Patty's coming to know Seth's love for her. This, then, is how trust contributes to the acquisition of knowledge through testimony.

But someone might object and inquire as to why this knowledge attained or received by her should count as a product of an intellectual virtue since little intellectual work is being done by her. It seems the work is done by the sender, Seth; not by the receiver, Patty. But it is just this assumption about knowledge and the processes leading to it that recent neurobiological research on mind-reading questions. Indeed, this research shows that there are cognitive systems that are "we-centric." Because humans are social animals, some of our excellences come about only in operation with other persons.[199] The mind-reading system is one of these. It operates virtuously only when it manages to appropriately connect two minds in some sort of unity, whose unity provides the basis for the transmission of knowledge. This social or communal excellence is one that is not designed to operate successfully in isolation, on one's own, as it were, but in community.

If Patty were impaired with respect to this capacity, she would not succeed in gaining knowledge through testimony via trust. Obviously, the mind-reading capacity is not infallible. But such is the condition of most other humanly reliable cognitive capacities. Like perceptual or memory faculties, it can be used in ways not suited for its success, so that it yields delusions about other people. Like reasoning abilities, it too can be used in epistemically careless ways; it can be dull or untrained. Thus, the mind-reading capacity does not guarantee knowledge. Deception, even self-deception, is surely possible. If we accept some externalist, reliabilist account of knowledge, as Aquinas does, then we can understand why the testimonial transmission of knowledge sometimes results in knowledge, assuming the mind-reading process is applied appropriately and successfully.

So Patty might be deceived, but as it happens, she is not. What Seth is testifying about is a state in himself to which Patty potentially has partial access to through mind-reading under the appropriate circumstances and proper function of her capacities. First, she is in a position to assess Seth's trustworthiness where she is concerned; and second, she mind-reads Seth's emotions and or intentions toward her. In some cases, there is no iterated use of the mind-reading capacity (e.g., in the previous illustration about directions given by the older student). Instead, there will only be an initial use, not two uses, involved in the transmission of knowledge via testimony.

Further, Patty's case presupposes Seth is a reliable testifier of his own inner states and is likewise a reliable self-reporter. Thus, operative presuppositions are that Seth's report of his love for Patty should be both true and based on reliable cognitive processes in Seth; likewise Seth's belief about himself underlying and underwriting his self-report is likewise based on similar reliable introspective and communicative processes. As in the case of Patty, there is an important role for faith and mind-reading to play in discerning the goodness of the testifier, Seth, or in Aquinas's case, God. In

---

199. Goldberg, *Relying on Others*; Plantinga, *God and Other Minds*.

both cases there is a willingness to be open that is an important part of the process of the deepening relationship whose willingness is a consequence of the dynamic interaction of the intellect and the will, whereby the will exercises causal control over the intellect.

Another potential objection, that mind-reading is prone to give false results when there is strong wish-fulfillment, is apparent yet without substance. For mind-reading to be reliable, it might be thought that there should be some more reliable connection between apparent and real goodness. Aquinas would maintain that one acquires reliably true beliefs about God by mind-reading or joint-attention, which is brought about by the presence of the Holy Spirit. This process cannot rule out wish fulfillment. In considering how the mirror neuron system works to explain the capacity to read minds, it should be noted that the system cuts both ways since it has a "common space." So it allows us to project our own emotions, thoughts, and intentions onto others. Even though mind-reading allows us to take on others' mental states, it also allows us to communicate or (more skeptically) project (via "transference") our own mental states (and wishes).[200] Research indicates that "the notions of projective identification and the interpersonal dynamic related to transference . . . can be viewed as instantiations of the implicit and pre-linguistic mechanisms of the embodied simulation-driven mirroring mechanisms."[201] Thus, the system may take incoming data and process it as content from the inside, but it also allows one to take one's own internal content and project it (imagine it) onto another as though it is their feelings. But a possible failure in a form of knowledge (whether testimonial, perceptual, mind-reading, etc.) does not entail its unreliability. One may also object that such mind-reading capacities as have been discussed rely on relationships that take time to develop, but this is not always the case. The illustrations earlier of the scientist or older student serve to rebut this.[202] Research at this early stage in neuroscience and social science regarding mind-reading and joint-attention seem to be well grounded and are helpful to elucidate Aquinas's pneumatically relational model of spiritual formation.[203]

---

200. Oelsner, *Transference and Counter-Transference*.
201. Gallese, "Mirror Neurons," 519–36.
202. Bockmuehl, "Aquinas on Abraham's Faith," 39–51.
203. Pasnau, *Thomas Aquinas on Human Nature*.

Conclusion

For Aquinas, faith is a factor in epistemic and salvific justification and is required. When it comes to the virtue of faith being functionally akin to the bifurcating notion of *phronesis*, the master virtue in Aristotle, relative to living the good life with significant salvific implications in Aquinas, the consequences seem severe. Given the universality of depravity, this seems initially crippling for Aquinas's viewpoint regarding the possibility for people to experience the good life. But given the robust notion of grace, such a factor is greatly mitigated.

There is something that stands out for Aquinas. Even after considering his views of the universality and gravity of total depravity, the resolution for the good life seems to be quite ubiquitous, at least in principle, in that even young children, women, slaves, and those intellectually disabled have access. His position overcomes the esotericism found in both Aristotle and Maimonides, being far more egalitarian than either one of them.[1] The fact that his faith epistemology is grounded ultimately in God's self-revelation and on a very immanent level (something Aquinas cannot avoid, nor would he want to, given the doctrine of the Incarnation and the role of the Holy Spirit in human life), accompanied by the infused virtues and gifts of the Spirit, such an evaluation seems to make Aquinas's view more motivationally attractive than Maimonides's view which suffers from a sort of spiritual autism by comparison. At best, Maimonides can autistically know of God's presence via God's ways, his actional attributes, and perhaps even imitate some of them. But this is worlds apart from knowing God, empathizing, or adopting a shared stance with God.

Maimonides's version of *via negativa* reveals a sort of knowledge of God that may or may not be any more motivational than that of Aristotle's.

---

1. I should point out that egalitarianism may be a misguided sentiment if taken in full. Rather than fairness, justice is what concerns Aquinas as characteristic of God. For Aquinas, God is just, but God is not necessarily fair. See Matt 20:1–16 and Aquinas's related comments.

Indeed, at least for Aristotle, something about his God can be positively known. But it seems that for the best life to obtain, some richer theology than Aristotle's, and perhaps richer than Maimonides's, is required for motivation (or at least a richer theology provides greater motivation).[2] There is no greater motivation in life than religious motivation grounded in love.[3] But Maimonides's agnosticism and esotericism elicits questions about the fundamental elusiveness of the good life for the masses, especially those outside of Judaism, and also for those within whose knowledge of God in light of *via negativa* seems somewhat perplexing, to say the least, in terms of motivation for the good life. These are areas for criticism. But this does not appear to be the case for Aquinas where opportunity is broad and motivation abounds.[4]

As is universally acknowledged, Aquinas thinks faith is reasonable. It is reasonable in that it allows the good life to be available to the masses and not just to the elite, and also because he thinks it is consistent and buttressed by evidence for God via general and special revelation that is readily available (Rom 4:16; Gen 15:6). Aquinas's famous five proofs for God's existence, often the sole item university students are exposed to when reading Aquinas, are explicated in but a single article (one and onehalf pages) of the massive *Summa's* approximately 3500 pages. By stark contrast, there are over one thousand articles (one-third of the *Summa*) dedicated to the accounts of the virtues and related matters. His emphasis is elsewhere. Aquinas spoke much more about issues pertinent to the good life than to those concerning evidence for God's existence. Perhaps this irony is because Aquinas's views, and especially his ethics, are traditionally understood as a mere baptism of Aristotle and so are ignored. But as we saw, Aquinas does not consider Aristotle's virtue theory to be *genuinely* virtuous.

In drawing this exploration to a close, I would like to recap and then consider a direction for further implications and research regarding the spirituality of Aquinas. Like Aristotle, whose understanding of the good life ultimately proved elusive to most, Maimonides's and Aquinas's understanding give a similar albeit different appearance as well, at least at first glance. Initially, for Maimonides, it was thought that perhaps natural law theory could come to the rescue, not just as an aid to reasoning for God's existence (since Maimonides already believed he had that demonstrated through cosmological arguments), but significantly because moral perfection is a

2. Nagel, *View from Nowhere*, 219.
3. Jacquette, "Aristotle," 371–89.
4. Swinburne, "What Difference Does God Make to Morality?," 151–66; Adams, "Moral Arguments for Theistic Belief," 125–27.

necessary condition for intellectual perfection, and it might be thought that natural law ethics could be of assistance for the majority who are non-Jews. However, in the end it is not clear that this has helped Maimonides given certain statements by him concerning the authoritativeness behind one's reasons for keeping the law, which is relevant to the moral perfection of the individual. Further, in terms of connecting one's *telos* to one's understanding of imitating God, the problem is that Maimonides, in seeking to divest God of any and all anthropomorphic qualities, goes too far. If there is no likeness between the Creator and creation such that terms like "wise," "lives," and "powerful," are totally ambiguous when applied to God and us, then the concept of God that remains is too thin for the average worshipper to appreciate. But of course, Maimonides does not see himself as the average worshipper. He is an elitist. Closeness to God is measured by the amount of knowledge one has or can acquire. For a variety of reasons, then, most are precluded and so cannot be near to or love God. Right or wrong, this offends modern egalitarian notions. His philosophy demonstrates what results from removing all anthropomorphic content from the deity: virtually all content is removed. Consequently, we are left with a God that is unknowable, indescribable, and ineffable such that we might question what the possible value is in such a conception either to philosophy or religion.[5]

For Aquinas, we have seen that his philosophy goes in a different direction from Maimonides in terms of his conception of God not being radically transcendent but instead being remarkably immanent, making a divine-human relationship widely available. The pneumatic element is indispensable for characterizing Aquinas's viewpoint. This not only aids in knowing about God more broadly, but also in knowing God more deeply on both philosophical and religious levels. This spiritually formative moral epistemology illuminates implications for future research in virtue theory, philosophy, Trinitarian theology, and social cognition. This comparative exploration has served to both highlight a Thomistic metaphysics that "recognizes the absolute primacy of persons,"[6] all persons—including divine, women, children, and the intellectually impaired[7]—as well as to illuminate the relational and motivational structure of the good life for Aquinas. The comparative approach has helped bring this to light in ways otherwise missed outside of such an approach where Aquinas theology is sometimes seen as dry and a bit stoic.

---

5. Seeskin, "Maimonides."
6. Pinsent, *Second-Person Perspective*, 104.
7. Aquinas, *ST* II-II.47.14.ad3.

CONCLUSION

We are reminded of a story told about Aquinas, the quintessential Dominican and one of the greatest philosophers and theologians in the West. "After a religious vision he quit writing. He said that by comparison with what he had seen of God, the theories and arguments in his work were nothing but straw."[8] Given the breadth and depth of Aquinas's prolific works in philosophy, theology, and biblical studies, one can only imagine what kind of overwhelming experience he might have had with the Holy Spirit in order for him to consider his own previous works as straw. Salient in our study is the notion that, for Aquinas, "living a good life ends with, but, more important, begins with God."[9]

---

8. Guillaume de Tocco quoted in Stump, *Wandering in the Darkness*, 62. Aquinas wrote nearly one hundred volumes prior to the printing press and before he died at age forty-nine. That is quite a bit of work to consider "straw."

9. Ryan, "Second-Person Perspective," 62.

Bibliography

Primary Sources

Aquinas, Thomas. *Aquinas's Shorter Summa: St. Thomas's Own Concise Version of His Summa Theologica*. Translated by Cyril Vollert. 1993. Reprint, Manchester, NH: Sophia Institute, 2002.

———. *Commentary on the Gospel of St. John*. Translated by James Weisheipl and Fabian Larcher. Albany: Magi, 1998.

———. *Commentary on the Letter of St. Paul to the Romans*. Translated by Fabian Larcher. Latin/English Edition of the Works of St. Thomas Aquinas 37. Lander, WY: Aquinas Institute for the Study of Sacred Doctrine, 2012.

———. *Commentary on the "Nicomachean Ethics."* Translated by C. I. Litzinger. 2 vols. 1964. Reprint, Notre Dame: Dumb Ox, 1993.

———. *Commentary on St. Paul's Letters to the Galatians and Ephesians*. Translated by Fabian Larcher and Matthew L. Lamb. Latin/English Edition of the Works of St. Thomas Aquinas 39. Lander, WY: Aquinas Institute for the Study of Sacred Doctrine, 2012.

———. *Disputed Questions on Truth*. Translated by Robert W. Mulligan, et al. 3 vols. 1954. Reprint, Indianapolis: Hackett, 1994.

———. *Faith, Reason, and Theology: Questions I–IV of His Commentary on the De Trinitate of Boethius*. Translated by Armand Maurer. Toronto: Pontifical Institute of Mediaeval Studies, 1987.

———. *The Literal Exposition on Job: A Scriptural Commentary Concerning Providence*. Translated by A. Damico and M. Yaffe. Classics in Religious Studies 7. Atlanta: Scholars, 1989.

———. *On Evil*. Translated by Jean T. Oesterle. Notre Dame: University of Notre Dame Press, 1995.

———. "On the Principles of Nature." In *Thomas Aquinas: Selected Writings*, edited and translated by Ralph McInerny, 18–29. Harmondsworth: Penguin, 1998.

———. *Summa Contra Gentiles*. Translated by Lawrence Shapcote. https://aquinas.institute/operaomnia/summa-contra-gentiles.

———. *Summa Theologiæ*. Translated by Fathers of the English Dominican Province. Edited by Kevin Knight. *New Advent*. 2017. Online. http://www.newadvent.org/summa.

Aristotle. *The Complete Works of Aristotle*. Edited by Jonathan Barnes. 2 vols. Princeton: Princeton University Press, 1984.

———. "De Anima." In *The Basic Works of Aristotle*, edited by Richard McKeon, 535–603. New York: Random House, 1941.

———. "Metaphysics." In *The Basic Works of Aristotle*, edited by Richard McKeon, 689–926. New York: Random House, 1941.

———. *Nicomachean Ethics*. Translated by Terence Irwin. 2nd ed. Indianapolis: Hackett, 1999.

Maimonides, Moses. *The Code of Maimonides*. Translated by Abraham M. Hershman. New Haven: Yale University Press, 1949.

———. "Eight Chapters." In *The Ethical Writings of Maimonides*, edited by Raymond Weiss and Charles Butterworth, 59–104. New York: Dover, 1975.

———. *The Ethical Writings of Maimonides*. Translated, edited, and compiled by Raymond Weiss and Charles Butterworth. New York: Dover, 1975.

———. *The Guide of the Perplexed*. Translated by Shlomo Pines. Chicago: University of Chicago Press, 1963.

———. *The Guide of the Perplexed*. Translated by Chaim Rabin. Indianapolis: Hackett, 1995.

———. "Laws Concerning Character Traits." In *The Ethical Writings of Maimonides*, edited by Raymond Weiss and Charles Butterworth, 27–58. New York: Dover, 1975.

———. *Maimonides: The Book of Knowledge*. Translated by M. Hyamson. Jerusalem: Feldheim, 1974.

———. *A Maimonides Reader*. Edited and compiled by Isadore Twersky. West Orange, NJ: Behrman House, 1972.

———. *Mishneh Torah*. Edited by S. Frankel. 12 vols. Jerusalem: Hotzaat Shabse Frankel, 2000.

———. "Treatise on the Art of Logic." In *The Ethical Writings of Maimonides*, edited by Raymond Weiss and Charles Butterworth, 155–64. New York: Dover, 1975.

Plato. "The Republic." In *Complete Works*, edited by John Cooper, 971–1223. Translated by G. M. A. Grube. Revised by C. D. C. Reeve. Indianapolis: Hackett, 1997.

Secondary Sources

Ackrill, J. L. "Aristotle on *Eudaimonia*." In *Essays on Aristotle's Ethics*, edited by Amélie Oksenberg Rorty, 15–34. Berkeley: University of California Press, 1980.

Adams, Robert Merrihew. *Finite and Infinite Goods: A Framework for Ethics*. Oxford: Oxford University Press, 1999.

———. "Involuntary Sins." *The Philosophical Review* 94 (1985) 3–31.

———. "Moral Arguments for Theistic Belief." In *Rationality and Religious Belief*, edited by C. F. Delaney, 116–40. Notre Dame: University of Notre Dame Press, 1979.

Aertsen, Jan. "The Convertibility of Being and Good in St. Thomas Aquinas." *New Scholasticism* 59 (1985) 449–70.

———. "Thomas Aquinas on the Good: The Relation between Metaphysics and Ethics." In *Aquinas's Moral Theory*, edited by Scott MacDonald and Eleonore Stump, 235–53. Ithaca, NY: Cornell University Press, 1999.

Annas, Julia. *The Morality of Happiness*. Oxford: Oxford University Press, 1993.

Anscombe, G. E. M. "Modern Moral Philosophy." *Philosophy* 33 (1958) 1–19.

Anselm. "The Ontological Argument." In *Philosophy of Religion: An Anthology*, edited by Louis Pojman, 70–72. Belmont, CA: Wadsworth, 1998.
Ariel, David. *What Do Jews Believe?* New York: Schocken, 1996.
Augustine, Aurelius. *The Confessions*. Translated by Edward Pusey. New York: Pocket Books, 1952.
Barnes, Jonathan. *The Cambridge Companion to Aristotle*. Cambridge: Cambridge University Press, 1995.
Benor, Ehud. *Worship of the Heart: A Study of Maimonides's Philosophy of Religion*. Albany: State University of New York Press, 1995.
Berg, Jonathan. "How Could Ethics Depend on Religion?" In *A Companion to Ethics*, edited by Peter Singer, 525–34. Oxford: Blackwell, 1991.
Bergmann, Michael. "Epistemic Circularity: Malignant and Benign." *Philosophy and Phenomenological Research* 69 (2004) 709–727.
Berman, Lawrence. "Maimonides, the Disciple of Al-Farabi." *Israel Oriental Studies* 4 (1974) 154–78.
———. "Maimonides on the Fall of Man." *AJS Review* 5 (1980) 1–15.
———. "The Political Interpretation of the Maxim: The Purpose of Philosophy Is the Imitation of God." *Studia Islamica* 15 (1961) 53–61.
Bland, Kalman. "Moses and the Law According to Maimonides." In *Mystics, Philosophers, and Politicians: Essays in Jewish Intellectual History in Honor of Alexander Altmann*, edited by J. Reinharz and D. Swetschinski, 67–84. Durham: Duke University Press, 1981.
Bleich, David. "Judaism and Natural Law." *Jewish Law Annual* 7 (1988) 5–42.
Bockmuehl, Markus. "Aquinas on Abraham's Faith in Romans 4." In *Reading Romans with St. Thomas Aquinas*, edited by Matthew Levering and Michael Dauphinais, 39–51. Washington, DC: Catholic University of America Press, 2012.
Boguslawski, Steven C. *Thomas Aquinas on the Jews: Insights into His Commentary on Romans 9–11*. Mahwah, NJ: Paulist, 2008.
Boyle, John F. "On the Relation of St. Thomas's Commentary on Romans to the Summa theologiae." In *Reading Romans with St. Thomas Aquinas*, edited by Matthew Levering and Michael Dauphinais, 75–82. Washington, DC: Catholic University of America Press, 2012.
Bradley, Denis. *Aquinas on the Twofold Human Good: Reason and Human Happiness in Aquinas's Moral Science*. Washington, DC: Catholic University of America Press, 1997.
Broadie, Alexander. "Maimonides and Aquinas." In *History of Jewish Philosophy*, edited by Daniel H. Frank and Oliver Leaman, 224–34. Routledge History of World Philosophies 2. New York: Routledge, 1997.
———. "Maimonides and Aquinas on the Names of God." *Religious Studies* 23 (1987) 157–70.
Brock, Stephen. *Action and Conduct: Thomas Aquinas and the Theory of Action*. Edinburgh: T&T Clark, 1993.
Brunt, P. A. "Aristotle and Slavery." In *Studies in Greek History and Thought*, by P. A. Brunt, 343–88. Oxford: Oxford University Press, 1993.
Buber, Martin. "Imitatio Dei." In *Contemporary Jewish Ethics*, edited by Menachem Kellner, 152–61. New York: Sanhedrin Press, 1978.
Buckle, Stephen. "Natural Law." In *A Companion to Ethics*, edited by Peter Singer, 161–74. Malden, MA: Blackwell, 1991.

Buijs, Joseph. "A Maimonidean Critique of Thomistic Analogy." *Journal of the History of Philosophy* 41 (2003) 449–70.
———. "The Negative Theology of Maimonides and Aquinas." *The Review of Metaphysics* 41 (1988) 723–38.
Burnett, Charles. "Arabic into Latin: The Reception of Arabic Philosophy into Western Europe." In *The Cambridge Companion to Arabic Philosophy*, edited by Peter Adamson and Richard C. Taylor, 370–404. Cambridge: Cambridge University Press, 2005.
Burrell, David B. *Aquinas: God and Action*. Notre Dame: University of Notre Dame Press, 1979.
———. "Aquinas's Debt to Maimonides." In *A Straight Path: Studies in Medieval Philosophy and Culture*, edited by R. Link-Salinger, 37–48. Washington, DC: Catholic University of America Press, 1987.
———. *Freedom and Creation in Three Traditions*. Notre Dame: University of Notre Dame Press, 1993.
———. *Knowing the Unknowable God: Ibn-Sina, Maimonides, Aquinas*. Notre Dame: University of Notre Dame Press, 1986.
———. "A Philosophical Foray into Difference and Dialogue: Avital Wohlman on Maimonides and Aquinas." *American Catholic Philosophical Quarterly* 76 (2002) 181–94.
———. "Review of *On a Complex Theory of a Simple God: An Investigation in Aquinas's Philosophical Theology*, by Christopher Hughes." *The Journal of Religion* 72 (1992) 120–21.
Cairns, Earle C. *Christianity through the Centuries: A History of the Christian Church*. Grand Rapids: Zondervan, 1996.
Casey, John. *Pagan Virtue: An Essay in Ethics*. Oxford: Oxford University Press, 1990.
Celano, Anthony. "Medieval Theories of Practical Reason." *Stanford Encyclopedia of Philosophy*, edited by Edward N. Zalta. 2003. Online. http://plato.stanford.edu/archives/win2003/entries/practical-reason-med.
Chappell, Timothy. *Understanding Human Goods: A Theory of Ethics*. Edinburgh: Edinburgh University Press, 1998.
Chesterton, G. K. *Orthodoxy*. Garden City, NY: Image, 1959.
Ching, Julia. *Chinese Religions*. Maryknoll, NY: Orbis, 1993.
Code, Alan. "Aristotle: Essence and Accident." In *Philosophical Grounds of Rationality: Intentions, Categories, Ends*, edited by R. Grandy and R. Warner, 411–39. Oxford: Oxford University Press, 1983.
———. "On the Origins of Some Aristotelian Theses about Predication." In *How Things Are: Studies in Predication and the History of Philosophy*, edited by James Bogen and James E. McGuire, 101–131. Dordrecht: Reidel, 1985.
Cook, J. Thomas. "Deciding to Believe without Self-Deception." *The Journal of Philosophy* 84 (1987) 441–46.
Coolman, Holly. "Romans 9–11: Rereading Aquinas on the Jews." In *Reading Romans with St. Thomas Aquinas*, edited by Matthew Levering and Michael Dauphinais, 101–112. Washington, DC: Catholic University of America Press, 2012.
Cooper, J. M. "Aristotle on the Goods of Fortune." *Philosophical Review* 94 (1985) 173–96.
Copan, Paul. "Original Sin." *Philosophia Christi* 5 (2003) 519–41.

Copleston, Frederick. *Medieval Philosophy: From Augustine to Duns Scotus*. Vol. 2 of *A History of Philosophy*. New York: Image, 1993.

Craig, William Lane. *The Cosmological Argument from Plato to Leibniz*. London: Macmillan, 1980.

———. "'No Other Name': A Middle Knowledge Perspective on the Exclusivity of Salvation through Christ." In *The Philosophical Challenge of Religious Diversity*, edited by Philip Quinn and Kevin Meeker, 38–53. Oxford: Oxford University Press, 2000.

Crosby, John. "Are Being and Good Really Convertible: A Phenomenological Inquiry." *New Scholasticism* 57 (1983) 493–94.

Crowe, Michael B. *The Changing Profile of the Natural Law*. The Hague: Nijhoff, 1977.

Curzer, H. "Aristotle's Much Maligned *Megalopsychos*." *Australasian Journal of Philosophy* 69 (1991) 131–51.

———. "A Great Philosopher's Not So Great Account of Great Virtue: Aristotle's Treatment of 'Greatness of Soul.'" *Canadian Journal of Philosophy* 20 (1990) 517–38.

D'Anconca, Cristina. "Greek into Arabic: Neoplatonism in Translation." In *The Cambridge Companion to Arabic Philosophy*, edited by Peter Adamson and Richard C. Taylor, 10–31. Cambridge: Cambridge University Press, 2005.

Davies, William. *Paul and Rabbinic Judaism*. 4th ed. Philadelphia, PA: Fortress, 1980.

Davis, Stephen. "Three Conceptions of God in Contemporary Christian Philosophy." In *Readings in the Philosophy of Religion*, edited by Kelly James Clark, 491–508. 2nd ed. New York: Broadview, 2008.

Dawkins, Richard. *The Selfish Gene*. 30th anniversary ed. Oxford: Oxford University Press, 2006.

DeWeese-Boyd, Ian. "Self-Deception and Moral Responsibility." PhD diss., St. Louis University, 2001.

Diamond, James A. *Maimonides and the Hermeneutics of Concealment: Deciphering Scripture and Midrash in the Guide of the Perplexed*. Albany: State University of New York Press, 2002.

Dobbs-Weinstein, Idit. *Maimonides and St. Thomas on the Limits of Human Reason*. Albany: State University of New York Press, 1995.

Dooyeweerd, Herman. *In the Twilight of Western Thought*. Nutley, NJ: Craig, 1980.

———. *A New Critique of Theoretical Thought*. Translated by David H. Freeman and William S. Young. 4 vols. Philadelphia: Presbyterian and Reformed, 1953–58.

Doyle, Tom. *Dreams and Visions: Is Jesus Awakening the Muslim World?* Nashville: Thomas Nelson, 2012.

Draper, Paul. "The Skeptical Theist." In *The Evidential Argument from Evil*, edited by Daniel Howard-Snyder, 175–92. Bloomington: Indiana University Press, 1996.

Duns Scotus, John. *Duns Scotus on the Will and Morality*. Edited by Allan Wolter. Washington, DC: Catholic University of American Press, 1997.

Dupuis, Jacques. *Toward a Christian Theology of Religious Pluralism*. Maryknoll, NY: Orbis, 1997.

Emery, Gilles. "The Holy Spirit in Aquinas's Commentary on Romans." In *Reading Romans with St. Thomas Aquinas*, edited by Matthew Levering and Michael Dauphinais, 126–62. Washington, DC: Catholic University of America Press, 2012.

———. "Theologia and Dispensatio: The Centrality of the Divine Missions in St. Thomas's Trinitarian Theology." *The Thomist* 74 (2010) 515–61.
Erickson, Millard. *Introducing Christian Doctrine*. Edited by L. Arnold Hustad. Grand Rapids: Baker, 1992.
Evans, G. R. *Augustine on Evil*. Cambridge: Cambridge University Press, 1982.
Evans, Robert F. *Pelagius: Inquiries and Reappraisals*. 1968. Reprint, Eugene, OR: Wipf and Stock, 2010.
Fakhry, Majid. "Maimonides on Religious Language." In *Perspectives on Maimonides: Philosophical and Historical Studies*, edited by Joel Kraemer, 175–91. London: Littman Library of Jewish Civilization, 1996.
———. "Neoplatonic Currents in Maimonides's Thought." In *Perspectives on Maimonides: Philosophical and Historical Studies*, edited by Joel Kraemer, 115–40. London: Littman Library of Jewish Civilization, 1996.
Faur, José. *Homo Mysticus: A Guide to Maimonides's Guide for the Perplexed*. Syracuse: Syracuse University Press, 1999.
Finnis, John. *Aquinas: Moral, Political, and Legal Theory*. Oxford: Oxford University Press, 1998.
———. *Fundamentals of Ethics*. Washington, DC: Georgetown University Press, 1983.
———. *Natural Law and Natural Rights*. Oxford: Oxford University Press, 1980.
Finnis, John, and Germain Grisez. "The Basic Principles of Natural Law: A Reply to Ralph McInerny." *American Journal of Jurisprudence* 26 (1981) 21–31.
Flannery, Kevin. *Acts Amid Precepts: The Aristotelian Logical Structure of Thomas Aquinas's Moral Theory*. Washington, DC: Catholic University of America Press, 2001.
Flew, Antony. "My Pilgrimage from Atheism to Theism." *Philosophia Christi* 6 (2004) 197–212.
———. "The Presumption of Atheism." *Canadian Journal of Philosophy* 2 (1972) 29–46.
Flew, Antony, and Roy Varghese. *There Is a God: How the World's Most Notorious Atheist Changed His Mind*. New York: HarperCollins, 2007.
Flint, Thomas. *Divine Providence: The Molinist Account*. Ithaca, NY: Cornell University Press, 1998.
Foot, Philippa. *Natural Goodness*. Oxford: University Press, 2000.
Fox, Marvin. *Interpreting Maimonides: Studies in Methodology, Metaphysics, and Moral Philosophy*. Chicago: University of Chicago Press, 1990.
———. "Maimonides and Aquinas on Natural Law." *Dine Israel* 3 (1972) v–xxxvi.
Franck, Isaac. "Maimonides and Aquinas on Man's Knowledge of God: A Twentieth Century Perspective." *Review of Metaphysics* 38 (1985) 591–615.
Frank, Daniel H. "Anger as a Vice: A Maimonidean Critique of Aristotle's Ethics." *History of Philosophy Quarterly* 7 (1990) 269–81.
———. "The Development of Maimonides's Moral Psychology." *American Catholic Philosophical Quarterly* 76 (2002) 89–106.
———. "The End of the Guide: Maimonides on the Best Life for Man." *Judaism* 34 (1985) 485–95.
———. "Humility as a Virtue: A Maimonidean Critique of Aristotle's Ethics." In *Moses Maimonides and His Time*, edited by E. Ormsby, 89–99. Washington, DC: Catholic University of America Press, 1989.

———. "Idolatry and the Love of Appearances: Maimonides and Plato on False Wisdom." In *Proceedings of the Academy for Jewish Philosophy*, edited by David Novak and Norbert M. Samuelson, 155–68. Lanham, MD: University Press of America, 1992.
———. "Introduction." *American Catholic Philosophical Quarterly* 76 (2002) 3.
———. "Maimonides and Medieval Jewish Aristotelianism." In *The Cambridge Companion to Medieval Jewish Philosophy*, edited by Daniel H. Frank and Oliver Leaman, 136–56. Cambridge: Cambridge University Press, 2003.
———. "On Defining Maimonides's Aristotelianism." In *Medieval Philosophy and the Classical Tradition in Islam, Judaism, and Christianity*, edited by John Inglis, 231–44. London: Curzon, 2002.
———. "Prophecy and Invulnerability." In *The Jewish Philosophy Reader*, edited by Daniel H. Frank, et al., 79–86. New York: Routledge, 2000.
———. "Reason in Action: The 'Practicality' of Maimonides's Guide." In *Commandment and Community: New Essays in Jewish Legal and Political Philosophy*, edited by Daniel H. Frank. Albany: State University of New York Press, 1995.
Frank, Daniel H., et al., eds. *The Jewish Philosophy Reader*. New York: Routledge, 2000.
Freud, Sigmund. *The Future of an Illusion*. New York: Norton, 1961.
Frost, Ronald. "Aristotle's 'Ethics': The 'Real' Reason for Luther's Reformation?" *Trinity Journal* 18 (1997) 223–41.
———. "Richard Sibbes's Theology of Grace and the Division of English Reformed Theology." PhD diss., King's College of the University of London, 1996.
Gallagher, Shaun. *How the Body Shapes the Mind*. Oxford: Clarendon, 2005.
———. "Neural Simulation and Social Cognition." In *Mirror Neuron Systems: The Role of Mirroring Processes in Social Cognition*, edited by Jaime Pineda, 355–71. New York: Springer, 2009.
———. "The Practice of Mind: Theory, Simulation or Interaction." In *Between Ourselves: Second-Person Issues in the Study of Consciousness*, edited by Evan Thompson, 83–108. Charlottesville, VA: Imprint Academic, 2001.
Gallese, Vittorio. "'Being Like Me': Self-Other Identity, Mirror Neurons, and Empathy." In vol. 1 of *Perspectives on Imitation: From Neuroscience to Social Science*, edited by Susan Hurley and Nick Chater, 101–18. Cambridge: Massachusetts Institute of Technology Press, 2005.
———. "Mirror Neurons, Embodied Simulation, and the Neural Basis of Social Identification." *Psychoanalytic Dialogues* 19 (2009) 519–36.
Garcia, Robert K., and Nathan L. King. *Is Goodness without God Good Enough? A Debate on Faith, Secularism, and Ethics*. Lanham, MD: Rowman and Littlefield, 2009.
Gauthier, David. *Morals by Agreement*. Oxford: Oxford University Press, 1986.
Geisler, Norman. *Thomas Aquinas: An Evangelical Appraisal*. Grand Rapids: Baker, 1991.
George, Robert. "Natural Law." In *A Companion to Philosophy of Religion*, edited by Philip Quinn and Charles Taliaferro, 460–65. Malden, MA: Blackwell, 1999.
Goldberg, Sanford. *Relying on Others: An Essay in Epistemology*. Oxford: Oxford University Press, 2012.
Goldman, Alvin. "Mirroring, Mindreading, and Simulation." In *Mirror Neuron Systems: The Role of Mirroring Processes in Social Cognition*, edited by Jaime Pineda, 311–30. New York: Springer, 2009.

———. "Two Routes to Empathy: Insights from Cognitive Neuroscience." In *Empathy: Philosophical and Psychological Perspectives*, edited by Amy Coplan and Peter Goldie, 31–44. Oxford: Oxford University Press, 2011.

Gomez-Lobo, Alfonso. *Morality and the Human Goods: An Introduction to Natural Law Ethics*. Washington, DC: Georgetown University Press, 2002.

Greco, John. *Achieving Knowledge*. Cambridge: Cambridge University Press, 2010.

Grisez, Germain. "The First Principle of Practical Reason: A Commentary on the *Summa Theologiae*, 12, Question 94, Article 2." *Natural Law Forum* 10 (1965) 168–201.

———. "Natural Law and Natural Inclinations: Some Comments and Clarifications." *New Scholasticism* 61.3 (1987) 307–320.

———. "Natural Law, God, Religion, and Human Fulfillment." *American Journal of Jurisprudence* 46 (2001) 3–36.

———. *The Way of the Lord Jesus*. Vol. 1 of *Christian Moral Principles*. Chicago: Franciscan Herald, 1983.

Guttmann, Julius. "Commentary." In *The Guide of the Perplexed*, edited by Julius Guttmann, 203–226. Translated by Chaim Rabin. London: East and West, 1952.

———. "Editor's Introduction." In *The Guide of the Perplexed*, edited by Julius Guttmann, 1–36. Translated by Chaim Rabin. London: East and West, 1952.

Halevi, Judah. "Lord, Where Shall I Find You?" In *The Penguin Book of Hebrew Verse*, edited by T. Carmi, 338. Philadelphia: Penguin; JPS, 1981.

Harak, G. Simon. *Virtuous Passions: The Formation of Christian Character*. New York: Paulist, 1993.

Hardie, W. F. R. "'Magnanimity' in Aristotle's Ethics." *Phronesis* (1978) 63–79.

Hare, John E. *God and Morality: A Philosophical History*. Malden, MA: Blackwell, 2007.

———. *God's Call*. Grand Rapids: Eerdmans, 2001.

———. "Is Moral Goodness without Belief in God Rationally Stable?" In *Is Goodness without God Good Enough?*, edited by Robert K. Garcia and Nathan L. King, 85–100. Lanham, MD: Rowman and Littlefield, 2009.

———. *The Moral Gap: Kantian Ethics, Human Limits, and God's Assistance*. New York: Oxford University Press, 1996.

———. "Naturalism and Morality." In *Naturalism: A Critical Analysis*, edited by William Lane Craig and J. P. Moreland, 189–212. New York: Routledge, 2000.

Harvey, Steven. "Islamic Philosophy and Jewish Philosophy." In *The Cambridge Companion to Arabic Philosophy*, edited by Peter Adamson and Richard C. Taylor, 349–69. Cambridge: Cambridge University Press, 2005.

Heil, John. "Belief In and Belief That." In *A Companion to Epistemology*, edited by Jonathan Dancy and Ernest Sosa, 48. Oxford: Blackwell, 1992.

Helm, Paul. "Maimonides and Calvin on Divine Accommodation." In *Referring to God: Jewish and Christian Philosophical and Theological Perspectives*, edited by Paul Helm, 149–69. New York: Routledge, 2000.

———. *The Providence of God: Contours of Christian Theology*. Downers Grove, IL: InterVarsity, 1993.

Henry, Douglas V. "Does Reasonable Nonbelief Exist?" *Faith and Philosophy* 18 (2001) 75–92.

Herberg, Will. *Judaism and Modern Man*. New York: Antheneum, 1970.

Heschel, A. J. *God in Search of Man*. New York, 1977.

Hobbes, Thomas. *Leviathan*. Oxford: Oxford University Press, 2009.

Horner, David. "What It Takes to Be Great." *Faith and Philosophy* 15 (1998) 415–44.
Hughes, Christopher. *A Complex Theory of a Simple God*. Ithaca, NY: Cornell University Press, 1989.
Hutchinson, D. S. "Ethics." In *The Cambridge Companion to Aristotle*, edited by Jonathan Barnes, 195–232. Cambridge: Cambridge University Press, 1995.
Irwin, Terence. *The Development of Ethics*. 3 vols. Oxford: Oxford University Press, 2007–2009.
———. "The Metaphysical and Psychological Basis of Aristotle's Ethics." In *Essays on Aristotle's Ethics*, edited by Amélie Oksenberg Rorty, 35–50. Berkeley: University of California Press, 1980.
Ivry, Alfred. "Islamic and Greek Influences on Maimonides's Philosophy." In *Maimonides and Philosophy*, edited by Shlomo Pines and Yirmiyahu Yovel, 139–56. Dordrecht: M. Nijhoff, 1986.
Jacobs, Jonathan. "Aristotle and Maimonides: The Ethics of Perfection and the Perfection of Ethics." *American Catholic Philosophical Quarterly* 76 (2002) 145–63.
———. *Choosing Character: Responsibility for Virtue and Vice*. Ithaca, NY: Cornell University Press, 2001.
———. *Dimensions of Moral Theory: An Introduction to Metaethics and Moral Psychology*. Malden, MA: Blackwell, 2002.
———. *Law, Reason, and Morality in Medieval Jewish Philosophy*. Oxford: Oxford University Press, 2010.
———. "Maimonides (1138–1204)." Internet Encyclopedia of Philosophy. Online. https://www.iep.utm.edu/maimonid.
———. "Plasticity and Perfection: Maimonides and Aristotle on Character." *Religious Studies* 33 (1997) 443–54.
———. "Some Tensions between Autonomy and Self-Governance." *Social Philosophy and Policy* 20 (2003) 221–44.
———. "Taking Ethical Disability Seriously." *Ratio* 11 (1998) 141–58.
Jacquette, Dale. "Aristotle on the Value of Friendship as a Motivation for Morality." *Journal of Value Inquiry* 35 (2001) 371–89.
Jaffa, Harry. *Thomism and Aristotelianism*. Chicago: University of Chicago Press, 1952.
James, William. "The Will to Believe." In *Philosophy of Religion: An Anthology*, edited by Louis Pojman, 404–412. Belmont, CA: Wadsworth, 1998.
Jammer, Max. *Einstein and Religion*. Princeton: Princeton University Press, 1999.
Jenson, Robert. *The Triune God*. Vol. 1 of *Systematic Theology* New York: Oxford University Press, 1997.
Jones, John. *On Aristotle and Greek Tragedy*. London: Chatto and Windus, 1962.
Jordan, Mark. "The Names of God and the Being of Names." In *The Existence and Nature of God*, edited by Alfred Freddoso, 161–90. Notre Dame: University of Notre Dame Press, 1983.
———. *Ordering Wisdom: The Hierarchy of Philosophical Discourses in Aquinas*. Notre Dame: University of Notre Dame Press, 1986.
———. "Theology and Philosophy." In *The Cambridge Companion to Aquinas*, edited by Norman Kretzmann and Eleneore Stump, 232–51. Cambridge: Cambridge University Press, 1993.
Kaiser, Walter C., Jr. "Is It the Case that Christ is the Same Object of Faith in the Old Testament? (Genesis 15:1–6)" *Journal of the Evangelical Theological Society* 55 (2012) 291–98.

Kant, Immanuel. *Groundwork of the Metaphysic of Morals*. Translated by H. J. Paton. New York: Harper and Row, 1964.

Kaplan, Lawrence. "Maimonides on the Miraculous Element in Prophecy." *Harvard Theological Review* 70 (1977) 233–56.

Keaty, Anthony. "The Holy Spirit Proceeding as Mutual Love." *Angelicum* 77 (2000) 533–57.

Kellner, Menachem. "Heresy and the Nature of Faith in Medieval Jewish Philosophy." *Jewish Quarterly Review* 77 (1987) 299–318. Reprinted in *The Jewish Philosophy Reader*, edited by Daniel H. Frank, et al., 114–19. New York: Routledge, 2000.

———. "Is Maimonides's Ideal Person Austerely Rationalist?" *American Catholic Philosophical Quarterly* 76 (2002) 125–44.

———. "Jewish Ethics." In *A Companion to Ethics*, edited by Peter Singer, 82–90. 1991. Reprint, Malden, MA: Blackwell, 2000.

———. *Maimonides on Human Perfection*. Atlanta: Scholars, 1990.

———. *Must a Jew Believe Anything?* Portland, OR: Littman Library of Jewish Civilization, 2006.

———. "Spiritual Life." In *The Cambridge Companion to Maimonides*, edited by Kenneth Seeskin, 273–99. Cambridge: Cambridge University Press, 2005.

———. "The Virtue of Faith." In *Neoplatonism and Jewish Thought*, edited by Lenn E. Goodman, 195–205. Albany: State University of New York Press, 1992.

Kelly, J. N. D. *Early Christian Doctrines*. Rev. ed. San Francisco: Harper & Row, 1978.

Kenny, Anthony. "Aquinas on Aristotelian Happiness." In *Aquinas's Moral Theory*, edited by Scott MacDonald and Eleonore Stump, 15–27. Ithaca, NY: Cornell University Press, 1999.

———. *Aristotle on the Perfect Life*. Oxford: Clarendon, 1996.

———. *What Is Faith?* Oxford: Oxford University Press, 1992.

———. *Will, Freedom, and Power*. New York: Barnes & Noble, 1975.

Kerr, Fergus. *After Aquinas: Versions of Thomism*. Malden, MA: Blackwell, 2002.

Kierkegaard, Soren. *Fear and Trembling*. Translated by Walter Lowrie. 1941. Reprint, Princeton: Princeton University Press, 1974.

King, Peter. "Aquinas on the Passions." In *Aquinas's Moral Theory: Essays in Honor of Norman Kretzmann*, edited by Scott MacDonald and Eleonore Stump, 101–132. Ithaca, NY: Cornell University Press, 1998.

Klein-Braslavy, Sara. "Bible Commentary." In *The Cambridge Companion to Maimonides*, edited by Kenneth Seeskin, 245–72. Cambridge: Cambridge University Press, 2005.

Koester, Helmut. "The Concept of Natural Law in Greek Thought." In *Religions in Antiquity*, edited by Jacob Neusner, 521–41. 1968. Reprint, Eugene, OR: Wipf and Stock, 2004.

Kosman, Aryeh L. "Divine Being and Divine Thinking in 'Metaphysics' Lambda." *Proceedings of the Boston Area Colloquium in Ancient Philosophy* 3 (1987) 165–88.

———. "What Does the Maker Mind Make?" In *Essays on Aristotle's De Anima*, edited by Martha Nussbaum and Amélie Oksenberg Rorty, 343–58. Oxford: Oxford University Press, 1995.

Kraemer, Joel, ed. *Perspectives on Maimonides: Philosophical and Historical Studies*. Oxford: Oxford University Press, 1991.

Kreisel, Haim (Howard). *Maimonides's Political Thought: Studies in Ethics, Law, and the Human Ideal*. Albany: State University of New York Press, 1999.

Kretzmann, Norman. "Abraham, Isaac, and Euthyphro: God and the Basis of Morality." In *Hamartia: The Concept of Error in the Western Tradition*, edited by D. V. Stump, 27–50. New York: Edwin Mellen, 1984.

———. "God among the Causes of Moral Evil: Hardening of Hearts and Spiritual Blinding." *Philosophical Topics* 16 (1988) 189–214.

———. *The Metaphysics of Theism: Aquinas's Natural Theology in Summa Contra Gentiles I*. Oxford: Clarendon, 1997.

———. *The Metaphysics of Theism: Aquinas's Natural Theology in Summa Contra Gentiles II*. Oxford: Clarendon, 1999.

———. "Warring Against the Law of My Mind: Aquinas on Romans 7." In *Philosophy and the Christian Faith*, edited by Thomas Morris, 172–95. Notre Dame: University of Notre Dame Press, 1988.

Kretzmann, Norman, and Eleonore Stump, eds. *The Cambridge Companion to Aquinas*. Cambridge: Cambridge University Press, 1993.

Kries, Douglas. "Thomas Aquinas and the Politics of Moses." *Review of Politics* 52 (1990) 1–21.

Kuhn, Thomas. *The Structure of Scientific Revolutions*. 2nd ed. Chicago: University of Chicago Press, 1970.

Kyle, Richard. "Semi-Pelagianism." In *Evangelical Dictionary of Theology*, edited by Walter Elwell, 1089–90. 2nd ed. Grand Rapids: Baker, 2001.

Lachterman, D. R. "Maimonidean Studies 1950–1986: A Bibliography." *Maimonidean Studies* 1 (1990) 197–216.

Lackey, Jennifer. "Testimony: Acquiring Knowledge from Others." In *Social Epistemology: Essential Readings*, edited by Alvin Goldman and Dennis Whitcomb, 71–91. Oxford: Oxford University Press, 2011.

Lahey, Stephen. "Maimonides and Analogy." *American Catholic Philosophical Quarterly* 67 (1993) 219–32.

Leaman, Oliver. "Ideals, Simplicity, and Ethics: The Maimonidean Approach." *American Catholic Philosophical Quarterly* 76 (2002) 107–123.

———. *Moses Maimonides*. Rev. ed. Surrey: Curzon, 1997.

Lear, Jonathan. *Aristotle: The Desire to Understand*. Cambridge: Cambridge University Press, 1988.

Leftow, Brian. "Anselm's Perfect-Being Theology." In *The Cambridge Companion to Anselm*, edited by Brian Leftow and Brian Davies, 132–56. Cambridge: Cambridge University Press, 2004.

———. "Concepts of God." In *The Encyclopedia of Philosophy*, edited by Edward Craig, 4:93–102. New York: Routledge, 1998.

Leibowitz, Yeshaiahu. *The Faith of Maimonides*. New York: Adama, 1987.

Lerner, Ralph. *Maimonides's Empire of Light: Popular Enlightenment in an Age of Belief*. Chicago: University of Chicago Press, 2000.

Levine, Michael. "Maimonides: A Natural Law Theorist?" *Vera-Lex* 10 (1990) 11–15.

Lisska, Anthony. *Aquinas's Theory of Natural Law: An Analytic Reconstruction*. Oxford: Oxford University Press, 1996.

Lobel, Diana. "Silence Is Praise to You: Maimonides on Negative Theology, Looseness of Expression, and Religious Experience." *American Catholic Philosophical Quarterly* 76 (2002) 25–49.

Loewe, Raphael. "The Medieval History of the Latin Vulgate." In *The Cambridge History of the Bible*, edited by G. W. H. Lampe, 146–49. Cambridge: Cambridge University Press, 1988.
Luther, Martin. "Disputation against Scholastic Theology." In *Career of the Reformer I*, edited by Harold Grimm, 9–16. Vol. 31 of *Luther's Works*. Augsburg: Fortress, 1959.
MacDonald, Scott. "Aquinas's Libertarian Account of Free Choice." *Revue Internationale de Philosophie* 52 (1998) 309–328.
———. "Egoistic Rationalism: Aquinas's Basis for Christian Morality." In *Christian Theism and the Problems of Philosophy*, edited by Michael Beaty, 327–54. Notre Dame: University of Notre Dame Press, 1988.
———. "Practical Reasoning and Reasons-Explanations: Aquinas's Account of Reason's Role in Action." In *Aquinas's Moral Theory: Essays in Honor of Norman Kretzmann*, edited by Scott MacDonald and Eleonore Stump, 133–59. Ithaca, NY: Cornell University Press, 1999.
———. "Primal Sin." In *The Augustinian Tradition*, edited by Gareth Matthews, 110–39. Berkeley: University of California Press, 1999.
———. "Ultimate Ends in Practical Reasoning: Aquinas's Aristotelian Moral Psychology and Anscombe's Fallacy." *The Philosophical Review* 100 (1991) 31–65.
MacDonald, Scott, and Eleonore Stump, eds. *Aquinas's Moral Theory: Essays in Honor of Norman Kretzmann*. Ithaca, NY: Cornell University Press, 1998.
MacIntyre, Alasdair. *After Virtue*. 2nd ed. Notre Dame: University of Notre Dame Press, 1984.
———. *First Principles, Final Ends, and Contemporary Philosophical Issues*. Milwaukee: Marquette University Press, 1990.
———. *Whose Justice? Which Rationality?* Notre Dame: University of Notre Dame Press, 1984.
Mahdi, Muhsin. "Al-Farabi on Philosophy and Religion." *Philosophical Forum* 4 (1972) 5–25.
Maitzen, Stephen. "Divine Hiddenness and the Demographics of Theism." *Religious Studies* 42 (2006) 177–91.
Mann, William, "Augustine on Evil and Original Sin." In *The Cambridge Companion to Augustine*, edited by Eleonore Stump and Norman Kretzmann, 40–48. Cambridge: Cambridge University Press, 2001.
Marshall, Bruce. "Action and Person: Do Palamas and Aquinas Agree about the Spirit?" *St. Vladimir's Theological Quarterly* 39 (1995) 379–408.
———. "What Does the Spirit Have to Do?" In *Reading John with St. Thomas Aquinas: Theological Exegesis and Speculative Theology*, edited by Michael Dauphinais and Matthew Levering, 62–77. Washington, DC: Catholic University of America Press, 2010.
Marx, Karl. "Critique of the Hegelian Philosophy of Right." In vol. 3 of *Marx & Engels Collected Works*, 3–129. London: Lawrence & Wishart, 1975.
Matthews, Gareth B. "It is No Longer I That Do It . . ." *Faith and Philosophy* 1 (1984) 44–49.
McDowell, John. "The Role of *Eudamonia* in Aristotle's *Ethics*." In *Essays on Aristotle's Ethics*, edited by Amélie Oksenberg Rorty, 359–77. Berkeley: University of California Press, 1980.

McFall, Michael. "Can We Have a Friend in Jesus?" *Philosophia Christi* 14 (2012) 315–34.

McGrath, Alister. *Iustitia Dei: A History of the Christian Doctrine of Justification*. 2nd ed. Cambridge: Cambridge University Press, 1998.

McInerny, Ralph. *Aquinas Against the Averroists: On There Being Only One Intellect*. West Lafayette, IN: Purdue University Press, 1993.

———. *Aquinas and Analogy*. Washington, DC: Catholic University of America Press, 1996.

———. *Aquinas on Human Action: A Theory of Practice*. Washington, DC: Catholic University of America Press, 1992.

———. *Ethica Thomistica: The Moral Philosophy of Thomas Aquinas*. Washington, DC: Catholic University of America Press, 1997.

———. "The Principles of Natural Law." *American Journal of Jurisprudence* 25 (1980) 1–15.

———, ed. *Thomas Aquinas: Selected Writings*. Translated by Ralph McInerny. Harmondsworth: Penguin, 1988.

McInerny, Ralph, and John O'Callaghan. "Saint Thomas Aquinas." *Stanford Encyclopedia of Philosophy*, edited by Edward N. Zalta. 2005. Online. http://plato.stanford.edu/archives/spr2005/entries/aquinas.

McMyler, Benjamin. *Testimony, Trust, and Authority*. Oxford: Oxford University Press, 2011.

Miller, Corey. "A Critique of Marx's Philosophy of Religion from Religious Epistemology." *International Philosophical Quarterly* 49 (2009) 351–59.

———. "Review of *Natural Law in Judaism*, by David Novak." *Philosophia Christi* 11 (2009) 488–92.

———. "Review of *The Second-Person Perspective in Aquinas's Ethics: Virtues and Gifts*, by Andrew Pinsent." *American Catholic Philosophical Quarterly* 87 (2012) 207–211.

Miller, Corey, and Paul Gould, eds. *Is Faith in God Reasonable? Debates in Philosophy, Science, and Rhetoric*. New York: Routledge, 2014.

Miner, Robert. *Thomas Aquinas on the Passions*. Cambridge: Cambridge University Press, 2009.

Moore, Derek G., et al. "Components of Person Perception: An Investigation with Autistic, Non-Autistic Retarded and Typically Developing Children and Adolescents." *British Journal of Developmental Psychology* 15 (1997) 401–423.

Morris, Thomas. *The Logic of God Incarnate*. Ithaca, NY: Cornell University Press, 1986.

Moser, Paul. *The Elusive God: Reorienting Religious Epistemology*. Cambridge: Cambridge University Press, 2008.

Muller, Richard. "Scholasticism, Reformation, Orthodoxy, and the Persistence of Christian Aristotelianism." *Trinity Journal* 19.1 (1988) 81–96.

Murphy, Mark C. *Natural Law and Practical Rationality*. Cambridge: Cambridge University Press, 2001.

Nagel, Thomas. "Aristotle on *Eudaimonia*." In *Essays on Aristotle's Ethics*, edited by Amélie Oksenberg Rorty, 7–14. Berkeley: University of California Press, 1980.

———. *The Last Word*. Oxford: Oxford University Press, 1997.

———. *The View from Nowhere*. New York: Oxford University Press, 1986.

———. "What Is It Like to Be a Bat?" *The Philosophical Review* 83 (1974) 435–50.

Novak, David. "Election." In *The Jewish Philosophy Reader*, edited by Daniel H. Frank, et al., 126–27. New York: Routledge, 2000.

———. *The Image of the Non-Jew in Judaism: An Historical and Constructive Study of the Noahide Laws*. New York: Edwin Mellen, 1983.

———. *Natural Law in Judaism*. Cambridge: Cambridge University Press, 1998.

Nussbaum, Martha. *The Fragility of Goodness: Luck and Ethics in Greek Tragedy and Philosophy*. Cambridge: Cambridge University Press, 1986.

Oberman, Heiko A. *Archbishop Thomas Bradwardine: A Fourteenth-Century Augustinian*. Utrecht: Kemink & Zoon, 1957.

———. *Forerunners of the Reformation: The Shape of Late Medieval Thought*. 1966. Reprint, Philadelphia: Fortress, 1981.

———. *Luther: Man between God and the Devil*. Translated by Eileen Walliser-Schwarzbart. London: HarperCollins, 1993.

O'Callaghan, John. *Thomist Realism and the Linguistic Turn: Toward a More Perfect Form of Existence*. Notre Dame: University of Notre Dame Press, 2003.

Oelsner, Robert. *Transference and Counter-Transference Today*. New York: Routledge, 2013.

Okholm, Dennis, and Timothy Phillips, eds. *Four Views on Salvation in a Pluralistic World*. Grand Rapids, MI: Zondervan, 1995.

Owens, Joseph. "Aristotle and Aquinas." In *The Cambridge Companion to Aquinas*, edited by Norman Kretzmann and Eleonore Stump, 38–59. Cambridge: Cambridge University Press, 1993.

Pasnau, Robert. *Thomas Aquinas on Human Nature*. Cambridge: Cambridge University Press, 2002.

Pelikan, Jaroslav. *Reformation of Church and Dogma (1300–1700)*. Chicago: University of Chicago Press, 1984.

Pinckaers, Servais. *Morality: The Catholic View*. South Bend, IN: St. Augustine's, 2001.

Pines, Shlomo. "Adam's Disobedience in Maimonides's Interpretation and a Doctrine of John Philosoponus." *Proceedings of the Israel Academy of Sciences and Humanities* 5 (1971–76) 105–125.

———. "The Limitations of Human Knowledge according to Al-Farabi, Ibn Bajja and Maimonides." In vol. 1 of *Studies in Medieval Jewish History and Literature*, edited by Isadore Twersky and Jay M. Harris, 82–109. Cambridge: Harvard University Press, 1979.

Pines, Shlomo, and Yirmiyahu Yovel, eds. *Maimonides and Philosophy*. Dordrecht: M. Nijhoff, 1985.

Pinsent, Andrew. "Gifts and Fruits of the Holy Spirit." In *The Oxford Handbook to Thomas Aquinas*, edited by Brian Davies and Eleonore Stump, 475–90. Oxford: Oxford University Press, 2012.

———. *The Second-Person Perspective in Aquinas's Ethics: Virtues and Gifts*. New York: Routledge, 2012.

Plantinga, Alvin. "Essence and Essentialism." In *A Companion to Metaphysics*, edited by Jaegwon Kim and Ernest Sosa, 138–40. Malden, MA: Blackwell, 1995.

———. "Evolutionary Argument against Naturalism." In *Knowledge of God*, edited by Alvin Plantinga and Michael Tooley, 31–51. Oxford: Blackwell, 2008.

———. *God and Other Minds: A Study of the Rational Justification of Belief in God*. Cornell: Cornell University Press, 1967.

———. *Warrant and Proper Function*. Oxford: Oxford University Press, 1994.

———. *Warranted Christian Belief.* Oxford: Oxford University Press, 2000.
Plantinga, Cornelius. *Not the Way It's Supposed to Be: A Breviary of Sin.* Grand Rapids: Eerdmans, 1995.
Pope, Stephen. *The Ethics of Aquinas.* Washington, DC: Georgetown University Press, 2002.
Price, H. H. "Belief 'In' and Belief 'That.'" *Religious Studies* 1 (1965) 5–28.
Quinn, Philip. "Sin and Original Sin." In *A Companion to Philosophy of Religion*, edited by Philip L. Quinn and Charles Taliaferro, 541–55. Oxford: Blackwell, 1997.
Raith, Charles. "Portraits of Paul: Aquinas and Calvin on Romans 7:14–25." In *Reading Romans with St. Thomas Aquinas*, edited by Matthew Levering and Michael Dauphinais, 238–61. Washington, DC: Catholic University of America Press, 2012.
Rand, Ayn. *The Virtue of Selfishness.* New York: Signet, 1962.
Rawidowicz, Simon. "On Interpretation." In *Studies in Jewish Thought*, edited by Nahum N. Glatzer, 45–80. Philadelphia: JPS, 1974.
Rea, Michael. "The Metaphysics of Original Sin." In *Persons: Human and Divine*, edited by Dean Zimmerman and Peter van Inwagen, 319–56. Oxford: Oxford University Press, 2007.
Reddy, Vasudevi. *How Infants Know Minds.* Cambridge: Harvard University Press, 2008.
Reeve, C. D. C. *Practices of Reason: Aristotle's Nicomachean Ethics.* New York: Oxford University Press, 1992.
Regan, Richard, and William Baumgarth, eds. *Thomas Aquinas: On Law, Morality, and Politics.* Indianapolis: Hackett, 2003.
Reymond, Robert L. "John H. Gerstner on Thomas Aquinas as a Protestant." *Trinity Review*, May 2001. 1–5.
Rhonheimer, Martin. *Natural Law and Practical Reason: A Thomist View of Moral Autonomy.* New York: Fordham University Press, 2000.
Richardson, Don. *Eternity in Their Hearts.* 2nd ed. Ventura, CA: Regal, 1984.
Rorty, Amélie O., ed. *Essays on Aristotle's Ethics.* Berkeley: University of California Press, 1980.
Rosati, Connie S. "Moral Motivation." *Stanford Encyclopedia of Philosophy*, edited by Edward N. Zalta. 2014. Online. http://plato.stanford.edu/archives/spr2014/entries/moral-motivation.
Ross, Jacob Joshua. "The Hiddenness of God—a Puzzle or a Real Problem?" In *Divine Hiddenness: New Essays*, edited by Daniel Howard-Snyder and Paul K. Moser, 181–96. Cambridge: Cambridge University Press, 2002.
Ruse, Michael. "Darwinism and Christianity Redux: A Response to My Critics." *Philosophia Christi* 4 (2002) 189–94.
———. "Not Reasonable but Not Unreasonable." In *Is Faith in God Reasonable? Debates in Philosophy, Science, and Rhetoric*, edited by Corey Miller and Paul Gould, 112–21. New York: Routledge, 2014.
Russell, Bertrand. *On God and Religion.* Edited by Al Seckel. Buffalo: Prometheus, 1986.
———. "The Talk of the Town." *New Yorker*, February 21, 1970. 29.
Ryan, Tom. "Second-Person Perspective: Virtues and the Gifts in Aquinas's Ethics." *Australian eJournal of Theology* 21 (2014) 49–62.

Sayre-McCord, Geoffrey. "Introduction: The Many Moral Realisms." In *Essays on Moral Realism*, edited by Geoffrey Sayre-McCord, 1–26. Cornell: Cornell University Press, 1988.

Schaeffer, Francis. *Escape from Reason*. Downers Grove, IL: InterVarsity, 1968.

Schellenberg, John L. "'Breaking Down the Walls That Divide': Virtue and Warrant, Belief and Nonbelief." *Faith and Philosophy* 21 (2004) 195–213.

———. *Divine Hiddenness and Human Reason*. Ithaca, NY: Cornell University Press, 1993.

Schwarzschild, Steven S. "Do Noachites Have to Believe in Revelation?" *Jewish Quarterly Review* 52 (1962) 297–308.

———. "Moral Radicalism and 'Middlingness' in the Ethics of Maimonides." *Studies in Medieval Culture* 11 (1977) 64–95.

Searle, John. "How to Derive 'Ought' from 'Is.'" *The Philosophical Review* 73 (1964) 43–58.

Seeskin, Kenneth, ed. *The Cambridge Companion to Maimonides*. New York: Cambridge University Press, 2005.

———. "Judaism and the Linguistic Interpretation of Jewish Faith." In *Studies in Jewish Philosophy: Collected Essays of the Academy for Jewish Philosophy, 1980–85*, edited by Norbert Samuelson, 215–34. Lanham, MD: University Press of America, 1987.

———. "Maimonides." *Stanford Encyclopedia of Philosophy*, edited by Edward N. Zalta. 2014. Online. http://plato.stanford.edu/archives/spr2014/entries/maimonides.

———. "Metaphysics and Its Transcendence." In *The Cambridge Companion to Maimonides*, edited by Kenneth Seeskin, 82–104. Cambridge: Cambridge University Press, 2005.

———. "The Middle Way in Maimonides's Ethics." *Proceedings of the American Academy for Jewish Research* 54 (1987) 31–72.

———. "The Positive Contribution of Negative Theology." In *Jewish Philosophy in a Secular Age*, by Kenneth Seeskin, 31–69. Albany: State University of New York Press, 1990.

———. "Sanctity and Silence: The Religious Significance of Maimonides's Negative Theology." *American Catholic Philosophical Quarterly* 76 (2002) 7–24.

———. *Searching for a Distant God: The Legacy of Maimonides*. New York: Oxford University Press, 1999.

Shalkowski, Scott. "Atheological Apologetics." *American Philosophical Quarterly* 26 (1989) 1–17.

Shanley, Brian *The Thomist Tradition*. Dordrecht: Kluwer Academic, 2002.

Shapiro, David. "The Doctrine of the Image of God and *Imitatio Dei*." In *Contemporary Jewish Ethics*, edited by Menachem Kellner, 127–51. New York: Sanhedrin, 1978.

Shatz, David. "Freedom, Repentance, and Hardening of the Hearts." In *The Jewish Philosophy Reader*, edited by Daniel H. Frank, et al., 51–57. New York: Routledge, 2000.

———. "Maimonides's Moral Theory." In *The Cambridge Companion to Maimonides*, edited by Kenneth Seeskin, 167–92. Cambridge: Cambridge University Press, 2005.

Shelley, Bruce. "Pelagius, Pelagianism." In *Evangelical Dictionary of Theology*, edited by Walter A. Elwell, 897. 2nd ed. Grand Rapids: Baker, 2001.

Sherwin, Michael. "Infused Virtue and the Effects of Acquired Vice: A Test Case for the Thomistic Theory of Infused Cardinal Virtues." *The Thomist* 73 (2009) 29–52.

Smith, Janet E. "Come and See." In *Reading John with St. Thomas Aquinas: Theological Exegesis and Speculative Theology*, edited by Michael Dauphinais and Matthew Levering, 194–211. Washington, DC: Catholic University of America Press, 2010.

Snell, R. J. "Thomism and Noetic Sin, Transposed: A Response to Neo-Calvinist Objections." *Philosophia Christi* 12 (2010) 7–28.

Sokolowski, Robert. *The God of Faith and Reason*. Notre Dame: University of Notre Dame Press, 1982.

Sosa, Ernest. "Testimony." In *A Companion to Epistemology*, edited by Jonathan Dancy and Ernest Sosa, 503–5. Oxford: Blackwell, 1998.

Stenger, Victor J. "Faith in Anything Is Unreasonable." In *Is Faith in God Reasonable? Debates in Philosophy, Science, and Rhetoric*, edited by Corey Miller and Paul Gould, 55–68. New York: Routledge, 2014.

Stern, Josef. "Maimonides's Epistemology." In *The Cambridge Companion to Maimonides*, edited by Kenneth Seeskin, 115–27. Cambridge: Cambridge University Press, 2005.

Strauss, Leo. "How to Begin Study: *The Guide of the Perplexed*." In *Moses Maimonides, The Guide of the Perplexed*, edited by Shlomo Pines, xi–lvi. Translated by Shlomo Pines. Chicago: University of Chicago Press, 1963.

———. "The Literary Character of the *Guide for the Perplexed*." In *Persecution and the Art of Writing*, by Leo Strauss, 38–94. Glencoe, IL: Free Press, 1952.

———. *Philosophy and Law: Contributions to the Understanding of Maimonides and His Predecessors*. Translated by Eve Adler. Albany: State University of New York Press, 1995.

Striker, Gisela. "Origins of the Concept of Natural Law." *Proceedings of the Boston Area Colloquium in Ancient Philosophy* 2 (1986) 79–94.

Stump, Eleonore. *Aquinas*. London: Routledge, 2003.

———. "Aquinas's Account of Freedom: Intellect and Will." *Monist* 80 (1997) 576–97.

———. "Biblical Commentary and Philosophy." In *The Cambridge Companion to Aquinas*, edited by Norman Kretzmann and Eleonore Stump, 252–69. Cambridge: Cambridge University Press, 1993.

———. "Faith, Wisdom, and the Transmission of Knowledge through Testimony." In *Religious Faith and Intellectual Virtue*, edited by Laura Frances Goins and Timothy O'Connor, 204–230. Oxford: Oxford University Press, 2014.

———. "The God of Abraham, Saadia, and Aquinas." In *Referring to God: Jewish and Christian Philosophical and Theological Perspectives*, edited by Paul Helm, 95–119. New York: Routledge, 2000.

———. *Hamartia: The Concept of Error in the Western Tradition*. New York: Edwin Mellen, 1983.

———. "The Non-Aristotelian Character of Aquinas's Ethics: Aquinas on the Passions." *Faith and Philosophy* 28 (2011) 29–43.

———. *Wandering in Darkness: Narrative and the Problem of Suffering*. Oxford: Oxford University Press, 2010.

———. "Wisdom: Will, Belief, and Moral Goodness." In *Aquinas's Moral Theory: Essays in Honor of Norman Kretzmann*, edited by Scott MacDonald and Eleonore Stump, 28–62. Ithaca, NY: Cornell University Press, 1999.

Stump, Eleonore, and Norman Kretzmann. "Being and Goodness." In *Being and Goodness: The Concept of the Good in Metaphysics and Philosophical Theology*, edited by Scott MacDonald, 98–128. Ithaca, NY: Cornell University Press, 1991.

Swinburne, Richard. "What Difference Does God Make to Morality?" In *Is Goodness without God Good Enough?*, edited by Robert K. Garcia and Nathan L. King, 151–66. Lanham, MD: Rowman and Littlefield, 2009.

Taylor, Richard C. "Averroes: Religious Dialectic and Aristotelian Philosophical Thought." In *The Cambridge Companion to Arabic Philosophy*, edited by Peter Adamson and Richard C. Taylor, 180–200. Cambridge: Cambridge University Press, 2005.

———. "Truth Does Not Contradict Truth: Averroes and the Unity of Truth." *Topoi* 19 (2000) 3–16.

Ten Elshof, Gregg. "The Problem of Moral Luck and the Parable of the Land Owner." *Philosophia Christi* 3 (2001) 139–52.

Tertullian, Quintus. "The Prescription against Heretics." Translated by Peter Holmes. Christian Classics Ethereal Library. 1850. Online. http://www.ccel.org/ccel/schaff/anf03.v.iii.vii.html.

Tugwell, Simon, ed. *Albert and Thomas: Selected Writings*. Translated by Simon Tugwell. Classics of Western Spirituality. Mahwah, NJ: Paulist, 1988.

Twersky, Isadore. *Introduction to the Code of Maimonides (Mishneh Torah)*. New Haven: Yale University Press, 1980.

Urmson, J. O. "Aristotle's Doctrine of the Mean." *American Philosophical Quarterly* 10 (1973) 223–30.

Van Inwagen, Peter. *An Essay on Free Will*. Oxford: Clarendon, 1983.

Van Til, Cornelius. *The Defense of the Faith*. Philadelphia: Presbyterian and Reformed, 1963.

Vos, Arvin. *Aquinas, Calvin, and Contemporary Protestant Thought*. Grand Rapids: Eerdmans, 1985.

Wallace, Daniel. *Greek Grammar Beyond the Basics*. Grand Rapids: Zondervan, 1996.

Weinandy, Thomas. *Aquinas on Scripture: An Introduction to His Biblical Commentaries*. London: T&T Clark, 2005.

Weisheipl, James. *Friar Thomas D'Aquino: His Life, Thought, and Works*. Washington, DC: Catholic University of America Press, 1983.

Weiss, Raymond L. "The Adaptation of Philosophic Ethics to a Religious Community: Maimonides's Eight Chapters." In *Proceedings of the American Academy for Jewish Research* 54 (1987) 261–87.

———. *Maimonides's Ethics: The Encounter of Philosophic and Religious Morality*. Chicago: University of Chicago Press, 1991.

Weiss, Raymond L., and Charles E. Butterworth, eds. *Ethical Writings of Maimonides*. New York: New York University Press, 1975.

Whiting, Jennifer. "Aristotle's Function Argument: A Defense." *Ancient Philosophy* 8 (1988) 33–48.

Wiggins, David. "Weakness of Will, Commensurability, and the Objections of Deliberation and Desire." In *Essays on Aristotle's Ethics*, edited by Amélie Oksenberg Rorty, 241–66. Berkeley: University of California Press, 1980.

Willard, Dallas. "Spiritual Formation and the Warfare between the Flesh and the Human Spirit." *Journal of Spiritual Formation and Soul Care* 1 (2008) 1–6.

Williams, Bernard. *Moral Luck*. Cambridge: Cambridge University Press, 1981.

Witherington, Ben. *New Testament Rhetoric: An Introductory Guide to the Art of Persuasion in and of the New Testament*. Eugene, OR: Cascade, 2009.

Wohlman, Avital. *Maimonide et Thomas d'Aquin: un dialogue impossible.* Fribourg: Editions universitaires, 1995.

———. *Thomas d'Aquin et Maimonide: un dialogue exemplaire.* Paris: Cerf, 1988.

Wolfson, Harry A. "The Knowability and Describability of God in Plato and Aristotle." *Harvard Studies in Classical Philology* 56–57 (1947) 233–49. Reprinted in vol. 1 of *Harry A. Wolfson: Studies in the History of Philosophy and Religion*, edited by Isadore Twersky and George H. Williams, 98–114. Cambridge: Harvard University Press, 1973.

———. "Maimonides on Negative Attributes." In vol. 2 of *Harry A. Wolfson: Studies in the History of Philosophy and Religion*, edited by Isadore Twersky and George H. Williams, 195–230. Cambridge: Cambridge University Press, 1973.

———. "Maimonides on the Unity and Incorporeality of God." In vol. 2 of *Harry A. Wolfson: Studies in the History of Philosophy and Religion*, edited by Isadore Twersky and George H. Williams, 433–57. Cambridge: Cambridge University Press, 1973.

———. *Structure and Growth of Philosophical Systems from Plato to Spinoza.* Vol 2. of *Philo: Foundations of Religious Philosophy in Judaism, Christianity, and Islam.* Cambridge: Harvard University Press, 1962.

Wood, W. Jay. *Epistemology: Becoming Intellectually Virtuous.* Downers Grove, IL: InterVarsity, 1998.

Zagzebski, Linda. "Intellectual Motivation and the Good of Truth." In *Intellectual Virtue: Perspectives from Ethics and Epistemology*, edited by Linda Zagzebski and Michael De Paul, 135–54. Oxford: Oxford University Press, 2003.

www.ingramcontent.com/pod-product-compliance
Lightning Source LLC
Chambersburg PA
CBHW070325230426
43663CB00011B/2224